ROUTLEDGE LIBRARY EDITIONS:
TRANSPORT ECONOMICS

Volume 9

THE ECONOMICS OF ROAD TRANSPORT

THE ECONOMICS OF ROAD TRANSPORT

K.G. FENELON

Routledge
Taylor & Francis Group
LONDON AND NEW YORK

First published in 1925 by George Allen & Unwin Ltd

This edition first published in 2017
by Routledge
2 Park Square, Milton Park, Abingdon, Oxon OX14 4RN

and by Routledge
711 Third Avenue, New York, NY 10017

Routledge is an imprint of the Taylor & Francis Group, an informa business

British Library Cataloguing in Publication Data
A catalogue record for this book is available from the British Library

ISBN: 978-0-415-78484-9 (Set)
ISBN: 978-1-315-20175-7 (Set) (ebk)
ISBN: 978-1-138-63066-6 (Volume 9) (hbk)
ISBN: 978-1-315-20927-2 (Volume 9) (ebk)

THE ECONOMICS OF ROAD TRANSPORT

BY

K. G. FENELON, M.A.

LONDON : GEORGE ALLEN & UNWIN LTD.
RUSKIN HOUSE, 40 MUSEUM STREET, W.C. 1

TO

MY FATHER AND MOTHER

First published in 1925

Printed in Great Britain

CONTENTS

ACKNOWLEDGMENTS

THE Author desires to express his indebtedness to Professor J. S. Nicholson, who read over the MS. and offered valuable suggestions for its improvement; to Messrs. William Younger & Co., Ltd., and to Messrs. Hovis, Ltd., for kind permission to publish tables of their costs; to their respective Transport Managers, Mr. G. S. Vickary and Mr. C. F. Roberts for the necessary facts and figures; to Mr. Willcox, Editor of *The Tramway and Railway World*, for the statistics on pages 129 and 162; and to Mr. W. L. Sleigh, Jnr., for aid in obtaining cost records.

The MS. and proofs have been read over by the Author's father, and to his suggestions many improvements are due.

To those friends who have aided and encouraged him in the writing of the book the Author desires to express his appreciation and gratitude.

The Economics of Road Transport

CHAPTER I

INTRODUCTION

EVEN in an age accustomed to the rapid commercial exploitation of new inventions, the great and extensive development of mechanical road transport stands out conspicuously. The motor car, not so many years back, was unknown, while the commercial motor van or lorry occupied but a very minor place in the transport system of this country up to the outbreak of war in 1914.

During the nineteenth century road transport had been under a cloud. The railways had overshadowed the road, and it seemed that no great scope was left to the older method of animal traction on roadways or even for the application of the steam engine to road vehicles. Now once more, however, as a result of the development of the new mechanical power, the road has come into its own again.

The new recruit to the commercial methods of transportation has already done a great deal to improve internal communications, and in the future, we may rest assured, it will do yet more.

On the importance of transportation much has been written, and here little need be said to stress further the significance of the vital service rendered by transport in the intricate and interdependent economic organization of modern times. "It is in the development of transport and the means of communications that the present century most overtops its predecessors." [1]

Transport is an essential link in the industry and commerce of the world; indeed the whole fabric of industry rests upon the assumption that raw materials or finished products can readily be sent to the places where they are required. Industry, commerce and transport are bound up together, for the extension or the development of the one reacts upon the others.

Though in the modern world transport has assumed an increasing importance, it has long been recognized as an essential instrument in the economic life of the community. Thus Adam Smith, writing in the pre-railway age, declared that "good roads, canals and navigable rivers, by diminishing the expense of carriage, put the remote parts of the country more nearly upon a level with those in the neighbourhood of the town. They are upon that account the greatest of all improvements." [2] Porter, in his *Progress of the Nation*,[3] speaks with pride of our "viabilité immense." "The advantages to a commercial people of roads upon which they can pass at all times with comfort and celerity between distant markets can hardly be appreciated too highly." [4] Later economic writers have likewise insisted upon the importance of transportation.[5]

It must not be forgotten that road transport has had a long history and that it has done its full share to help on the progress of civilization. In the past the highways of Europe have been an important factor in the development of trade, industry and commerce, and in the spread of culture. In the growth of towns and markets the influence of the road is clearly to be seen. The highways of Imperial

[1] Nicholson, *Principles of Political Economy*, vol. iii, book iv, ch. iv, p. 94.

[2] *Wealth of Nations*, book i, ch. xi, p. 62 (Nicholson's edition).

[3] *Progress of the Nation*, New Edition, 1851, section vi, ch. i, p. 288.

[4] Op. cit., p. 288.

[5] E.g., Marshall, *Principles of Economics* and *Industry and Trade*; Knowles, *Industrial and Commercial Revolutions in Great Britain*.

Rome are well known to have played a great part in the history of that Empire and in the spread of civilization.

In Britain, Thorold Rogers has shown that road communications during the mediæval period played an important part in the economy of the time.[1] Water carriage, it is true, was less expensive and more convenient, but waterways did not penetrate to all parts. On the roads, it would appear, " common carriers " were to be found plying on regular routes and undertaking the carriage of all kinds of commodities at moderate charges. Even in early times such carriers traversed long stretches of road, and instances are to be found of services between such towns as Oxford and Newcastle, Oxford and Winchester, etc.

Thorold Rogers maintains that the rates charged were low and that communications were easy and probably regular.[2] The rates varied, it is true, since rudimentary forms of " classification " or " charging what the traffic could bear " would seem to have been imposed.[3] But though the rates varied with the article carried, it is demonstrable that they fell below an average of 2d. per ton per mile ; grain, for instance, was carried for 1d. per ton per mile. Of course, the mediæval penny was a much more valuable coin than its modern counterpart, probably twelve times as valuable, yet considering all things, these rates were not high for the period.

Compared with the mediæval period, the most striking developments of road transport are, on the one hand, the great decrease in the cost of transit, and, on the other hand, the great increase in the speed of conveyance. Cost and speed are the two vital factors in modern transport.

[1] *History of Agriculture and Prices*, vol. i, ch. xxviii, on " The Cost of Carriage."

[2] Opinions differ as to the condition of mediæval roads. It is well known, however, that the Church did a great deal to improve roads in the mediæval period. To help travellers and to repair roads was regarded as an important form of charity, while certain religious societies or Gilds were founded for the purpose of improving roads or building bridges, e.g. The Gild of the Holy Cross at Birmingham.

[3] Nicholson, *Principles of Political Economy*, vol. iii, p. 91.

Characteristics and Analysis of Road Transport.

The outstanding characteristic of road transport is its flexibility. Road vehicles are not tied down to particular routes like the railway or the canal, because our road system is very extensive and the highways penetrate almost everywhere. If necessary, a road vehicle can be transferred readily to another district or to a new route. Anyone is free to put a vehicle on the King's highway and operate it as he wishes, provided only that it complies with certain regulations as to axle weight, speed, etc., and on payment of the appropriate tax. Road transport is the only form of inland transport where door-to-door services can be operated without any special construction of sidings, wharves, terminals, etc., which would be essential to other forms of transport. It is true, of course, that yards, loading devices, etc., may prove a useful aid in expediting road transit, but the point is that these are not absolutely essential, as witness the frequent services to shops, farms, private houses, etc., where no attempt is made to provide terminal facilities. In any case, such terminal works are far less expensive than with other systems of transport. The keynotes of road transport are thus flexibility and freedom.

It is usual in any analysis of transport services to distinguish four essential elements :—

1. The vehicle or vessel.
2. Motive power.
3. The highway.
4. Terminals.

Every method or system of transport—road, rail, river, canal, sea or air—depends on a combination of these four elements, though as between the various systems marked differences are to be found.

In some cases one or more of the essential elements are provided free by nature, e.g. the highway of the air or the oceans.

In the case of the railway the proprietors furnish all the requirements—power, vehicles, permanent way and terminals. This was not the intention of the earliest promoters, who thought that it would suffice to provide the permanent way only, charging tolls on all those who wished to utilize the track for running their own vehicles. In practice, however, this was found to be unworkable after the introduction of steam operation, though certain exceptions still remain to the general rule that a railway owns and operates the whole system, e.g. " private owners' wagons " in Britain ; in some other countries, the leasing of a state-constructed permanent way to private companies.

A very different practice is exemplified by British canals, which charge tolls for the use of their specialized way, but do not, with a few exceptions, undertake the work of carriers. In France the State-owned waterways are toll free.

Road transport resembles the railway or the canal, but differs from air or ocean transport in that it is dependent on an artificial highway, though this is not so specialized as the canal or railway track. However, with the development of mechanical traction and the growth of heavier traffic travelling at high speeds, the road is tending to become more costly and more highly specialized.

In Britain there is a marked divergence between railway and canal practice on the one hand and road construction and maintenance on the other. The responsibility for road construction and maintenance devolves on the community and not upon private individuals or companies. The system of direct payment for use, through the imposition of turnpike tolls, after an extensive trial was found liable to abuse and unsatisfactory in practice. Since the coming of the modern mechanical road vehicle, however, there has been a partial return to a system of payment for use in an indirect form that avoids the main evils of the older toll system. The former petrol tax and the more recent vehicle tax, though the latter is not proportioned to road usage, may be regarded, as indeed they are, a payment for special services rendered.

Recently, projects have been put forward for the construction of wide, high-speed "motorways" on a commercial basis, the expense of construction and maintenance to be defrayed by tolls on the vehicles that use them. These projects confirm the view that the road is becoming a more highly specialized way. They are interesting also as a revival of the turnpike road, in a form somewhat different, it is true, and modified to suit modern traffic. Was not the initial reason for the turnpike road that it was hoped to better road standards by the application of private enterprise? It must be admitted, it is only fair to note, that the much abused Turnpike Trusts, with all their glaring faults, did something to improve the roads and to introduce a new standard of maintenance.

From the fact that those responsible for road maintenance are not coextensive with the direct users—though all benefit greatly from our road system—it follows that a conflict of interests may arise, as it has arisen all through the history of our roads.

There are thus two sides to the economic problems of road transportation—the vehicle is useless without the road, and the purpose of the road is to serve the vehicle.

On the one hand, there are the economic problems of road usage—the carriage of goods and passengers; the economics of the various types and systems of road transport; questions of rates and fares; monopoly or competition; organization of road transport services; and the like.

On the other hand, there are the administrative, economic and financial problems of road construction and maintenance, and the consideration of how the charges involved are to be met.

Finally, each of these two sides of the question has its own technical problems, the construction of vehicles, cost accounting, engine efficiency, road surfacing, foundations, etc.; but these fall outside the scope of the present work.[1]

In the sequel attention will be mainly confined to the transportation side, though something will have to be said of the economics of the roadway.

[1] On the technical side of the subject there is an extensive literature. It is difficult to select from the mass of material available, but perhaps the following may be indicated as providing much useful information and as suggestive of further reading :—

Conradi, *Mechanical Road Transport* (Macdonald & Evans).

Phillimore, *Motor Road Transport for Commercial Purposes* (Sir Isaac Pitman).

Grupp, *Economics of Motor Transportation* (Appleton) (deals mainly with the U.S.A.).

An excellent bibliography will be found in the Readers' Bulletin of the Coventry Public Libraries (1923-24).

See also the Glasgow Public Libraries Joint Technical Catalogues, "Motor Vehicles," 1922.

CHAPTER II

HISTORICAL SURVEY

1. The Development of Mechanical Road Transport.

The application of mechanical power to road vehicles dates back further than is sometimes supposed, for it was in 1769 that the first successful steam-driven carriage was built by a Frenchman, Nicholas Joseph Cugnot. Mounted on three wheels, his carriage was driven by two single-acting cylinders, and could attain a speed of 2¼ miles per hour with a load of four persons. Cugnot's boiler, however, proved to be too small, for with it only a sufficient head of steam could be maintained for fifteen minutes, after which it was necessary to wait till sufficient pressure was again available to propel the vehicle.

To remedy the defect Cugnot constructed another machine, with a larger boiler, and this was completed by 1770. Cugnot, however, met with misfortune, as his machine overbalanced when turning a corner in the streets of Paris near where the Madeleine now stands, and in consequence the trials were abandoned. But though Cugnot carried his experiments no further, they were sufficient to demonstrate the practicability of mechanical traction on roads, and entitle him to be ranked as the first successful pioneer of mechanical road transport.

For the next phases in the evolution of the power-driven road vehicle we have to turn to Great Britain. In 1784 Watt obtained a patent for the construction of a steam carriage, but he did not proceed with the actual building of a vehicle.

Before the nineteenth century successful working models were constructed by Murdoch (1782), Symington (1786), and others. In the United States inventors were also busy planning the construction of steam road carriages, e.g. Evans (1787), Read (1790); but it was not till 1804 that the first American road locomotive was built by Evans. Two years before this Trevithick and Vivian constructed a machine which they ran with success on the roads of London, attaining a speed of 8 or 9 miles per hour. The trials, however, were not continued, maybe on account of the bad state of the roads, and Trevithick turned his inventive genius to other experiments.

Some years after this the state of the roads was greatly improved, and a fresh impetus was given to mechanical road traction. During the period 1821–40 numerous patents were filed and many steam carriages were built and put into operation on the ordinary roads. Patents were taken out by Griffiths (1821), Gordon (1822), Burstall and Hill (1824), James (1824 and 1825), Gurney (1825, 1826 and 1827), Hancock (1829), Scott Russell (1840), and others. Many of the earlier inventors thought that wheels would not give sufficient adhesion on the road surface for propulsion purposes, and they constructed their vehicles with legs imitating the action of a horse's feet and working on the principle of a punting pole. It soon came to be found, however, that plain wheels could be utilized, and nearly all the later or more successful machines were operated on this principle.

Many of the inventors confined their attention to experiment only, but Gurney, Hancock, Scott Russell, and a few others produced vehicles that were used for public services on ordinary roads.

As early as 1831 Hancock inaugurated a regular road service between Stratford and London. In the same year Sir Charles Dance, utilizing a steam coach built by Gurney, ran a regular service, four times a day, between Gloucester and Cheltenham for a period of four months, and during that time it covered over 3,500 miles and carried over 3,000 passengers.

In 1834 Scott Russell constructed six steam coaches and put them into regular operation between Glasgow and Paisley, a distance of 7½ miles. These worked on the route with considerable success and great regularity, but as a result of an accident caused by the breaking of a wheel they had to be taken off the road by order of the Court of Session.

For a number of years in the Metropolis, Hancock, undoubtedly the most successful of the early inventors, ran a fleet of several steam omnibuses, each of which seated from 14 to 22 passengers.[1] He put them on fairly constant service in the streets as early as 1832, which, be it noted, was but a few years later than the introduction for the first time of horse-drawn buses by Shillibeer (1829).

Some of his coaches ran longer journeys on occasion, as from London to Brighton, London to Reading, etc.

It is interesting to notice that practically all of these early mechanical vehicles were designed and utilized for the conveyance of passengers. They were in effect the ordinary stage coach adapted for mechanical propulsion, the boiler generally being placed at the back and the engine either there or under the coach. It is a valid generalization that all forms of transport are first utilized for the carriage of high-grade traffic, often passengers, because it is only

[1] In Young's *Steam on Common Roads* (1860) Hancock is stated to have constructed the following vehicles :—

Experimental carriage, seating four outside, exclusive of steersman, engineer and fireman.

Infant carriage, seating ten outside, exclusive of steersman, engineer and fireman.

Infant carriage (enlarged), seating fourteen outside, exclusive of steersman, engineer and fireman.

Era carriage, seating sixteen inside, two out, exclusive of steersman, engineer and fireman.

Enterprise carriage, seating fourteen inside, exclusive of steersman, engineer and fireman.

Autopsy carriage, seating nine inside, five out.

Erin carriage, seating eight inside, six out.

German drag carriage, seating six inside, others in drawn wagon.

Automaton carriage, seating twenty-two outside.

Steam phaeton (for private use).

such traffic that can afford to bear the cost at the initial stages, and to this generalization the history of mechanical road transport is no exception.

In 1831 a Committee of the House of Commons was appointed to investigate the subject of steam carriages on common roads and to consider, amongst other matters, the question of tolls imposed on steam carriages.[1] They reported that the introduction of mechanical power for road vehicles was one of the most important improvements ever introduced in the means of internal communication, and they considered that its practicability had been fully established. They stated also that they were convinced that the tolls enforced on steam carriages were excessive, and that legislative protection should be introduced to protect the new form of locomotion with the least possible delay. Nothing, however, was done by Parliament, and a Bill to give effect to the Committee's recommendations was rejected.

In view of the measure of success achieved by the new vehicles, it may seem strange that after 1840 no further attempts were made to develop the new form of transport, and that, on the contrary, the mechanically operated carriage disappeared from our roads, not to be revived till the end of the century.

The reasons are to be found in the hostility of the rural interests, the indifference of the public, the growth of railways, along with the exorbitant tolls charged on such vehicles by the Turnpike Trusts.

As regards the amount of the tolls, which did more than anything else to strangle the new system in its early days, Gurney, in his evidence before the Committee of 1831, gave the following examples : On the Ashburton and Totnes road his steam carriage would have to pay £2, while a four-horse coach would only pay 5s. On the Liverpool and Prescot road a stage coach paid 4s., but the steam carriage had to pay £2 8s.

[1] This Select Committee was appointed to inquire into "the present state and future prospects of land carriage by means of wheeled vehicles propelled by steam or gas on common roads."

As a consequence of the early failure to establish steam carriages, practically nothing further was done in this country between 1840 and 1895, except in the direction of the evolution of the cumbrous traction engine, stringently limited as to its activities by the law, but from 1861 protected against excessive tolls. For the development of the lighter motor vehicle we have to thank the engineers and experimenters of France and other countries, where legislation was not so oppressive as that enforced in Britain by the Acts of 1861 and 1865. (For an account of this legislation see below.)

In 1873 Bollée, a Frenchman, built a steam car, and in 1880 constructed an omnibus that embodied several improvements over his first vehicle.

From about 1890 attention was turned to the utilization of some means of propulsion other than steam, and the adoption of electricity and internal combustion engines began to be experimented with.

When Gottlieb Daimler in 1884 constructed his epoch-making light internal combustion engine, the first step in the evolution of the modern petrol motor vehicle may be said to have been taken. Not long after an experimental motor bicycle was built and fitted with one of Daimler's engines. About the same time a petrol-driven tricycle was constructed independently by Benz in 1885. In 1891 a motor car was built by Panhard and Lavassor, who had acquired the rights to build Daimler engines in France and Belgium.

In these early days the motor vehicle was necessarily an expensive vehicle, and only the wealthy enthusiast or the large firm recognizing a good advertising medium could afford to own one. However, the motor soon grew in popularity, and by 1895 a considerable number were in operation on the streets of Paris. The success of the motor vehicle was due not a little to the adoption of the pneumatic tyre, first introduced, it would appear, by R. W. Thomson of Edinburgh, and later commercially adapted for the bicycle and motor by the Dunlop firm.

In Britain restrictive legislation hindered the development of motor transport, though in spite of it a number of vehicles were running in 1894. A strong agitation against the restrictions was commenced, and in 1896 a certain measure of success was obtained, and again in 1903 a further instalment of reform in the law was achieved after renewed agitation.

An important factor in the subsequent development of the motor in Britain was the popularity already achieved by the ordinary bicycle. The cycle pioneered the way for the motor, for it opened up the roads to through traffic. The main routes had become almost deserted except for purely local traffic since the decay of the stage coach. The established position of the cycle industry gave a basis for the new manufacture of motor cycles and cars.

The modern cycle dates back only to 1867, though the "dandy horse," or velocipede, was introduced in 1770. In 1870 the invention of the low or "safety bicycle," and in 1888 the adoption of the pneumatic tyre, gave a great stimulus to the use of cycles. In the years 1895–97 a great boom took place in cycle manufacture, and though a slump followed till 1900, a very considerable addition was made to the ranks of the cyclists, and the now popular machine was to be seen in thousands on the roads throughout the country. The cyclist devotees of the open road provided a large number of recruits for the mechanical mount.

To return to the road motor, in 1900 a London–Edinburgh and return trial of 1,000 miles was arranged, which occupied eleven days, and the journey was successfully completed by twenty cars, a striking demonstration of the reliability of the new method of transport for those days.

From 1900 to 1914 the development of the motor cycle, the private motor car and the taxi-cab proceeded rapidly. They soon became a common method of travel for pleasure or business purposes among those who could afford them, instead of being novelties rather resented by the general public. In the year 1911–12, for instance, there were 175,588 motor vehicles licensed in England and Wales.

In the same period the motor omnibus also increased greatly in popularity. Even as early as 1904 several such vehicles were running in London and elsewhere. During the years 1911 and 1912 a very large number of new vehicles were put into operation in and around London, while by 1913 the capital invested in motor buses in the Metropolis alone was about four million pounds.

2. The Evolution of the Highway.

Turning now to consider the history of road transport, not from the point of view of the vehicle, but from that of the highways, it will be found that it is a valid historical generalization to state that the introduction of a new method of road usage leads to bitter quarrels between the new users and those responsible for road maintenance. There is indeed no better approach to the study of present-day problems of the road than by way of a historical survey, but the limits of space and proportion forbid us to linger in this interesting field and the briefest summary must suffice.[1]

The new users of the roads have one after the other demanded a new and better standard of road construction and repair. "The roads," they have declared, "must be made to suit the traffic."

But, on the other hand, those who had to maintain the roadway have demanded that the new vehicles should be made to suit the existing roads or else be denied admission to the fraternity of the King's highway. Bitter has been the opposition, loud and prolonged the complaints. The new vehicles go at excessive speeds, they create dust, they destroy the roads, they are a danger to life and limb.

Yet in the end the new methods have generally won the day despite restrictive legislation. In the end the roads have had to be accommodated to the new traffic. We witness

[1] On the whole subject see S. and B. Webb, *Story of the King's Highway*; and Pratt, *Inland Transport and Communication in England*.

a gradual improvement in road construction and the setting up of a new standard of maintenance. Thus in the seventeenth century the coming of the wheeled vehicle, and in the eighteenth century the great expansion in its use, evolved a storm of opposition.

Though they may have sufficed in earlier times for the horsemen, the droves of cattle or the pack-horse, the narrow, stone-paved causeways or the soft unmade roads were quite unsuited to the new traffic. Faced with innumerable and angry petitions, Parliament, sorely perplexed, passed a bewildering series of Highway Acts restricting the new road users.

Eventually a way out was found by means of Turnpike Trusts, with statutory powers to levy tolls. The turnpikes, it is true, were lax in their finance, burdensome and restrictive in practice, unconsolidated, unco-ordinated and decidedly unpopular—witness the Rebecca Riots of 1842–43 in South Wales, when numerous toll-gates and toll-houses were demolished—yet, despite all their faults, they did help to provide the new highways so urgently required. The problem of road-building was solved for the time by the labours of Sir Henry Parnell,[1] Telford,[2] and Macadam,[3] just before the railways began to supersede the coach and

[1] Sir Henry Parnell (1776–1842), an Irish M.P. and author of a *Treatise on Roads* (1833), as well as of several other works, notably one on Financial Reform, did a great deal to improve the standard of road administration His *Treatise on Roads* was for a long time the authoritative account of the subject.

[2] Thomas Telford (1757–1837), son of an Eskdale shepherd, became a celebrated engineer. He is best known as the constructor of the Suspension Bridge over the Menai Strait, and achieved fame as a road constructor in Scotland and as the builder of the Holyhead Road. A believer in a solidly constructed roadway, with firm foundations, his method had the disadvantage at the time of being more costly than that popularized by Macadam.

[3] James Loudon Macadam (1756-1836), perhaps the best known of the nineteenth-century road-makers, did a great deal to improve road-building. The "Macadamized road" has become known to everyone, though he did not invent the method, nor does the present type of construction follow his specifications. He believed in building a good *surface*, formed from small broken angular stones, without water or mud binding. His roads had the great advantage of being cheap to construct.

stage-wagon proprietors. The new methods of road construction furnished both the technical and financial solutions that were required.

The opposition to the steam coaches in their early days has been described, but in the last century not even the humble and inoffensive cyclist escaped. To us of a younger generation the opposition against this new intruder on the King's highways seems incredible. The cyclist was a pest, he "scorched," he raised clouds of dust, he frightened horses, he was a nuisance on the highway and a danger to the King's lieges. Not till 1895, indeed, can it be said that he obtained a secure place on the road.

The opposition to the motor car in its early years, and a little later to the motor bus, is the history of our own times, and since the war the old worn debate between road user and maintainer has received new zest, consequent on the expansion of the motor transport industry and especially of the heavy commercial motor.

3. The Evolution of Legislation.

The development of road transport is bound up with the development of the laws and regulations relating to our highways, and consequently no account of road transport can be complete unless some notice be taken of the highway laws. The development of mechanical road transport in Britain has been circumscribed, hindered, and retarded by laws framed under earlier and consequently different conditions, and therefore unsuited to changes in the method of road transportation. It is thus that the slow development of road motors is to be explained in Britain, and hence it was that the pioneer work was largely undertaken in other countries where the laws looked with less disfavour on any new use of the highways.

But not only has the law reacted on the progress of mechanical road traction, the development and actual achievements of road motors have also reacted on the law. The new traffic has gradually led to changes in the law, and has obtained amendments to the law that have given it a legal right, and not merely a right on sufferance, to the use of the King's highway.

For an account of the earlier struggles between road user, road maintainer and landlord for legal recognition of their respective rights or duties the reader must be referred to *The Story of the King's Highway* and to Professor Cannan's *History of Local Rates*, as here only the evolution of the law in regard to mechanically propelled road vehicles can be traced.

The earliest recognition by Parliament of the presence of mechanical vehicles on the roads would appear to have been in 1831, when the Select Committee of the House of Commons was appointed to inquire into "the present state and future prospects of land carriage by means of wheeled vehicles propelled by steam or gas on common roads," and to investigate the tolls imposed on such vehicles by the Turnpike Trusts.[1]

It was not till thirty years after this that the first general statute dealing with mechanical road transport was passed. This was the Locomotive Act, 1861, and was framed for the heavier type of steam road engine—the precursors of the traction and agricultural engines—that were since 1840 the only type of mechanical traction utilizing the roads. The Act presumed that all road power-driven vehicles were of the traction engine type, and limited speed to a maximum of 10 miles per hour, and in villages or towns to 5 miles per hour. Their weight was not to exceed 12 tons, and other provisions were inserted relating to width, wheels, number of attendants, and the use of bridges. Protection against excessive tolls, however, was granted by a section of the Act.

Later certain amendments were made by the Locomotives Act, 1865, and again in 1875 by other legislation.

The Act of 1865 reduced the maximum speed allowable from 10 to 4 miles per hour, while in towns or villages

[1] Shortt Committee Report, Cmd. 5. 1918

2 miles per hour was not to be exceeded. Further, every locomotive was to be in charge of three persons, one of whom was to walk in front carrying a red flag. By the Acts of 1878 powers were given to local authorities to recover the expenses caused through damage to roads by "excessive weight" or "extraordinary traffic."

The effect of this restrictive legislation was to hinder the evolution of the light mechanical vehicle, since it was treated exactly in the same manner as the cumbrous traction engine, and no advantage could be obtained from its possible speed, as the legal maximum was 4 miles per hour.

In 1898 another Locomotives Act was passed as a result of the increased use of roads by traction engines. By this Act certain roads and bridges could be closed to road locomotives.

Before the passing of this last Act, however, the light locomotive or motor car gained legal recognition as the result of a vigorous and prolonged agitation. By an Act of 1896—the so-called "Magna Carta" of the motorist—relaxations in favour of lighter vehicles were made in the regulations as to the use of roads. Many of the more stringent provisions of earlier legislation were now removed, for by this Act—the Locomotives on Highways Act, 1896—the "light locomotive" was granted special privileges. Speeds up to 14 miles per hour might be allowed provided that the vehicle was not used for drawing more than one trailer and that the unladen weight was under 3 tons and that no smoke or visible vapour was emitted except from accidental or temporary causes. If a trailer was drawn the combined unladen weight was not to exceed 4 tons.

To the Local Government Board in England and Wales and the Secretary for Scotland was left the duty of prescribing detailed regulations. These regulations were subsequently issued in 1896, and dealt with such matters as width, brakes, tyres and conditions of use. As regards speed, a limit of 12 miles per hour was imposed instead of the permissible 14, and for vehicles of unladen weight greater than $1\frac{1}{2}$ tons, or where a trailer was utilized, still lower speed limits were enforced.

As a result of the passing of this Act a great increase took place in motor traffic, and a fresh agitation was commenced by the motorists and others to secure amendment of the law as it stood. On the one hand motor manufacturers and users declared that the Act was too oppressive. On the other it was complained that the new transport was dangerous and a nuisance to other road users and that the regulations laid down were not obeyed.

To meet these various demands a new Act—The Motor Car Act, 1903—was passed, and in this the "light locomotive" of 1896 is now recognized as the "motor car." This statute still remains the basis of the present legislation that determines and regulates the use of motor cars on our roads, though now a further agitation is under way with the object of obtaining amendments and consolidation of the law and regulation of motor transport that will bring the legal requirements more into accordance with the recent developments of road transport.

The main provisions of the 1903 Act are as follows: A maximum speed of 20 miles per hour was imposed, though in certain cases, e.g. through villages, lower limits could be enforced. On narrow roads not exceeding 16 feet in width motor cars could be prohibited. To meet the objections brought against motor cars, it was deemed under Section 1 of the Act a legal offence to drive "recklessly or negligently, or at a speed or in a manner which is dangerous to the public, having regard to all the circumstances of the case, including the nature, condition and use of the highway and to the amount of traffic which actually is at the time, or which might reasonably be expected to be, on the highway."

Under this Act all motor cars were required to be registered and drivers licensed by County Councils or County Boroughs in England and Wales, and by County Councils or certain Burghs in Scotland.

The Local Government Board and the Secretary for Scotland were authorized by the Act to increase by regulations the permissible maximum unladen weight of motor cars and to impose special limitations on the speed of the heavier vehicles over 2 tons unladen weight.

After a report was presented by a Departmental Committee this clause of the Act was given effect to in 1904 by the Heavy Motor Car Order, 1904. In this Order the "heavy motor car" is differentiated from its smaller brethren, and is defined as a vehicle which exceeds 2 tons unladen weight, but which does not come into the category of "road locomotives."

By this Order the permissible unladen weight was raised from the 3 tons of the 1896 Act to 5 tons, or, where a trailer was utilized, to a maximum combined unladen weight of 6½ tons, in substitution of the former limit of 4 tons. In no case, however, was the total weight of vehicle and load together to exceed 12 tons, and special provisions were laid down as to axle weights, which were not to exceed 8 tons on any axle, or, in the case of a trailer, 4 tons.

A variety of other restrictions were also imposed, and these dealt with wheels, tyres, width, use of bridges, etc., while maximum speeds of 5, 8 and 12 miles per hour were fixed for these heavy vehicles, dependent on the weight of the vehicle and the nature of its tyres.

Since 1904 a number of other Orders have been issued; for instance, those of 1907 and 1911, the former dealing with the use of bridges by heavy motor cars and the latter with military motor cars.

During the period of the war the Local Government (Emergency Provisions) Act, 1916, imposed temporary restrictions, since withdrawn, on the use of roads by certain vehicles. No motor bus was to be put into service on a new route without the consent of the highway authorities concerned, and this consent might be given upon conditions. The object of this regulation was to prevent the growth of road traffic, as road maintenance was difficult and expensive owing to shortage of labour and materials. It became general for local authorities to charge for their consent, as they could do under the Act, on a mileage basis, i.e. so much per bus-mile run, varying in practice from three-eighths of a penny to threepence or more, as a contribution towards road maintenance.

By the Roads Act, 1920, and the Provisional Regulations made under it—the Heavy Motor Car (Amendment) Order, 1921—the maximum unladen weight was increased from 5 to 7¼ tons, or for a heavy motor car and trailer from 6½ tons to 9¾ tons.

By another Order the maximum weight of "locomotives" (e.g. traction engines) was raised from 14 tons to 15½ tons, with certain further increases in special cases, e.g. cable ploughing machines, those carrying permanent fittings as cranes, dynamos, etc., or those fitted with rubber or resilient tyres.

The Finance Act, 1920, made considerable modification of the former regulations concerning motor cars, but these need not be recapitulated here, as they are dealt with under the heading of Taxation.

In 1922, by the Heavy Motor Car (Amendment) Order of that year, the six-wheeler was given a definite legal position and axle loads and permissible load considerably increased.[1]

4. The History of the Tramway.

A brief account of the development of the tramway seems called for, since the tramway is a road user, though in other respects its nature and economic characteristics are more akin to the railway.

The modern street tramway was first employed in the United States, though in this country "tramways" were utilized for the haulage of coal from pits to the docks or canal wharves at a much earlier date. "Tramways" or

[1] For a more detailed survey of Legislation see the excellent account given in the Shortt Report, Cmd. 5, 1918, and in the 1922 Report of the Departmental Committee on the Taxation and Regulation of Road Vehicles (Second Interim Report).

"rail-ways" were indeed laid down in the early years of the seventeenth century.

In America during the first part of the nineteenth century the streets and roads of the large towns and cities were in a very bad condition, and this gave a great impetus to the construction of passenger-carrying tramways, just as did the poor state of the highways in Britain at the commencement of the industrial revolution of the eighteenth century, when the early tramways were developed as a means of improving goods haulage.

The New York and Haarlem line was the pioneer of the American passenger-carrying tramways. The first section, running through the main streets, was opened in 1832, but it proved unpopular, and it was some time before the idea was revived. Tramways, however, were constructed in large numbers in New York and other American cities from about the middle of the nineteenth century. The poor condition of roads and streets, the long distances to be traversed, and the scarcity of other vehicles all combined to popularize the tramway, despite the fact that at first the rails were of formidable proportions. One witness indeed went so far as to describe them as "rails which have a sort of iron gutter attached to each on their inside edge."

In Britain the modern passenger tramway was introduced by Train at Birkenhead in 1860. The early experiments, however, did not meet with much success, because the projecting rails were troublesome and dangerous to other traffic, for as yet the modern type of grooved tramway rail laid flush with the roadway had not been evolved. Further, the conditions that favoured the American tramways did not operate in Britain, since by the mid-nineteenth century the roads were fairly good and cabs and omnibuses were in common use.

In the 'seventies, however, the rails were considerably improved and the number of tramways laid down increased greatly in a few years. All the earlier tramways were operated by horse, but it was not long before attempts were made to utilize mechanical traction. The first steam car was constructed in America for the Cincinatti tramways in 1859, and in 1860 steam power was employed on five or six systems.

In Britain after 1870 the steam car was frequently adopted, while on the Continent the steam tramway still retains a prominent place in street transportation. Steam power, however, was found to have several important disadvantages for the purpose of street locomotion, especially as the modern refinements as are now fitted to the road "steamer" of the motor vehicle type had not been evolved. The steam trams were noisy, they emitted overmuch smoke and sparks, and they frightened horse traffic, consequently attention was turned towards the substitution of other types of mechanical motive power. The hot-water locomotive—such as is still employed in oil refineries, brickette factories, and other dangerous areas—attained a fair degree of popularity. The working of the hot-water locomotive depends on the phenomenon that steam will be spontaneously formed in a boiler filled with water heated previously to a high temperature and kept under high pressure if the pressure is released through the opening of the regulator. Though they suffered from certain disadvantages, these fireless locomotives were not open to the objections brought against the orthodox type when used for street traffic.

Other kinds of motive power also obtained some degree of popularity, for instance, compressed air and ammonia gas. Tramways propelled by underground cable secured a considerable vogue, and in certain towns they have been utilized up to the present day, e.g. in parts of Melbourne, and till very recently Edinburgh. The cable is operated from a central power house, while each car is furnished with a "gripper" attachment.

The introduction of electric power led to the rapid supersession of most other systems, and it gave a great impetus to tramways. Power was supplied to the tramcars either by overhead trolley or conduit system. Surface contact systems were also experimented with, as this method seemed cheaper than the conduit system and, like it, did not interfere with the amenities of the streets. It had, however, the great disadvantage of necessitating complex automatic switch gear to cut the contacts in and out as a car passed. Obviously it would be dangerous to leave live contacts exposed on the roadway. Nowadays the overhead trolley system is all but universal.

The first line to be operated on the overhead trolley system was at Kansas City in 1884, while in this country the method was introduced in 1891 on the Leeds system, and after the experience thus gained it was adopted in many other towns and cities.

Tramway Legislation.—The basis of tramways' legislation in Britain is still the Act of 1870, entitled "An Act to facilitate the Construction and to regulate the Working of Tramways." Framed at a time when horse-drawn trams were practically the only type as yet evolved, this Act has been of the first importance in shaping and conditioning the development of our tramways. For the tramways it was unfortunate that the Act was drafted at a time when local authorities were aggrieved with the water and gas companies because it was asserted that the charges imposed by the companies were extortionate and that they could not buy the companies out except at an excessive price. To the local authorities it seemed that the tramways were yet another "monopoly," which must be prevented from achieving the same position as the gas or water companies.

Consequently a provision was inserted in the Act by which the assent of the local and road authorities had to be obtained before a tramway could be constructed. Further, the original concession was only to be granted for a period of twenty-one years, after which, or at the end of any subsequent period of seven years, the local authorities were to have the option of purchasing the tramway at its then value. The limitation of tenure was of less importance in the days of horse-drawn trams because the capital outlay was not very great and the horses could be sold for a fair price ; but with the introduction of electric traction the clause tended to retard conversion to the newer method and hastened on municipalization. Electric traction would involve a very considerable outlay of capital, but a company could only expect to earn dividends on it for twenty-one years, or, if their tenure was partially expired before conversion, for a shorter period, because at the expiry of the concession their system could be purchased at " scrap iron " rates.

Towards the end of a tenure it has been general to find that systems were allowed to fall into a neglected state, as the companies would grudge any additional expenditure on which they would not obtain an adequate return.

The veto on construction possessed by the local authorities has sometimes led to unnecessary expenditure and the placing of difficulties in the way of tramway construction. In some places the veto has been used to obtain terms from the companies, which have had to undertake extensive street widenings and improvements, while in a few notorious cases the local authorities have greatly abused this power of veto.

These provisions of the 1870 Act were responsible for stimulating the municipalization of tramway systems. In the Act itself it was assumed that while local authorities might construct or acquire tramways, the operation of any system so constructed would be leased out to private companies very much in the manner at present prevalent in France and certain other countries. Till 1882 this was indeed the general rule, and in many large cities, e.g. Manchester, Glasgow, Liverpool, Birmingham, etc., the Corporation leased out their lines to private companies for an annual rent. Huddersfield, however, found itself in 1882 in the unhappy position of having constructed a tramway which no one would lease. Eventually Parliament allowed the Board of Trade to license the Corporation to operate the system itself. Ten years later the plan was made general, and the " Huddersfield Clause " could be inserted in any Act authorizing the construction of a tramway. In 1896 all restraints were removed and local authorities became free to operate or construct in their area either by Private Act or Provisional Order.

To return now to the other provisions of the 1870 Act, the important clauses relating to road maintenance have next to be considered. The Act lays down that a tramway must maintain not only the space between the rails but also 1 foot 6 inches on either side, and in such a manner that the top of the rails are on a level with the road surface. If a double track is laid down the roadway between the two sets of rails must be kept in repair. In the event of a tramway being abandoned, the roadway must be reinstated to as good a state as it was before the tramway was constructed.

The Act, however, also conferred certain benefits as well as imposed the disabilities before mentioned. Promoters were granted the exclusive use of their tramway and the requisite procedure for obtaining powers to construct was simplified and cheapened. It was no longer essential to procure a Private Act, for now a Provisional Order may be granted by the Board of Trade (since 1919 by the Ministry of Transport), which, on formal confirmation by Parliament, has the same force as a Private Act.

During recent years the process of transferring tramways from private to municipal ownership has gone on continuously, and the various local authorities have made considerable use of the powers obtained in 1870 and 1896. A Ministry of Transport Return for 1922 shows that of 250 tramway undertakings in Great Britain, 170 were owned and operated by municipalities and only 80 by private companies. Of a total route mileage of 2,579 miles open for traffic, 1,756 were worked by local authorities and only 823 by companies in that year. The municipalities are thus the chief operators of tramways in this country. In America company ownership and operation is the more common by far, while on the Continent both private and public ownership are to be found, though in some countries, notably Germany, the municipalities lease out the working to companies.

CHAPTER III

THE RECENT DEVELOPMENT OF ROAD TRANSPORT

BETWEEN 1900 and 1914 considerable progress had been made by mechanical road transport, but this was chiefly in the direction of passenger vehicles. The private car, the motor cycle, the taxi-cab and the motor bus had become well-established users of our highways.

The development of commercial road haulage of merchandise, however, was much slower. Indeed, little was done except by some few traders for delivery purposes, by a few road haulage contractors and by certain railway companies, e.g. the North-Eastern, the Great North of Scotland, and the Lancashire and Yorkshire Railways. The early utilization of road transport by the railways is interesting in view of the recent agitations concerning road powers for the railways. Some of these road services were established almost twenty years back, and were utilized as feeders to the railway system catering not only for passengers but also for goods, parcels and mails.

Contrasting present conditions with those of the years previous to 1914, none can fail to perceive the very striking increase in road transport of goods and merchandise as well as of passengers. Formerly practically all goods traffic went by rail, the only competitors the railways had to fear were the coasting vessels on certain traffic routes, horse cartage on the shortest journeys, and the very limited rivalry of the canals. But since the Armistice the road has come into its own again, and a very considerable volume of goods traffic has been carried by the new enterprises.[1]

In the Report of the 1922 Traffic Census issued in 1924 by the Ministry of Transport, interesting statistics are given which clearly indicate the considerable volume of mechanical road vehicles that utilize Class I roads. Though in pre-war years there was no comprehensive traffic census, yet some figures are available for the years 1910–11 when the Road Board obtained statistics of traffic on certain roads. In nearly all cases where these figures are available a great increase is observable in the amount of road traffic, and in every case the proportion of horse traffic shows an absolute decrease. To quote from the Report: "The records secured by the Road Board prior to the war make it possible in a few isolated cases to obtain some idea of the increase in the weight of traffic by road during the past ten years. For example: At a point on the London–Folkestone Road (A 20) between Eltham and Sidcup the weight of traffic has increased from 2,519 tons per day in 1910 to 5,609 in 1922, and the proportion due to mechanically propelled vehicles has risen from 41 to 95 per cent.

"Still more striking are the figures for a point at Sankey Bridges, near Warrington, on the Liverpool–Manchester Road (A 57). Here the increase in tonnage between 1911 and 1922 has been from 1,167 to 8,250 tons per day, and the proportion due to mechanically propelled vehicles has risen from 26 to 98 per cent.

"Again in a rural area such as Hensingham in Cumberland, on the Carlisle–Whitehaven–Dalton-in-Furness Road (A 595), though the weight of traffic has only increased from 560 to 826 tons per day, the increase in the proportion due to

[1] As an indication, though, of course, not an exact measurement of this growth, the number of concerns operating road vehicles (goods or passenger) that are recorded in the *Motor Transport Year Book* may be cited.

Year.	Number of Undertakings.	Year.	Number of Undertakings.
1916	331	1920	800
1918	395	1921–22	1,888
1919	486	1922–23	2,406

mechanically propelled vehicles is from a mere 14 per cent. in 1911 to 91 per cent. in 1922."

The figures available in other cases show a very definite increase in the number of vehicles and the tonnage passing by the census points as well as a marked decline in the number of horse vehicles. Thus at a point on road A 1 in Durham the average daily number of vehicles is shown to have increased from just under 400 in 1912 to about 1,250 in 1922. The number of horse-drawn vehicles shows a decrease from about 220 to 100.[1]

In the same Report the approximate number of motor vehicles in use in the calendar year 1922 is given as 979,000, and of these 378,000 were motor cycles, 315,000 private cars taxed on horse power, and 151,000 commercial goods vehicles, while motor hackneys account for 78,000. For the calendar year 1921 it has been estimated elsewhere that the total number of mechanically propelled vehicles was about 874,000. In 1908 there were about 12,000 commercial vehicles and 17,000 private cars. It must, however, be borne in mind that it is impossible to give exact figures because a considerable number of licences that are issued are quarterly or part year, and so it is only possible to estimate approximately the number of vehicles to which the licence figures refer.

As a guide to the considerable increase of road vehicles the following table (see page 38) of the number of licences issued may be of interest.

In 1921 the value of the licences issued totalled £9,735,832, while in 1922 the total proceeds of motor taxation rose to £11,013,861, and in 1923 it increased still further to £12,757,550, the basis of taxation being unchanged throughout the period.[2]

What reasons are to be assigned for this great and rapid advance in the utilization of road transport ?

[1] See diagram in Appendix V of the Report for further examples.

[2] The latest Ministry of Transport Return for the nine months, January to August, 1924, shows that 1,312,357 motor vehicles were licensed in that period. Of these 203,156 were commercial goods vehicles. The nine months revenue amounts to £13,892,879.

The war may be said to have demonstrated the possibilities of the modern road vehicle. Motor lorries were utilized in great numbers both in the war areas and at home, and indeed at times motor services were responsible for the complete victualling of the forces and for the supply of material, ammunition, fodder, etc., between the railhead and the troops over very long distances after a rapid advance. Under very adverse conditions, motor lorries rendered valuable and indeed indispensable services.

In 1919 the prestige gained during the war by motor traction was still further enhanced as a result of the important work performed by fleets of road vehicles during the railway strike. The work of food distribution was

	Estimated Number of Vehicles for which Licences were issued.		
	1921.	1922.	1923.
Motor cars	250,000	293,740	382,538
Cycles	355,000	352,340	391,097
Invalid vehicles	332	384	506
Commercial goods	135,000	158,856	181,235
Road locos., etc.	2,600	2,268	1,981
Motor ploughs, etc. ..	18,100	17,293	17,018
Motor tractors	1,550	1,301	1,420
Motor hackneys	76,000	72,263	78,358
Tramcars	13,583	13,797	14,147
General trade licences ..	10,000	9,527	11,989
Exempt vehicles	11.500	11,539	13,032

successfully carried out during the period of the strike by motor vehicles, and thus the latent possibilities of road transport became evident to commercial men. In short, the exigencies of the last few years have revolutionized road transport.

After the war, many persons turned to mechanical road haulage, and the new industry obtained a remarkable stimulus during the short boom period that followed the Armistice.

Another important factor that helped to establish the road haulage of goods on a wide scale was the dislocated state of the railways, the continued congestion due to shortage of rolling stock, and the high rates imposed on freight as a result of the disturbance of the war years. For a time, indeed, road transport could operate at lower rates than the railways for many classes of commodities that were placed not too low in the railway classification lists.

The provision of the necessary motor vehicles was facilitated by large sales of army surplus stock, while personnel was easily obtainable since during war-time large numbers of men had been trained in motor driving and repair. Moreover, road transport work was an enterprise congenial to many returned soldiers.

Post-war development, it is hardly necessary to state, has not been confined to goods carriage. Since the Armistice, passenger services by road—either motor bus or motor coach—have received a remarkable stimulus, and are now to be found in nearly every district, urban and rural. The motor coach or charabanc is practically a post-war development, and it appears to have secured public favour to a marked degree, especially at holiday resorts, though some part of its early popularity must no doubt be ascribed to its novelty.

The rapid development of these various forms of road transport—motor bus, motor coach and motor lorry—was at first somewhat artificial. Many new ventures, some of them on the smallest scale and run by men quite new to the business, were started, and not always where conditions were suitable. Competition became acute in consequence, and complaints about "rate cutting" below an economic level became frequent, for many of the new-comers in order to attract traffic to themselves quoted rates so low that only direct or running expenses could possibly be covered. They made no allowance for overhead charges, depreciation or interest on capital. With the bursting of the short-lived trade boom that followed the Armistice, the setting in of the prolonged trade depression, as it is natural to expect, had severe reactions on road transport, and many had to give up business. The industry of road transport, however, has been put on a more economic footing, and though the easy-profit making of the earliest period is now gone, the industry has continued to expand, and this expansion would be greatly increased if trade revived. In the face of the difficulties that have confronted motor transport operating concerns, it has been advocated that enterprises must resort to organization, if the difficulties are to be overcome. It is not, however, an easy matter to effect agreements as to rates among motor transport proprietors and contractors or to form combinations to prevent rate cutting, while to carry out the terms of such agreements when once they have been effected is still more difficult, as members are liable to break away or new competitors may arise. Any-one can put a vehicle on the road at but a small outlay of capital and thus compete with a combination.

Occasionally, it is true, combination may go farther, and a larger concern may obtain a practical monopoly, especially in the case of passenger traffic. In other cases a monopoly has been obtained in a few instances by municipalities. But in general it has not been found easy to obtain common action among a multiplicity of small firms. This is illustrated by the reports in motor journals of the frequent but not often successful attempts to bind owners of motor vehicles into some sort of Association that would regulate the rates charged and the condition of operation. In some districts, however, especially among motor coach proprietors, agreements as to rates and fares have been arrived at, and the rates fixed by the Association have been adhered to by the members. In others a greater or less degree of tacit agreement may occur, and no owner may be willing to go below the customary rates.

Freight Exchanges.—Organization in other directions, as, for example, freight exchanges, has not been so successful as might be expected. The freight exchange or road transport clearing house, as the name indicates, is simply an organization designed to provide return loads where possible, and otherwise co-ordinate the work of various road transport concerns. The idea is that these organizations would be able to put business men who required transport services in touch with those able to supply them, and especially to facilitate the obtaining of return loads for vehicles that otherwise might have to travel empty or half-loaded. The importance of providing some such organization that will eliminate unnecessary dead mileage on return journeys hardly requires to be stressed, as it is evident that otherwise much uneconomic operation will result. In the face of renewed railway competition the solution of the return freight problem is even more urgent to the road haulier.

The earliest attempts in this country to set up return load bureaux were, it would appear, the experimental offices set up during the war by the Road Transport Board (not to be confused, of course, with the Road Board, a totally different body). The Road Transport Board, of which Sir Evan Jones was Chairman, was set up in February 1918 to co-ordinate governmental road transport at home and to determine what measures were necessary to ensure the most economic use of road vehicles. The head office was established in London, while in addition local organizations were set up in various centres throughout the country. In all 84 Areas, each in charge of an Area Road Transport Committee, and grouped under 13 Divisional Road Transport Boards, were delineated. The chief problem before the Board was to meet a threatened disorganization of the transport of food, munitions and various materials of war, owing to a dangerous shortage of petrol and horse-provender. Hence their policy came to be one of eliminating, during the period of the war, all unnecessary use of transport due to overlapping or duplication of services. The efficiency of existing transport facilities was to be increased without increasing the number of vehicles on the road.

The Board therefore initiated schemes for the co-ordination of collections and deliveries of goods and, where possible, made provision for return loads, since economy demanded that where possible empty journeys or light loading should be eliminated. In particular the Board was forced to consider the question of the provision of return load bureaux or freight exchanges in the principal centres of the country. The first experiment in this direction was made about August 1918, when an office was opened at Bristol. It is recorded that in two months about 5,000 tons of goods were moved by utilizing transport that otherwise would have had to return empty or light.

Freight exchanges on similar lines were instituted at Birmingham, Coventry and the West Riding of Yorkshire, and in Manchester by the Chamber of Commerce.

After the Armistice the experiments of the Road Transport Board in building up a system of Clearing Houses were continued on commerical lines by private organizations or on a co-operative basis by local Chambers of Commerce. In the summer of 1920 an ambitious scheme was initiated by the Industrial Vehicle Section of the Automobile Association. Their aim was to establish a network of exchanges in five or six hundred districts by utilizing the services of the accredited agents of the Association. But the project did not meet with the success that was hoped for, and it has now, it would seem, been allowed to drop.

Several companies have been launched to provide clearing house facilities on commercial lines, while certain energetic Chambers of Commerce have made provisions to co-ordinate road transport work for their members in their own district. By 1920 road transport exchanges had been established by Chambers of Commerce at Manchester, Birmingham, Liverpool, Leicester, Nottingham, Bradford, Bristol, Sheffield, and several other towns. Of these latter, the outstanding example is that of the Nottingham Chamber of Commerce, whose venture has been attended with remarkable success, and has continued to transact a large volume of work, unlike some of the other ventures which have not maintained their operations on any scale. Since it is not run for profit, the commissions charged at Nottingham are only as much as is sufficient to defray administrative and office expenses.

Considerable difficulties have been found in the practical working of the various freight exchanges, though a few transact a large volume of business.

While it is only fair to mention that the good work of certain larger companies and Chambers of Commerce has not been called in question, yet many of the organizations have been subject from time to time to severe criticism, and against some exchanges strong expressions of disapproval have been uttered. On this matter a well-known transport periodical has expressed itself thus strongly and in measured terms: "The exchanges are liable to distribute traffic to suit their own purposes without regard to the interests of those engaged in the industry, of the working of which they do not possess a practical knowledge"; and again: "We are afraid that many of the clearing houses pay but little regard to the interests and welfare of the men who do the work, so long as they obtain their commission."

Many road haulage contractors dislike the exchanges because they fear that the establishment of such institutions may have the result of beating down return load rates, and this will react upon ordinary rates in those districts where return loads are sought, since what is a return load to an outside haulier is not one to a man established in the district. They assert that traders, manufacturers and others will only go to the trouble of seeking the aid of the exchanges if it is thought that the rates quoted will be lower.

From a different point of view the exchanges are also unpopular in certain circles. They are apt to be regarded with suspicion by the older and well-established road hauliers who are unwilling to encourage organizations that might aid their smaller rivals. The organization and the established position of the larger firm give it a great advantage and enable it to obtain return loads for its vehicles and to adjust journeys to the traffic available.

But whatever be the disadvantages and shortcomings of particular clearing houses, it is evident that some such organization to secure return loads is of the first importance, especially to the small man. Undoubtedly the problem of the return load is one of the most difficult that confronts road transport, for while it may be possible to obtain full loads both ways between large cities, it would not be so easy to build up organizations in less important centres. In this respect the railways have a considerable advantage over road transport concerns, for the railway organization is remarkably complete and can do much more to balance traffic requirements. Indeed, road transport in this respect is more akin to shipping than to rail. For instance, the cargo vessel often meets with a similar difficulty, and for return cargoes low rates or even ballast rates may be granted, if otherwise no traffic was offering. The possibility or the reverse of obtaining return cargoes has also an effect on the flow of shipping to the various world ports.

In road transport to make outward rates pay for returning empty is to exact a prohibitive charge for transit, and can only have the effect of turning traffic towards the railways.

In this respect road transport is not so well placed even as the cargo vessel, which can sometimes obtain rates that will compensate for the lack of return cargoes, since, unlike the road haulier, the tramp owner is not generally faced with the competition of an alternative type of transport. The road vehicle, however, can go to different parts of the country where traffic is to be had, though it is not quite so free in this respect as is the tramp steamer, since the latter is more self-complete, having quarters for the crew. The expenses of operating road vehicles mount up if the driver and mate are away from home, while garaging, overhaul and repair are also more expensive if the vehicles are operating at a distance from their base.

Unnecessary waste must be eliminated if road transport is to be put on an economic footing. To keep vehicles fully loaded all the time they are on the road means a reduction in the cost per ton-mile. For this purpose the great need of the time is adequate co-ordination and organization.

CHAPTER IV

ROAD TRANSPORT OF GOODS AND MERCHANDISE

1. The Sphere of Road Transport.

It is not easy to define the exact sphere that is to be assigned to the mechanical road haulage of merchandise, for its development is too recent, and, moreover, the peculiar conditions of the war and post-war period have somewhat obscured the issue between road transport and the alternative systems of transit.

It should be quite clear, however, despite the confident assertions of some enthusiasts to the contrary, that though road transport possesses certain important advantages, the railways are by no means likely to be superseded. Rail transport is quite capable of holding its own in regard to a large bulk of the traffic in this country. Facilities can be provided through the wide ramifications and the large scale of its operations that are impossible to other types of transport. For the carriage of certain classes of merchandise the railways are unrivalled, for example long-distance traffic; the movement of heavy commodities and low-grade traffic, especially if it passes in bulk. Even if substantial improvements be effected in mechanical road vehicles, the railways would still prove to be formidable competitors.

On the long haul, road transport cannot compete with the railway—except in the case of a few special commodities—since the speed of heavy road vehicles must be limited by law in the interest of public safety and to prevent excessive damage to road surfaces. But on the railway a muoh higher speed is practicable and tractive effort is more economically utilized, for a single powerful locomotive will carry many hundreds of tons. To take an exceptional case, compare this with the 12-ton load of a six-wheeler. and it should be obvious that the saving in labour cost alone per ton carried, is an important item. Nor can it be said that as yet the road vehicle is very economical either in running cost or in first cost when the limited load capacity is taken into account. Much possibly could be done by greater standardization of road vehicles and their parts, for this might lead to the economies of mass production and interchangeability of parts.

With the restored efficiency of the railways that is now under way, with improved organization and operation as a result of "grouping" and lower freight rates, there is little doubt that road hauliers will have to face renewed competition even in some of the fields they have made their own. Express freight services and a speeding up at terminals would greatly increase the advantages of the railways.

At the other end of the scale, the horse has not, as yet at any rate, been driven off the roads, though the new transport has greatly restricted the field for horse haulage. A motor vehicle represents a considerable capital outlay, and unless it is kept on the road, that capital is lying idle. Again, a petrol vehicle becomes expensive to run where stopping and starting are frequent. Motor vehicles are unsuitable and uneconomical where delays are frequent and where loading and unloading are responsible for much loss of time. Horse transport has the advantage where distances are very short, where streets are narrow and congested, where delays in loading and unloading are considerable, where traffic is too light to give full employment to a motor and where roads are very bad.

In some of these cases, however, especially where stopping and starting are frequent, the electric battery vehicle can be economically substituted for horse transport, and there is no doubt but that the development of the "electric" will lead to a further curtailment of the field suited to horse haulage. For example, in the house-to-house collection of refuse, many municipalities have turned to the electric vehicle, which is now tending to oust the old method of horse-cartage.

The position to be occupied by mechanical road haulage in our national system of transportation is thus seen to be an intermediate one For very short distances up to about 3 miles horse haulage is still in many cases the most economical. On the long haul the railway, on the other hand, has generally an advantage. The special field for mechanical road haulage would appear to lie between these two, and to be suited for distances up to about 30 miles or maybe longer, say up to 50 or 70 miles, where the traffic is suited to van loads and return cargo can be obtained. These figures must not, of course, be taken as true in all circumstances, for this is a subject on which it is impossible to dogmatize, because so much depends on the particular circumstances of each case.

2. The Advantages and Limitations of Road Transport.

Road transport possesses the great advantage of flexibility, for in this country the road leads everywhere. Rich is the legacy our ancestors have bequeathed us. The canal, the river and the railway, wide though the ramifications of the last-named, only provide facilities at special points or along the line of route. With these other systems there is a certain rigidity, since goods must be brought to the vehicle, but with road transport the vehicle can be brought to the goods and door-to-door services are possible. In consequence of this flexibility, road vehicles can pick up or deliver goods under more diverse conditions, and more easily than is possible with any other type of transport. Where traffic is seasonal, the flexibility of road transport is of great advantage. Thus, for example, Luton hat manufacturers have found the elasticity of road transport and the saving of time resulting from direct journeys between factory and market confer advantages of great importance. Their trade is largely dependent on the weather, and a few days of warm sunshine give a considerable stimulus to the industry, provided that the goods can be delivered in time before the weather changes.

Again, a road vehicle is free to go to any part of the country where traffic is to be had. A lorry utilized for the carriage of potatoes from Huntingdonshire may in the off season find remunerative work in transporting cabbages from Cambridgeshire. Sometimes, indeed, the same chassis is used for either passenger or goods according to seasonal demands by the simple device of changing the body. In the North Country this practice is said to be general among road-operating concerns.

As compared with the railways, mechanical road haulage possesses distinct advantages for the transport of moderate loads where the distance to be covered does not exceed, say, 30 to 50 miles. Where traffic is light, the road is the more economical form of transport, since a railway to achieve financial success requires a regular and fairly dense traffic, as otherwise sufficient revenue will not be earned to meet the heavy capital costs involved. In rural areas the traffic is often insufficient to justify the construction of even a light railway or "agrail." Yet the need for better transport facilities in such areas is immediate and urgent. But although the traffic may be quite insufficient to support a railway, it may suffice to give continuous and remunerative employment to a road motor.

Under certain conditions road transport may be more rapid and cheaper than rail for moderate distances. As regards saving of time, there is no loss due to the necessity of carting to and from stations, and terminal delays—incidental to rail traffic and often responsible for much wasted time—can be completely eliminated. Terminal delays on the railway are caused by waiting for full truck loads, the marshalling of wagons, transhipment and the like. Short distance traffic suffers proportionately more, since on the long haul the greater speed of the railway counterbalances these delays. To generalize, it may be said that the greater the time wasted by terminal delays on railways, the greater is the advantage of road transport. It has to be admitted, of course, that terminal delays may occur in road transport, either at loading point or destination, but it is not a parallel case to terminal delays on railways, since the latter are out with the control of the owner of the freight, and are occasioned by circumstances other than those connected with his business, while in any case rail transport generally involves cartage, and consequently the first class of terminal delay may operate as well as rail terminal delays.

Time may also be saved by road transport in other directions, since it is more amenable to direct control on the part of the consignor. Small lots sufficient for a van load can be sent off direct at any time, whereas with the railway the trains only depart at fixed times. For perishable commodities or to meet sudden demands, expeditious delivery is of the first importance.

The relative cost of road as compared with rail transport depends on a variety of circumstances. The principal factors that have to be taken into consideration can, however, be reduced to six in number. These are :—

(1) The length of the haul ;
(2) The possibility of obtaining return loads ;
(3) The liability of the goods carried to damage or pilferage ;
(4) The class of commodity to be transported ;
(5) The volume of traffic offering ; and
(6) The service rendered.

Considering these various factors in more detail, the first is of great importance, for it is quite clear that length of haul is in general the dominating consideration. As has already been stated, road transport can best compete with the railway on journeys of moderate length, say up to 50 miles, though it is impossible to give any exact limits, since the relative sphere of road and rail cannot yet be delineated with any exactitude. But though the question turns largely on the long versus the short haul, the position must needs be very disquieting to the railway companies, for in this country, unlike many other countries, the bulk of rail traffic is for short hauls only. On the other hand, while it be admitted that road and rail are to some extent competitive, it must be remembered that they are also partly complementary, and the growth of the traffic of the one tends to develop the traffic of the other. Road transport may act as a feeder to the railway system, and thus create as much or more traffic as it takes away. However, these considerations do not directly affect the question of relative cost, though in the long run they may become of paramount importance, for if a railway loses part of its traffic, the overhead charges become proportionately greater on what remains, and if the "standard revenue" fixed by the 1921 Railways Act is to be earned, freight rates might have to be raised.

To return to narrow considerations of cost, heavy lorries are slow when long distances are involved, owing to necessary limitations of speed, and, moreover, if the driver has to spend the night away from home, expenses begin to mount up. It is true that sometimes long journeys are undertaken, as, for instance, in the case of furniture removal, transport of motor tyres, sweets, etc. As the conditions under which these long journeys are undertaken emphasize the peculiar advantages of road transport, it may perhaps be instructive to go into a few details of furniture transport by road, for these demonstrate very clearly the type of considerations that determine the economy of road transport as compared with rail. In the case of furniture removal, distances up to 150 miles direct by road are often covered, while, indeed, journeys up to 400 miles or more are not unknown. Between

London and Newcastle, for instance, a regular weekly service is in operation. As compared with the older methods of furniture removal, road services offer great advantages, as it is often possible to give delivery on the same day as collection—a thing impossible with rail transport. The motor van scores over its competitors in convenience, economy, speed, reliability and the elimination of breakages. By rail or sea, careful and elaborate packing is essential, while expert packers may have to be sent to the destination to supervise unloading. In the case of road transport, much less elaborate packing is required, and the men can travel on the lorry.

To turn to the next factor, it requires no elaboration to prove that return loads must be arranged if road transport is to be provided at low cost. Hence traffic between important commercial centres, e.g. between Edinburgh and Glasgow, or between towns in closely settled manufacturing areas, e.g. in Lancashire or the Midlands, is usually well fitted to be carried on by road, since there is little difficulty in obtaining return loads. It is to promote economies of this nature that attempts have been made to organize a system of freight exchanges or clearing houses such as are described in the previous chapter.

In like manner road transport has been found very suitable and efficient for promoting the exchange of commodities between large towns and the surrounding country districts. Rural produce, such as milk, eggs, vegetables, etc., can be cheaply carried to the market and arrive there in fresher and better condition than if they were carried by rail. Return loads in the shape of manufactured commodities, farmers' requirements and the like, are generally obtainable, and thus otherwise dead mileage is eliminated.

In some types of transport work return loads are found ready to hand, and for transport of this nature road vehicles are well suited. Examples are those types of distributive work that necessitate the return of empties, e.g. petrol tins, biscuit tins, packing crates, etc. In other cases the raw materials required for manufacture may provide loads for vehicles returning to their starting town. For example, the motors that carry hats from Luton to the London market bring back millboard on their return journey. Where return loads are thus provided in one manner or another almost in the ordinary course of business, road transport is rendered the more economical, and can the more easily compete with alternative types of transport.

In regard to the third factor, liability of the goods carried to damage or pilferage, it should be noticed that claims against railway companies for damage or loss are a frequent cause of trouble and annoyance to traders. Under this heading considerable savings can be effected by utilizing road transport for easily damageable goods. Transhipments are eliminated, since road services go from door to door, and consequently considerable economy can be effected in the packing of such articles as fruit, groceries, aerated waters, sweets and other bottled goods, technical instruments, etc. Also there is less likelihood of pilferage, since the cargo is under the charge and control of the same man throughout the journey, and so responsibility can be determined and theft prevented. Many traders feel that the diminution in the number of claims for damage or loss and prolonged dispute is an important advantage in itself. Such savings often turn the scale in favour of road transport even if the cost is somewhat lower by rail. It has been found that goods of a very fragile nature, such as eggs, pastry, glass, etc., can be carried by road with practically no danger of breakage, while if vans specially fitted for the traffic are utilized no special packing may even be required. In the sphere of agricultural transport, the use of motor vehicles for bringing pedigree stock to market or to shows has marked advantages even if the cost be greater than by rail, since the stock does not lose the condition so necessary if good prices are to be obtained.

As regards the class of commodity carried, the higher a

commodity is placed in the railway's classification the more easily can the road compete. It is, of course, well known that railway rates are not flat rates of so much per ton per mile, applicable to all classes of goods, but on the contrary vary with the commodity carried.[1] Cost of service is naturally an element taken into consideration when tables of railway rates are drawn up, but speaking generally, the charges are largely based on "what the traffic can be expected to bear," i.e. in practice rates are fixed on the value of the article carried. The more valuable the commodity, the higher the rate. Now, it is obvious that those commodities which come into the highest classes on the railway's lists can be the more easily attracted to the road, provided only that they are not especially expensive to carry, due to such causes as great bulk in proportion to weight, etc. Among road hauliers who are in competition one with the other no classifications are adopted, and commodities are carried at rates approximating to cost of service.[2] The railways, indeed, complain that road hauliers select and choose their traffic, taking only the cream, but refusing to carry commodities of the lower classifications. The road haulage contractor is not a "common carrier," and so is not tied down to accept any commodity that may be offered for transport, even though he has not previously expressly announced that he will not convey that particular traffic.

Traders, manufacturers, wholesalers and others find the absence of a classification advantageous in several respects other than that of cost alone. It may simplify the keeping of accounts, since no elaborate check is required where flat

[1] For an account of Railway Rates, the reader should consult Acworth, *Elements of Railway Economics* and *The Railways and the Traders.* See also Colson, *Cours d'économie politique*, Livre sixième.

[2] Some variations, of course, will occur in road rates, since rates based on cost of service are not necessarily flat rates of so much per ton. For instance, some articles are very bulky in proportion to weight. Again, very valuable commodities involve greater risk, and so require a higher rate to cover the cost of insurance. Such rates, however, would not be differential charges, corresponding to railway classifications, because in these cases the cost of service is higher.

rates are charged per ton-mile irrespective of commodity. To traders such as large provision dealers and grocers who require transport for a considerable amount of miscellaneous merchandise, some savings may be effected, since they generally pay according to gross weight when their loads are sent by road.

The volume of traffic offering is an important consideration, since, though the flow of traffic may be too slight for a railway, it may be sufficient to remunerate a road motor service. Hence the motor van or lorry is especially suited to meet the requirements of rural areas.

As regards the last heading, quality of service, the special advantages of road transport may be of sufficient importance to outweigh even a greater cost of transport. It is often a great advantage to be able to have the goods delivered direct to the shop or warehouse. Transhipments are avoided and terminal delays eliminated, while, owing to our elaborate system of roads, places far removed from any railway station can be easily reached.

3. Road and Canal Competition.

In Britain the position occupied by inland water transport is far inferior to that of the railways. The canals suffer from obvious disadvantages, and, moreover, in Britain the canal system is badly organized, lacks uniformity, and is almost entirely unco-ordinated. Despite these disadvantages and the slow rate of transit, however, canals have advantages for transporting heavy commodities of low value.

In recent years, however, the canals have had to face the new competition of mechanical road transport. Much traffic would appear to have been attracted from the canals, especially where distances are short, despite the fact that in general road transport caters for the higher grades of traffic. On certain canals, even traffic in bricks, sand, pig-iron and road metal has been partially lost. The reason appears to lie in the advantage of flexibility enjoyed by road transport and the possibility of effecting deliveries direct from door to door. The savings in transhipment and labour costs thereby involved seem to outweigh the cheaper rates of water transport. There are, however, possibilities in road and canal co-operation, especially if demountable bodies or containers be utilized and mechanical loading and unloading appliances are provided at the wharves.

4. The Transport of Perishable Produce by Road.

The conveyance of perishable goods illustrates in a marked degree the special advantages that appertain to mechanical road transport. Over moderate distances, motor vehicles are especially suited to this type of traffic, and it is indeed not surprising that road transport of fruit, vegetables, poultry, milk or fish has become very popular. Motor transport is now the usual method of carrying fruit or vegetables and other market garden produce to London or other large towns from the surrounding area within a radius of about 30 miles.

Fish, it has also been found, can be best distributed from the ports to the various inland towns distant up to 50 miles by the use of road transport.

The transport requirements of dairy farmers, market gardeners, fruit growers, etc., are very exacting, since rapid, efficient and careful transit are absolutely essential. Unless fruit or vegetables can be brought to market in the minimum of time after picking, the " bloom " is lost and the produce in consequence will not obtain the best prices. In the case of some produce, if the early market can be reached, far higher prices than those of a day or two later can be obtained, and hence in such cases time is the all-important factor. For soft fruit very careful transport is required, if it is to remain undamaged.

Provided distances are not too long, motor transport is especially suited for such transport work. Vans can be loaded direct by the farmer or grower, and the produce need not be touched till the market is reached. Handling and transhipment are thus reduced to an absolute minimum, and this is a consideration of the first importance in the case of such fragile commodities. For the same reason packing costs, which for other systems of transport are an item of considerable expense, are greatly reduced.

Further, road transport is under the direct control of the grower, especially if he possesses a fleet of his own, and the vans or lorries can be dispatched immediately after the freshly gathered produce is loaded.

For distances from market up to about 30 miles, time is generally saved through the elimination of terminal delays, and since cartage to and from stations is done away with, a further saving of time is obtained. Thus by the use of motor transport produce can be brought to market in fresher and better condition and so fetch higher prices. Road transport also means the prompt and certain return of empties such as baskets, churns, etc., and these provide return loads for the vehicles.

Some of the firms engaged in contract work of this nature are able to arrange that empties are returned in fewer lorries than were required on the outgoing journeys, and by utilizing part of their fleet for bringing commodities from the town to the country are thus able to effect additional economies.

As regards the question of utilizing the services of road haulage contractors or providing their own fleets, the practice among farmers and growers varies. In some cases the work is done by firms specializing in the business, and these may often effect economies not easily obtained by the owner of a private fleet, by means of better organization; through arranging for return loads; by the more economical utilization of the capacities of their vehicles, etc.

On the whole, however, most farmers and growers prefer to utilize vans or lorries of their own, as it enables them to arrange journeys at their own time and convenience. Even men in quite a small way of business have bought 1-ton motor trucks. The 1-tonner is also favoured by larger farmers for general purposes, though for long-distance work and heavier loads 2- or 3-tonners have been found more suitable. During the off season the vehicles can find useful employment in the general haulage work incidental to farming operations, such as collection of manure, etc., or may be hired out for general transport work.

Other farmers in certain districts utilize the services of road transport firms engaged in haulage work from the towns to the country who are willing to take back agricultural produce at reduced rates rather than return empty.

Nowadays in many rural districts in the vicinity of large towns, e.g. London, Birmingham, Ashbourne, etc., it is a common sight to see milk churns or other agricultural produce stacked on platforms at the side of main roads. The goods are brought from the farms by local carriers or by the farmers themselves to the loading place situated on the route taken by the lorries that carry this produce to the markets.

CHAPTER V

TYPES OF VEHICLE—THEIR SPECIAL ECONOMIC CHARACTERISTICS AND ADVANTAGES FOR THE TRANSPORT OF GOODS AND MERCHANDISE

THE factors that determine the correct choice of the type of vehicle—petrol, petrol-electric, electric battery, steamer or horse—that will be best suited for any purpose depend entirely on the particular conditions of the case. The prospective user has to weigh and balance a variety of considerations if he is to obtain a vehicle that will give the best return on his outlay, perform the work at the lowest cost per ton-mile, and give the greatest satisfaction under the conditions of the case.

It must be admitted at the outset that there is no hard and fast line of demarcation between the various types. The petrol motor, for instance, is generally regarded as a high-speed machine for moderate loads, and the " steamer " as slower but suitable for heavy cargoes. Yet some " steamers " of the modern type, e.g. " The Sentinel," etc., are capable of high speed and are fitted with rubber tyres, while the latest development of the petrol vehicle, the petro six-wheeler, is capable of transporting loads of 10 to 12 tons.

Nevertheless there are particular cases when one type—steam, petrol, electric, etc.—is to be preferred, and which will give the most economical results for a particular class of work in particular local circumstances. That this is the case can be clearly seen from the fact that enterprising and go-ahead transport firms and certain large municipalities do employ various types for different classes of work, despite the difficulties that are involved in the organization and administration of a mixed fleet. They are of the opinion, and rightly so, that the savings effected by employing vehicles best suited to the varied kinds of transport work required, more than counterbalance the increased expense of a mixed fleet.

The Petrol Motor.—The petrol motor is by far the most generally utilized form of mechanical road transport. For small high-speed vehicles the petrol engine is universally employed, while for the heavier types of vehicle its use is very general. The internal combustion engine is capable of high speed, and on long runs where stops are not too frequent the petrol motor scores over its competitors. It can carry sufficient fuel in its tank for very long journeys, and even if supplies run short, the tank can be easily replenished almost anywhere, for the petrol supply companies have seen to it that fuel is to be obtained in all parts of the country.

It has a sufficient reserve of power, and by means of a gear-box it can tackle almost any route, however severe the gradients. It is reliable and has been brought to a high state of perfection, despite the complicated nature of engine and chassis.

It may be laid down as a general rule that the petrol motor should be employed unless the work required is of a nature that gives scope to the special characteristics and advantages of other types.

The Electric Battery Vehicle.—If frequent stopping and starting is necessitated, the petrol motor becomes expensive, and in this work the " electric " finds a limited but important field where it can show to advantage. Where distances to be covered are fairly short, where stops of short duration are frequent, and where a moderate speed suffices, the electric vehicle is hard to beat. On short journeys the petrol motor cannot show its speed, and further, if stopping and starting is frequent, it will mean a waste of fuel. The "electric" vehicle, however, is economical in congested traffic, and also for delivery rounds, because no energy is consumed when the vehicle is at rest.

The "electric" is simple in construction, having but few moving parts, has a smooth drive, requires no gears, and is possessed of rapid acceleration. Control is very simple, and horse-drivers can learn to manipulate it in a very short time. Since the mechanical construction is very simple, the vehicle has a longer life than other types of power vehicle, and consequently the amount that requires to be allowed for depreciation and maintenance per year is small. Another advantage of the "electric" is its reliability, for it gives constant service with the minimum of attention. In special cases the electric energy available can be utilized for other purposes, such as welding, track-grinding, etc., and "electrics" are sometimes used for such purposes by tramway companies.

Speed, however, is low, since battery weights are considerable, and the accumulators cannot be discharged too rapidly, but for city work maximum speed is not so important as average speed, and the "electric," owing to its rapid acceleration, can maintain a high average speed.

The "electric" is not suited to long-distance journeys, since continuous driving depletes the batteries and necessitates recharging. Its scope is in the sphere of transport intermediate between horse haulage and petrol or steam vehicles. On collection or delivery work the particular advantages of electric or petrol depend entirely on the position of the stopping places in the area served; if they are close together the "electric" is best, but if stretched out, then the petrol vehicle with its greater speed and capabilities for longer runs is the more suitable.

Thus short-distance work with frequent stops is most suited to "electrics," and it is often economical to substitute "electrics" for horse haulage under such conditions. The "electric" is also very suited to town work between definite centres, such as railway depots, where distance is not too great. For the transport of very fragile articles, "electrics" are almost ideal, since their acceleration is smooth, there is no vibration and running is very steady.

They are often utilized for the city delivery work of large London stores, for parcel delivery by the railway companies and carting firms, and by certain manufacturers, such as paper makers, engineers, textile manufacturers, etc.

In some spheres of municipal work, such as the collection of house refuse, the electric vehicle has proved itself most useful and very cheap to operate. The work of collecting refuse by house-to-house calls is especially suited to "electrics," since stops are frequent and runs are fairly short, and in this field horse cartage is gradually being superseded as less economical.

In Norwich an electric vehicle engaged on the work of refuse collection has been fitted with kerbside control, so that the driver can walk alongside his vehicle operating it from the pavement. A considerable saving is thus effected in working cost, as time is saved in getting in and out of the cab, which the driver would otherwise have to do if no loader were employed.

As regards charging, this is usually done at night, and occupies about six to seven hours. If a "boosting" charge be given say at the midday meal hour, or while a vehicle is loading, the daily mileage can be considerably increased.

The provision of the proper facilities by power stations would do not a little to increase the popularity of the vehicle, and if cheap rates were granted for night charging both parties would obtain an advantage, since the load factor of the generating station is low at that time.

The "Steamer."—Steam was the earliest form of power utilized for mechanical road transport, and to-day it continues to fill an important though restricted place in the field of road haulage. For the heaviest loads steam is the only form of traction employed on our roads, but no special account of the traction engine is required, as its advantages and limitations are obvious.

The "steamer," that is the lighter steam-driven vehicle like the "electric," has a special field of usefulness, and under satisfactory conditions it is preferred by many as being more economical than the petrol motor.[1] For heavy loads, and particularly where a trailer is utilized, the "steamer" often scores over petrol in economy of running when distances are of a fair length, for a "steamer" of good make can cover up to 70 miles in a day's work.

Coal merchants, brewers and others, whose loads are over 3 tons, frequently favour the "steamer," as do also those who require a serviceable and robust vehicle for special purposes such as tar-spraying. They are also frequently utilized for the transport of agricultural requirements, such as fertilizers, manures and feeding stuffs, from towns to the outlying country districts, and have proved themselves suitable for the work.

In the fairly sparsely populated districts of parts of Scotland, fleets of steam vehicles have been employed by the former Great North of Scotland Railway for cartage work to and from stations with continued success.

Britain may be said to be the home of the "steamer," for in other countries the steam vehicle is not used to anything like the same extent. This is due no doubt in some degree to the fact that in Britain there are ample supplies of cheap solid fuel in the shape of coal or coke.

The advantages of utilizing steam power are several, and of these the following appear to be the more important :—

(1) There is an ample reserve of power for tackling gradients even under heavy loads.
(2) A cheap and safe fuel is utilized.
(3) The engine is less complicated than an internal combustion engine, since there are fewer moving parts and also the piston speed is less.

[1] It has been estimated that there were about 1,000 steam-driven vehicles on our roads in 1903, 11,000 in 1918, and 30,000 in 1924.

The chief disadvantages are the risk of fire in warehouses or with inflammable cargo and the amount of attention required by the boiler, while in many areas there are difficulties in obtaining adequate water supplies.

The most important improvement made in the "steamer" during the last decade or two has been the evolution of a light efficient vehicle capable of travelling at a fair speed, fitted with rubber tyres, and able to carry a good load. Certain manufacturers are now experimenting with the construction of steam buses.

The "Petrol-Electric."—The essential characteristic of the "petrol-electric" is that the drive is not direct, for a petrol engine is utilized to drive a dynamo, and the current thus generated is harnessed to driving the vehicle.

The advantages of this type over the ordinary petrol motor vehicles are :—

(1) The smooth running obtained through the flexibility of the electric drive, since this means the elimination of transmission shocks, and both clutch and gear-box can be dispensed with ;
(2) There is as a result of the smooth drive less wear and tear on tyres and chassis ;
(3) Greater silence in running as compared with machines fitted with gear-box ;
(4) Greater braking power available ; and
(5) Greater simplicity of control.

The most popular field for the employment of the "petrol-electric" is for passenger transport, but they are also utilized to a limited extent for other purposes. The smooth get-away and travel, for instance, makes them suitable for "tramway tower wagons," as there is no clutch or gear change to cause jerks, and thus men can safely work on the elevated platform.

The current produced can be utilized for power purposes when the vehicle is stationary, and consequently the "petrol-electric" is often employed. e.g. for tramway maintenance, since the one lorry can be used for transport and for a variety of other purposes, e.g. welding, lighting, etc.

Horse Haulage.—The development of mechanical road transport has greatly limited the sphere of economic horse haulage, though as yet, at any rate, the horse is by no means completely displaced.

The disadvantages of horse haulage are obvious, for loads are limited, speed is low, and only a small daily mileage can be covered. This, however, is only one side of the question, and other factors may be of sufficient importance to counterbalance these drawbacks. The most important factor is that of capital cost. With a horse and wagon this is comparatively small as compared with the capital cost of a mechanical vehicle, while there is no heavy licence duty to pay and maintenance charges are very light. A "steamer," a petrol motor, or an electric battery vehicle, is an expensive piece of capital, and if it is to pay its way it must be kept on the move as much as possible; but with horse haulage, since the capital cost is so much smaller, delays are not so expensive. Again, one horse can operate several carts, one being in transit while others are loading or unloading.

Horse transport has the advantage where distances are very short, where streets are narrow and congested, where delays in loading and unloading are considerable, where traffic is too light to give full employment to a mechanical vehicle, and where roads are very bad.

The electric battery vehicle, it is true, has recently encroached considerably on the field still open to horse haulage, and no doubt in the future, as the advantages of the "electric" become better known as a suitable and economic substitute for horse haulage, the process of replacing horse vehicles is likely to extend considerably.

Horse haulage, however, still retains its position for most kinds of transport work other than passenger, where the radius of operation does not exceed 2 or 3 miles, and very often it is still the least expensive under those circumstances.

In dock traffic it will be found, for instance, that horse haulage is common, since congestion is usual, and delays in loading consume a large proportion of the duration of the working day, while distances are frequently quite short. Likewise in certain towns, where the warehouses are situated in narrow and congested streets, the local work is generally done by horse vehicles. Much of the transport required by the textile industry in Manchester, for instance, is still performed by horses, owing to the fact that narrow streets between warehouses only suffice to allow one vehicle to pass at a time.

Railway cartage, much of it of short distance, is still carried out largely by horse haulage, and in this field alone a vast annual tonnage remains open to the horse.

Amongst farmers the use of horse traction is general, since the fodder required may be raised on the farm, and the horse fits into the economy of farm organization more naturally and to a greater degree than does the motor vehicle.

It is also said that horse transport has some advantage over petrol motors or "steamers," in that the horse and cart is more manœuvrable, and so can be employed on work which necessitates entering warehouses with narrow entries at right angles to a narrow street that would present difficulties to other vehicles.

Again, where daily loads are small it would obviously in many cases be uneconomical to substitute motors for horse traction, since the motor might only find enough work to suffice for two or three journeys and would be standing idle for the rest of the day.

As regards the capacity of the horse, the heavier animals are able to transport loads of about 2 tons a distance of about 16 miles a day, while lighter animals can pull 1 to 1½ tons about 20 miles a day. In some towns, e.g. Liverpool, it is said that the heaviest type of dray horse can transport loads up to 5 tons for about 15 miles in the day, but under such conditions their useful life is rather short. It is impossible of course to give figures applicable to all conditions, for both load and mileage will vary with gradients, surfaces, etc.[1]

It has been urged that the conditions of the post-war period have been responsible for obscuring the issue between mechanical and horse transport, and that a wider field is left open to the horse than has been apparent on the surface, despite the advance in the technique of mechanical vehicles. It is asserted that sometimes motors were substituted where economic and operating conditions did not entirely justify the use of the more expensive vehicle, and that in consequence the field open to horse transport has appeared to be unduly narrowed. The issues it is declared were hidden by the scarcity of horses and the high price of provender, as well as by the greater available supply of motors at low prices as a result of the sale of surplus war vehicles.

Now, though the argument is sometimes put forward on too sweeping a basis, there may be some degree of truth in this, for it must be admitted that there is still a definite field to be filled by horse haulage, and it is a significant fact that some firms have recently reverted to horse transport consequent on the fall in the prices of horses and their food. However, it should not be forgotten that when horses and their food were dear, so also was the cost of operating motor vehicles. Cost, of course, is not the only factor ; a saving of time may also be of great importance.

Again, in many fields of horse cartage the true comparison is not between horses and petrol motors, but between horses and electric battery vehicles. If the latter comparison be substituted for the former, the case for horse haulage will not appear so strong in work that involves collections and deliveries, provided always that charging

[1] On the subject of horse haulage and its economies an interesting lecture has been reprinted in the *Journal of the Institute of Transport*, vol. v, No. 6, April 1924. E. Falconer, *Relative Efficiency of Horse and Mechanical Power for Road Transport*. See also comments on this lecture by the technical press.

facilities and cheap electric power are available. This is not to deny, of course, that horse transport has its legitimate sphere, for few would be so foolish as to suggest the immediate possibility of the entire supersession of horses by mechanical vehicles. Each form of transport has its own economic sphere.

From a more general point of view, two disadvantages of horse haulage call next to be considered.

The presence of horses in city streets does not conduce to the most hygienic condition of the towns, for horses and their stables are responsible for helping to spread disease. The coming of the motor, despite the sometimes obnoxious exhaust of the internal combustion engine, has done not a little to increase the cleanliness and healthiness of our streets. Secondly, in crowded thoroughfares the slow-moving horsed vehicle increases traffic congestion and holds up the faster traffic. It has therefore of late been suggested that horse vehicles should be debarred from using streets during certain hours of the day, especially in view of the increasing congestion and the general slowing down of traffic in our larger cities (see Chapter X, City Transport).

Some advocates of the horse base their arguments on sentimental grounds, and bewail the disappearance of the noble animal that has carried man's burdens for hundreds of years; but while such considerations are outside of the scope and nature of the present work, it might not be amiss to point out that perhaps the better friends of the horse are those who would relieve him of the heavy loads, sometimes up to 5 tons, that he is forced to drag through the hard-surfaced and noisy city streets.

Finally, a word or two must be said on the particular case of a firm contemplating the substitution of a few motor vehicles for part of a large horse fleet. In some special cases it must be admitted that it may be cheaper on the whole to keep horses on work that could be better done by mechanical vehicles, since overhead charges and the expense of operating a mixed fleet must be taken into account. To adapt the approaches, the premises, stabling, loading equipment, repair shops, etc., may involve considerable expense, and to do it for one or two motors while horses have to be retained for the bulk of the work may not be feasible. The interest charges may in some cases outweigh the saving in the running cost per ton-mile.

It is not of course suggested that this case is general, but in special circumstances the particular conditions require to be duly weighed.

Multi-wheel Vehicles, Creeper Track Vehicles and Trailers.

The Six-Wheeler.—As yet developments of motors in the direction of fitting a greater number of wheels than the orthodox four are in their infancy, but already in some types of haulage work the six-wheeled vehicle has proved both economical and satisfactory. Where goods require to be carried in bulk, or where large loads can be obtained with regularity for carriage over fair distance, it will be found that the six-wheeler possesses distinct advantages over other types of vehicle. Loads that a haulage contractor might find unremunerative if distributed over a number of smaller vehicles may be carried by a six-wheeler, and when thus bulked constitute a paying load.

The economies obtained by utilizing the larger capacity six-wheeled vehicle are due to the fact that operating costs can be considerably reduced per ton-mile when say 12 tons are carried on the one vehicle instead of the more usual three or four lorries. A large part of the savings effected obviously result from the economy in man power that is obtained, because the cost of labour, i.e. driver's and mate's wages, does not go up in proportion to the carrying capacity of the vehicle. Savings are also effected in petrol, oil, insurance, taxation, etc. The six-wheeler affords the advantage of a greater proportion of useful to total length of vehicle, and this may be an important factor for some kinds of load.

The type of six-wheeler that has made most advance in this country is what is termed the flexible six-wheeler, and the principle has been applied not only to the petrol lorry, but also to steam and electric vehicles. Essentially the flexible six-wheeler is a lorry fitted with a semi-trailer. A four-wheel tractor is utilized in connection with a two-wheeled trailer, the two portions being connected together by a turntable. This type of vehicle obtained a distinct legal status by the "Heavy Motor Car (Amendment) Order" of 1922. If fitted with soft tyres, these tractor and trailer combinations are permitted by that Order to travel at a speed of 12 miles per hour, as is a heavy motor car, provided certain requirements as to total length and weight are complied with. The Order, moreover, granted a substantial increase in legal axle-weights and allowed a reasonable length.

The main restrictions that remain are: (1) in relation to the drawing of a trailer by such units, and (2) the prohibition of tractor-trailers for passenger traffic. If a six-wheeler draws a trailer it becomes legally a "Road Locomotive," not a "Heavy Motor Car," and thus would be restricted to 5 miles per hour, In the near future undoubtedly a considerable development may be expected in the six-wheeler, since this type of vehicle has distinct possibilities. Already improvements are being effected, and the legal recognition obtained in 1922 and the growing popularity of the new type should hasten on developments.

Recently the air-brake, similar to railway appliances of that kind, has been fitted to some six-wheelers. Efficient braking by power removes one important objection to such heavy vehicles, and it should further their claim to be allowed to undertake passenger conveyance.

For certain classes of work, loading and unloading operations would be greatly facilitated if a number of separate trailer units were provided, capable of being quickly coupled or detached from the tractor unit. Time would be thus economized and a saving effected in labour costs. The expensive portion of the six-wheel unit—the power tractor—could be thus kept in full work and need not stand idle. Experiments of this nature have been carried out in France and Belgium, and they show that considerable economies can be obtained where loading and unloading delays are involved.

The problem of the multi-wheeled vehicle is being tackled in nearly all countries, and in some cases even more than six wheels have been successfully employed, while where the law permits six- and eight-wheeled buses are being constructed. The economy of mechanical road transport would be greatly increased, as would also the possible scope of its action, if improvements in this type of vehicle were continued.

From the point of view of road maintenance, the multi-wheeled vehicle also presents possibilities, for if a given weight is to be carried, the spreading of the load over more than four wheels should result in less damage to the roads.

Multi-unit Road Trains.—On the Continent interesting experiments have been carried out in the direction of evolving a multi-unit system of road transport that may be likened to a road train.

In a French invention—the Renard system—a high-powered tractor is used to draw a number of trailers, each of which has one pair of its wheels driven by power from the tractor. To transmit the power to each unit, a Cardan shaft set longitudinally is utilized, and by means of flexible couplings any number of trailers can be hitched on to the tractor. The steering of each trailer is worked from the tractor and thus no difficulties in this direction are met with, for the whole train is self-tracking.

A somewhat similar invention—the Muller system—is due to a German, but here the transmission of power is electrical. The tractor engine drives an electric generator on the same principle as works the familiar petrol-electric vehicle. Each of the trailers is provided with an electric motor, power being communicated to it by means of a flexible cable.

Another inventor, Durtnall, designed a number of road trains in 1906 on similar lines, driven by a petrol-electric tractor, and these were capable of transporting loads of great weight, being intended for military use or for transport in undeveloped regions.

Creeper Track or Track-laying Transport.—During recent years considerable attention has been devoted to creeper track vehicles, but it is not always realized that the system is not altogether new. Young, in his work on *Steam on Common Roads*, published 1860, gives a description of what he calls an "endless railway," which was a peculiar traction engine constructed by Boydell, and said to have given good results in actual working. To quote Young's description, "the peculiarities of this engine consist—First, in the shoes forming the endless railway, attached to the driving wheels, and revolving with them, and also attached to the steering wheels, if needed, by means of which it is enabled to pass over any ground, and to draw heavy loads on common roads without injuring them."

During the Great War the use of creeper tracks on military transport, of the so-called "Caterpillar" type, became well known, as it was utilized on "tanks" and for tractors used to drag guns over roads and across country. Such machines, indeed, were a common sight behind the lines in France. Since the war the same principles have been applied to commercial vehicles, and an interesting experiment has been performed by the crossing of the Sahara by such vehicles. In undeveloped countries, where roads are non-existent and routes are but soft earth tracks or even sand, there are striking possibilities for such vehicles. Though it can hardly be said that development has as yet gone much beyond that of successful trial and experiment, except in the case of military vehicles, there are distinct commercial possibilities in the type, since the machines have proved capable of maintaining a fairly high average speed over long distances, while load capacity is much greater than would be that of the orthodox motor under such difficult conditions.

The Trailer.—Unlike "steamers," most petrol lorries are not fitted with trailer gear, though of recent years the use of trailers has become more frequent. If a single trailer only is employed, the normal speed of 12 miles per hour is allowed under certain restrictions as to combined weight, and thus the use of trailer does not slow down the speed of transport. The utilization of a trailer, or, if speed is not a prime consideration, of several trailers, enables a haulage contractor to obtain a better return from his power vehicle, since costs do not under these conditions increase in proportion to the greater load. It has also the effect of reducing the capital outlay per ton of load capacity, for a trailer is comparatively inexpensive when compared with the power machine. For both these reasons, the use of trailers may mean a considerable reduction in the cost per ton-mile when a considerable volume of traffic has to be dealt with.

In recent years the trailer has developed considerably, and is now generally constructed of steel throughout, with motor car type of steering worked by the movement of the drawbar and rendering the vehicle self-tracking, while it is also often fitted with swivelling bogie trucks.

CHAPTER VI

THE ORGANIZATION OF ROAD TRANSPORT OF MERCHANDISE

THE road transport of merchandise falls naturally into two distinct classes of enterprise :—

(*a*) Haulage contracting (including that of common carriers), and

(*b*) The so-called "distributive" work of wholesalers, retailers and manufacturers who utilize their own private fleets.

Haulage Contracting.—In some cases, traders have found that it is more economical to utilize the services of outside contractors. Where goods are dispatched or collected at infrequent intervals, or where the amount of transport required is small, it would obviously be cheaper for the firms concerned to contract for their transport than to purchase vehicles which could not be utilized to their full capacity. Thus most of the hat manufacturers of Luton have found it better to send their products by independent transport firms, because the amount of goods they send away varies considerably from time to time, this being due to the nature of the trade. In this case a contractor providing transport facilities for a number of such firms is better able to equalize the demand for transport than could a single manufacturer, and, moreover, the contractors are in a better position to arrange for return loads from London, since they specialize in transport work, and are thus able to run regular services and work on a larger scale than would the various manufacturers.

Road hauliers may be further subdivided into two classes according as

(1) They act as "common carriers," or
(2) They contract independently with traders.

Some road haulage contractors only afford facilities to those desiring carriage for amounts of commodities affording a full van or lorry load, or maybe at the most, contract to carry part loads for two or three different traders requiring transit facilities to the same district.

The "Common Carrier."—If, however, a road haulier undertakes to carry goods for all persons who may care to send them by his vehicles, he becomes in law a "common carrier," with the obligations and legal disabilities thereby implied.

Since a "common carrier" exercises a public employment, he is bound to accept any goods that may be offered except he have a lawful excuse for refusing (such as lack of room on his vehicle). Further, he cannot charge more than a *reasonable* amount, and he is held to insure any goods that he carries. He is responsible for loss or damage, except it be due to—

(1) The act of God,
(2) The King's enemies, or
(3) The act of the consignor.

Thus he is responsible for any loss or damage caused by third parties, even if they are not within his control.

He is allowed, however, to demand payment in advance, while he may refuse the articles offered if they are improperly packed.

The responsibilities of the "common carrier" are imposed by the "custom of the Realm," and are thus enforceable without any contract.

If, however, he holds himself out to carry certain goods

only, then he is a "common carrier" in respect of these commodities, but not of any others. In such a case he could make contracts *with specific individuals* for the carriage of other goods, and in regard to these he would be bound by the special contracts, but not otherwise.

In 1830 "common carriers" obtained certain privileges by the "Carriers' Act" of that year, which limited their liability in the case of land carriage to some extent. This Act provided that they were not liable for loss of or damage to certain classes of goods specifically mentioned (e.g. gold or silver, watches, stamps, glasses, china, silks), when the value of such goods in any package "shall exceed the sum of Ten pounds, unless at the time of the delivery thereof . . . the value and nature of such Article or Articles or Property shall have been declared." They only became liable if an increased charge above the ordinary rate was agreed upon.

The Private Fleet.—Many advantages appertain to the possession of a private fleet, and hence firms that require transport services on a considerable scale prefer to run their own fleet rather than contract with others for their haulage or delivery work.

A compromise policy between owning and contracting is to be found in some cases, as, for instance, in Paris, where certain of the large stores do not own their fleets, but hire the vehicles by the year, and during that time every vehicle is under the firm's control and carries its name.

In this country, however, it is a general practice for traders and manufacturers to own their fleets. The advantages of this policy are obvious, and it means that the firm is secured of independence in the arrangement of its transport work. The owner can effect the delivery or collection of goods at times best suited to himself, and, moreover, he comes into more direct contact with his customers and can often arrange to suit their convenience, both facts of importance in business. A great attraction to traders is that a fleet of smart motor vehicles is of considerable publicity value, for they give an air of prosperity to the business and constitute a very valuable travelling advertisement. The trader finds possibilities to extend considerably his business area by the use of motor vehicles. The big firm is able by means of a private fleet not only to retain custom, but also to attract it over a wider area, and thus obtain business that otherwise would go to local firms. The work of collection and delivery, often very scattered and covering a wide area, is essential to many firms such as bakeries, laundries, etc. Such work is often very exacting, but in it mechanical road vehicles show marked advantages over rail. In both wholesale and retail trades it has been found also that petrol motors, and in some cases "steamers" or "electrics," are superior to horse haulage for almost any kind of delivery services. Expeditious delivery is of the first importance in these so-called "distributive trades," and thus the special advantages of a road vehicle may outweigh even a greater cost of service. Without motor vehicles much of the connection of the large stores could never have been built up. Frequently dead mileage can be cut down by providing for the return of empties, jars, bottles, biscuit tins, crates, etc., while if necessary the vans can be specially fitted for the type of goods carried, thus effecting savings in the packing department.

For all kinds of delivery work the motor vehicle has unquestionably proved its worth, and there are few trades which do not require the rapid, efficient and advantageous services that it can render.

Municipal Fleets.—In few spheres of activity has there been a more rapid and general adoption of mechanical road vehicles during recent years than in that of municipal work. Petrol, steam or electric battery vehicles have been utilized in all phases of municipal enterprise, and have proved eminently satisfactory. Some of the large municipalities employ as many as 100 to 200 motor vehicles of varied type in the ordinary routine of municipal work.

The *Municipal Year Book* for 1922 shows that over 5,000 mechanically propelled vehicles were employed by the various local authorities throughout the country, and since then many authorities have increased their fleets, while others have employed mechanical traction for the first time.

Perhaps the most difficult problem of civic administration in large cities is presented by the removal of household and street refuse. To this problem the adoption of mechanical transport presents a solution of no small value, and in this sphere the various types of vehicle, electric, petrol or steam, have achieved great success, and have been generally adopted by progressive municipalities. The horse is gradually being superseded in this work, and even the small sphere still left to horse traction is being encroached upon by the electric vehicle. Where municipalities operate an electrical generating station, the utilization of electric battery vehicles proves very economical, as the necessary charging of the accumulators can be carried on during the night hours of small "load," with considerable advantage to both departments. The horse can now only hold its own where the area of house-to-house collection embraces but a small district up to about a $\frac{3}{4}$-mile radius, or where the presence of tenements renders collection especially slow.

Some authorities at present employing both horsed and mechanical vehicles, however, are considering a change over to mechanical transport for all kinds of refuse collection on account of the expense entailed in a mixed fleet, requiring as it does a duplication of establishments.

Where horse vehicles only are employed, houses at a distance from the destructors may be neglected and collections only made once a week or so. In this and in other respects the use of mechanical vehicles would mean better sanitary conditions.

During recent years great advances have been made in the direction of providing specially constructed vehicles for special work, and as is shown by the wide adoption of such vehicles for these special purposes, their use has effected valuable economies. As examples of the special types of vehicle frequently employed there may be instanced those built for street sweeping, watering, road construction, cleansing, sprinkling and gully emptying. For fire brigade work, motors are now practically universal, and their greater speed over horses is here of the first importance. Likewise for tramway maintenance work, motor tower wagons, portable welding sets, etc., are to be found in the fleets of those municipalities that operate a tramway system.

For many kinds of municipal work the mechanical vehicle is of the greatest utility, as the power available can be used when required for purposes other than movement, as, for example, in emptying gullies, sprinkling streets, operating fire escapes, and with petrol-electrics in electric welding, etc. Multi-purpose machines have been evolved and are now utilized in many towns. The one machine may be used for fire fighting or street watering as occasion demands, while by the simple device of providing several bodies, the one chassis may be made to fit the various requirements of municipal work at a much lower initial cost than would be necessitated if separate vehicles were employed. The possibilities of these multi-purpose machines have induced many smaller municipalities to introduce mechanical transport for the first time. For them the provision of a varied fleet would be impossible, as the special types of machine would only find employment for part of the day; but a multi-purpose machine can be turned on another job when the first is finished, and thus the expensive power equipment is more fully utilized.

The Management of a Private Fleet.—For the successful operation of mechanical road transport it is necessary that running expenses should be kept as low as possible. For this purpose it is essential that systematic and full records of all expenses should be kept, and, indeed, the importance of such record-keeping cannot be too strongly emphasized.[1]

[1] See Appendix A for specimen cost sheets of a motor transport fleet.

Very often, however, this important work is neglected or perhaps inadequately performed, and the compilation of costs is obtained rather through guess-work than systematic investigation, with the result that waste is incurred and the possibilities of economizing are neglected. Records are of the first importance, because it is only by their means that the performance of individual vehicles can be checked. In this way the efficiency of a fleet can be kept up and any weak spot in the organization or any wasteful operations can be detected and the necessary steps taken to secure less costly running.

They prove valuable also in giving a guide as to the type or make of machine that is best suited for any special route or special purpose, and as an index when replacements come to be made as to what type or make of vehicle is best suited to the firm in question.

Other important matters of organization to which an efficient management will pay special attention are: The prevention of overloading; the care of tyres; the allotment of adequate time for garage inspection of vehicles; the economizing of fuel and oil.

The importance of securing the co-operation of drivers is so great that everything should be done that is possible to enable the men to take a pride in their vehicles, to realize the necessity of eliminating waste and to report at once any defect that is manifest. As an incentive to efficient work, many firms have found that some scheme of granting a bonus to drivers in addition to their wages is valuable.[1] The driver takes a greater interest in his vehicle, keeps it in better condition and reduces running costs. The types of bonus that are paid vary to a considerable extent, as some firms give separate bonuses for different savings

[1] Phillimore in his *Motor Road Transport for Commercial Purposes* attaches great importance to bonus systems. "If bonus systems," he states, "were more generally adopted, there is little doubt but that motor transport would be run on more economical lines. It is in the handling of vehicles that the greatest source of extravagance lies, yet it is the most neglected and least considered factor in their operation in this country" (p. 160, 1st Edition).

effected, while others grant a general bonus covering several items. Thus a bonus may be given for fuel economy, since a careful driver may effect considerable savings in this direction by attention to ignition, carburetter, shutting off engine while waiting, etc. In this type of bonus it is general to determine the normal fuel consumption of the vehicle in each case for a standard day's work under ordinary conditions Any economies of fuel as compared with this standard entitle the driver to a bonus based, say, at 25 per cent. of the value of the fuel saved.

Another type of bonus is employed in order to lengthen the life of tyres, and one firm for instance credit their drivers with 2s. 6d. immediately 4,000 miles have been run by any tyre, and for every 100 miles after that an additional penny is added to the bonus. Payment of such a bonus should encourage drivers to look after their tyres, as, for example, by giving immediate attention to gashes, small cuts, etc., or to change over rear tyres to the front wheels in the case of pneumatics after they show signs of wear.

Another bonus system is employed to encourage careful driving, and in this the firm grants a sum of money every six months in respect of each driver to meet any fines that may be incurred; but if at the end of the period none have been imposed, the sum is handed over to him, as would also any surplus after paying penalities imposed.

To obtain the full value of publicity from smart vans some firms give rewards for van appearance with good results.

If vehicles are to be kept in the best condition, however, it is not alone sufficient to give bonuses on wages, the necessary facilities and encouragement must also be given to drivers, such as allotting some portion of the week's work as shed time, so that the driver may effect minor adjustments and repairs.

Terminal Delays and Their Elimination.—One important advantage of road over rail transport has been seen to lie in the avoidance of terminal and transhipment delays, incidental to railway operations, but if time is wasted in the loading and unloading of road vehicles then this advantage is so far reduced.

Since a motor vehicle represents a considerable amount of locked-up capital, it is essential that the vehicle should be kept moving under load on the road as much as possible if the best results are to be obtained, quite apart that is from the necessity of rapid transportation which by itself is often just as important. Like all those forms of capital which the economist is accustomed to call "fixed capital," the mechanical vehicle ought to be worked hard so as to yield the maximum return. With the road vehicle, since the various overhead charges have to be met whatever the mileage, the greater the useful mileage under load, the lower is the cost per ton-mile for transport. Also, while a vehicle stands idle it should be remembered that the driver's time is wasted unless he be engaged in loading or unloading, though it is not perhaps a usual or indeed a sound practice to employ a highly skilled man on work that could be done by others.

With the general shortening of the hours of work during recent years, fixed capital must be kept going as much as possible, and especially is this the case where but one shift is worked per twenty-four hours, as in general is the case with motor vehicles.

To obtain the greatest advantage from a motor vehicle, delays of all kinds should be cut down to a minimum. As things are, vehicles often spend a considerable time waiting their turn for loading, and again at the other end for the reverse process, which operations are themselves often unnecessarily long. In many docks, for instance, congestion and delay are so considerable that it is often cheaper, though much slower, to employ the older method of horse haulage. In other cases, an undue advantage may be given to rail traffic.

The elimination of terminal and other delays is essentially

a question of organization, though in some forms of road transport, e.g. haulage contractors' work, greater difficulty is encountered, since unlike the railway it does not concentrate in one spot such as a goods station or depot. The problem calling for solution is the arrangement of some well-organized system of loading and unloading that will expedite the process and keep the vehicles on the roads as much as possible.

During recent years more attention has been devoted to the elimination of delays, though as yet there is a great deal to be done before the majority of firms or authorities can be said to have brought their terminal appliances and facilities fully up to date. Some progressive firms, dockyard authorities and others, have, however, introduced mechanical loading and unloading devices and other modern methods of cargo-handling. The adoption of these methods has been, under suitable conditions, fully justified by the economies obtained. At the busy centres of transhipment or at terminals, etc., the adoption of labour-saving devices does a great deal to expedite transport alike for road as for rail and steamship traffic.

The wages bill at such centres is a heavy item of expenditure, while the nature of the work is hard and involves considerable strain on the workers where heavy weights have to be lifted. It is neither desirable nor economic that men should still have to remain as beasts of burden transporting heavy weights from one vessel or vehicle to another. Nor can it be argued that the volume of traffic does not justify the introduction of mechanical appliances at these centres, since many warehouses, docks, goods depots, etc., are hard pressed to cope with the amount of traffic which has been increasing for a number of years. It is true, of course, where the amount of traffic handled is small that expensive appliances cannot be installed, but even in these cases some simple fixtures such as ropes and tackle, etc., could be usefully employed.

To facilitate quick loading and unloading, certain manufacturing firms, retail stores in London and Paris, and other large users of road transport, have introduced various mechanical devices that effect considerable economies.

Among those that have proved useful are spiral shoots for parcels, light goods, biscuit tins, etc., warping drums for larger commodities, such as barrels ; portable cranes ; hand trucks ; electric trucks, etc. Much can be done by the simple device of paying attention to the layout of the loading platform so that goods can be brought rapidly and easily to waiting vehicles. Other devices that have proved useful are travelling hoists, continuous conveyors and roller runways, as by their means the goods can be kept on the move with consequent saving of time.

Attention to the construction of the vehicle itself can go a long way to eliminate loading or unloading delays in many cases, and this special adaption to the nature of the work on which the vehicle is engaged has the important advantage that the special facilities, so to speak, travel with the vehicle, and are more or less independent of the place of loading or unloading.

Where the materials handled can be transported in bulk and are not easily damageable, such as stone, building material, road metal, coal, etc., an easy solution of the problem is at hand, for in all these cases tipping wagons can be used, thus saving the expense of a gang of unloaders and performing the work in the minimum of time. Many of the latest commercial lorries are fitted with tipping gear, either hand- or power-operated, and often constructed so that the load can be tipped to either side or the rear at will.

Where the goods to be transported are not suited to this treatment, the utilization of containers or demountable bodies, that can be lifted bodily from the vehicle, would mean that the vehicle was kept standing for as short a time as possible, while loading or unloading could be carried out when and as required. If transhipment, say, to another vehicle or to railway rolling stock, barges, steamships, etc., is necessitated, the "container" method is almost ideal, provided only that the goods in each container are bound for the same destination. This system has become very popular in the U.S.A., and in Britain it is gradually growing in favour, and has already been adopted by various railway companies, furniture removers, biscuit makers and other manufacturers.

Among other devices that may prove suitable for some purposes are lift-off tops, or the provision of side-doors, while for the transport of liquids specially constructed vehicles are frequently employed, and may effect considerable savings in time as well as in the cost of packing.

One obvious way of cutting down loss of time is through the utilization of a number of trailers, one being loaded at any time, while another is unloading at the other end, and a third is in transit. In this way the power unit would be kept more continuously on the road doing useful work, with a reduction in the cost per ton-mile.

Closely connected with the problem of eliminating terminal delays is that of internal transport in factories, railway termini, warehouses, docks, etc. In all these cases where there is a considerable volume of work to be handled small electric battery trucks can be utilized, and they have proved to be a good investment for such purposes. The electric truck has grown in favour during the past eight or ten years, and is displacing the hand barrow where a considerable volume of traffic has to be handled. They are now to be seen at many of the larger railway stations or depots, e.g. London, Edinburgh, Birmingham, at the dock side and in large factories, etc.

The introduction of electric transport for internal transit means a great increase in efficiency, a saving in cost and more rapid performance, as compared with the slow and laborious hand barrow. One power truck is quite capable of hauling a little train of trailers, as can be seen at the larger railway stations. New improvements and new types are continually being introduced, and the truck can be adapted to almost any kind of cargo by means of simple fitments for bales, parcels, barrels, etc. They can also, if necessary, be provide with a lifting platform for stacking heavy articles such as cotton bales.

A further refinement of the electric truck is the self-propelled runabout electric battery crane. This labour-saving device has many advantages and greatly simplifies the transference of goods at terminals, docks or warehouses.

CHAPTER VII

THE MOTOR CAR, THE MOTOR CYCLE, AND THE TAXI-CAB

The Motor Car and Motor Cycle.—Passenger motor cars were the first type of vehicle to be experimented with when, at the close of the last century, early attempts were made to utilize the internal combustion engine for transport purposes. Enthusiastic individuals pioneered the way, for it was not till success had been achieved with these earliest motors that the commercial application of the new mode of transport was attempted.

To-day the motor car and the motor cycle are well established as the ordinary type of vehicle among people who can afford to run a carriage of their own. In all countries, motor cars and motor cycles constitute by far the greatest proportion of all the mechanical vehicles utilizing the roads. In Great Britain during the calendar year 1922, out of a total of approximately 979,000 motor vehicles in use, about 315,000 were motor cars, 378,000 motor cycles, and 78,000 motor hackneys.[1] The number of horse-drawn vehicles licensed, totalled 237,342, of which 199,613 were private carriages and 37,729 hackneys.

In Canada, in the same year (1922), out of a total of nearly 514,000 motor vehicles registered, about 462,000 were passenger cars and about 9,000 motor cycles.[2]

In the U.S.A., for the corresponding period, registrations numbered over 12¼ million vehicles, and of these by far the greater proportion were motor cars.

[1] *Traffic Census*, 1922, Appendix II.
[2] *The Canada Year Book*, 1922–23, p. 650.

The rapid growth in the number of motor cars will be evident if a comparison is made with the year 1900; then the total number of motor cars in the world was under 11,000, and of these about 5,000 were French, only 700 being in use in the U.S.A.

In those early years the motor was a novelty, and was not looked upon with favour by the general public. However, it soon became a common luxury of the rich, while now a motor car is generally owned by most persons of moderate income. In the U.S.A. and Canada the automobile has become a not uncommon possession of the artisan. This great extension in the use of motor cars has been largely due to the mass production on standardized lines of a low-priced car by the Ford firm. Keen competition among manufacturers, the pushing of sales and the provision of varied facilities for the motor user, has resulted, especially in the United States, in the widespread ownership of automobiles among all classes. The Ford Company has paid special attention to the building up of an elaborate network of agencies, where large stocks of spare parts are always kept, and this has done a great deal to popularize the Ford car, the more especially as spares are cheap on account of the mass production of completely standardized parts. The American "hire-purchase" system, though from a wider point of view not always desirable, has been another important factor. As a result of these efforts and the popularity of the motor, there was one automobile for every nine persons in the U.S.A. in 1922. In Canada, despite the absence of any great mileage of roads suited to motor traffic, the proportion of cars to population in 1922 was in the ratio of one to 17·45. In the province of Ontario the proportion was as high as 12·4, while in the prairie and mainly agricultural province of Saskatchewan it was 12·8.

To business or professional men, such as doctors, clergymen, commercial travellers, etc., the motor car or motor cycle has proved to be of the greatest utility. The motor is now almost a necessity in those areas where population is scattered. Its speed and reliability enable the user to cover a wide area in the minimum of time and with the minimum of trouble, while there need be no unnecessary delays such as might be the case if the railway had to be utilized. Again, the motor user can travel direct from place to place in the course of his business. The economies thus effected in time or money often serve to more than offset the cost of upkeep.

For pleasure purposes, the motor car and the cheaper motor cycle have obtained a great vogue, and year by year the number of such motor users is increasing. On bank holidays and during week-ends an almost constant stream of cars and motor cycles can be seen passing along certain main roads near the larger towns. The amount of long-distance travel by road now undertaken is remarkable, and our country is rapidly being opened up to its inhabitants to an extent never before achieved. The motorist can penetrate almost everywhere, and can readily reach rural beauty spots or other places of interest that formerly were almost inaccessible. Incidentally, the motor car has been the cause of the revival of the country inn or hotel, which since the decline of the stage coach had almost ceased to cater for the traveller.

The motor cycle [1]—cheap in first cost and cheap in running costs—and the recently developed "light-car," with its modern high-efficiency, high-speed engine, combining the advantages of low cost and low taxation, have enabled many who could not afford to run a large car to participate in the pleasures of road travel.

It is indeed probable that during the course of the next few years a further considerable increase will take place in the use of motor cars in Great Britain. The mass production of cheap cars by the Ford, Morris, Citroën, Rover and other manufacturing firms, no doubt will do a great

[1] Britain may be said to be the home of the motor cycle, as 95 per cent. of the machines on our roads are of British manufacture, and in 1923 exports totalled 28,000 motor cycles—a world's record.

deal to bring the automobile within the reach of the many who at present do not own a car. The high percentage of cars to population in Canada and the U.S.A. indicates that the production of cheap cars should stimulate considerably the use of motors within this country, especially when trade and industry recover from the post-war slump.

One reason why Britain lags behind America would appear to lie in the fact that motors are still regarded as somewhat of a luxury of the richer and upper middle classes. The high initial price of a motor in Britain as compared with the U.S.A. and Canada has been a restrictive influence on the expansion of the motor market—despite the recent development of the "light car," almost unknown in the New World.

Further, in Great Britain there is a much better supply of public passenger services by train, tram and bus, while at the same time distances to be traversed are much shorter than in America. Again, in this country there has been somewhat of a shortage of sufficient garage accommodation at cheap rates in most towns and cities, and this fact has no doubt had a certain influence in hindering the more rapid development of road usage.

However, in more recent years considerable advance has been made in providing more adequate accommodation, and in many cities and towns motorists have recently been accorded permission to "park" vehicles in certain streets. The motor organizations have been allowed to erect signs notifying those places where cars may be allowed to stand. These increased facilities for garaging and parking should do something to encourage the more general use of motors.

One factor that has greatly encouraged the use of automobiles for pleasure or business travel has been the building up of a very extensive network of petrol supply facilities. In even the most out-of-the-way places it is possible to obtain petrol readily. The petrol supply companies by means of a thorough organization see that the retailers have a sufficient supply of fuel on hand at all times. The "petrol pump," despite certain assertions in some quarters as to its defects, has now become popular, and has further increased the ease of fuel replenishment, rendering that operation less tedious.

The Taxi-Cab.—Little need be said of the taxi-cab or motor hackney, which is now to be found in nearly all towns, having in recent years practically ousted the older horse-drawn cab. In the larger cities the number of such motor hackneys is very considerable, and they do a large business, providing a rapid and convenient means of communication. In New York City especially the number of taxi-cabs and the amount of work done by them is astonishing. The rates there charged are low, while the traveller is protected against excessive charges by the meter, which automatically prints a receipt showing the proper fare.

In many cities the provision of vehicles is largely in the hands of big firms, and the small owner-driver is in the minority. Some of the large American taxi-cab companies have spread over most parts of the States and into Canada, their distinctively marked vehicles being found in most of the larger towns and cities.

During recent years in Paris and in certain English towns attempts have been made to establish taxi-services at low rates by utilizing two-seater side-car outfits or very small cars. These, frequently operated by owner-drivers, have already obtained a certain amount of popularity on account of the cheaper fare charged.

Types of Motor Cars.—For the motor car, the petrol engine has pride of place and is all but universal as the power unit for passenger cars. In no country does any other type approach anywhere near to it in popularity. The continued labour of designers and manufacturers, aided by engineers and scientists over a number of years, has resulted in the evolution of a markedly efficient power unit, considering the conditions under which it has to operate. The numerous reliability and speed trials held each year have also helped to improve engines and chassis, since such trials show up any weak features, which where possible are subsequently eliminated.

No description of the orthodox motor vehicle need be attempted here, since the reader may be presumed to be familiar with at least the main features of the petrol-engined motor car. Recent developments have taken place along the lines of greater durability, greater efficiency and better braking.

Something, however, may be said of the types other than petrol which have proved satisfactory in use, since they are not so well known.

In the U.S.A. a certain number of "steam cars" are still being turned out, though none are now manufactured in this country. It might seem curious that Britain, the home of the commercial "steamer,"[1] should not produce passenger "steam cars." The former, however, burns solid fuel, while in the "steam car," oil, generally paraffin, is employed to heat the water, a "flash boiler" being utilized, which permits of the rapid generation of steam without necessitating undue weight. Boiler troubles in the "steam car" have retarded its development, despite the fact that it appears to have certain advantages in ease of operation, flexibility of control and cheapness in running cost.[2]

The "electric" vehicle, driven by storage batteries, would appear to possess many attractions for town driving. It is capable of rapid acceleration, is very silent in operation, light in weight, easy to control, and free from vibration, smoke or smell. Further, the rate of taxation on such vehicles is low, being only £6 per annum. In this country, however, the first cost of an electric passenger vehicle is high, and the facilities required for recharging the batteries are not readily obtainable in many districts. The scope of the "electric" is also limited to short-distance running, since it is hardly possible to cover much more than 100 miles on a charge of the accumulators.

[1] See Chapter V.

[2] See Conradi, *Mechanical Road Transport*, pp. 84 *et seq.*

The advantages of electric vehicles, however, taken together with their simplicity of control and general cleanliness, make them well suited for town driving. In the U.S.A. electric passenger vehicles have been and continue to be produced in considerable numbers. They are frequently used in the States for city driving both as private cars and as taxi-cabs.

Other types of vehicle manufactured in certain numbers are the petrol-electric and the car fitted with magnetic transmission, but for a description of these, which must necessarily be technical, the reader should consult works on the engineering side of automobilism.[1]

The Motor Organizations.—In Britain a number of motor and motor cycle clubs or associations have been founded with the object of organizing motorists, protecting their interests and providing means for increasing the amenities of travel by road. In most other countries, also, clubs with similar objects in view have been established.

The Automobile Association in Great Britain, with a membership of nearly 200,000 in 1923, was established to safeguard the interests of motorists generally. It provides a road patrol organization on many main roads for the help of its members. It is the duty of the patrol men, mounted on push cycles or motor cycles, to give members, recognized by a car badge, any information of interest about the road, to warn them of dangers ahead, and to give any assistance in their power in the case of accident or breakdown. Motor cycles fitted with a side-car containing tools, etc., for repair work are also supplied to some of the patrols, while recently some of these are operated during the night as well as during the day.

The Association has erected numerous village and road danger signs, which latter have done a great deal to decrease the perils of the highway. In addition a number of roadside telephones and fuel-supply stations have been set up at suitable spots for the convenience of members. Garages,

[1] E.g., a description is given in Conradi, *Mechanical Road Transport.*

agents and hotels are officially appointed, after inspection, so that members may be assured of attention and the best service. Finally, the Association aids its members in a number of ways, such as the giving of advice as to the best routes, the planning of tours, the provision of facilities for Continental trips, etc.

Very similar in objects and organization are the Royal Automobile Club, and in Scotland the Royal Scottish Automobile Club. The Royal Automobile Club is an influential body, and was founded as far back as 1897. It, too, has established a number of road patrols, has erected numerous road direction and warning posts, and aids its members with information as to routes, conditions of roads, etc. It also acts in the general interests of motorists when these are threatened by legislation or otherwise.

For motor cyclists, the Auto Cycle Union and other bodies carry out very similar work, though not on such a large scale, while in addition to these big centralized organizations many district or local automobile and motor cycle clubs have been established throughout the kingdom.

CHAPTER VIII

THE MOTOR COACH

SINCE the war the motor coach has become a prominent feature on our roads. At the seaside and other holiday resorts these vehicles are well in evidence, and indeed they have become a feature of the holiday season. They have greatly added to the attractions of pleasure places, as they provide a convenient method of seeing the local sights, and further, they help to increase the number of visitors to such resorts by putting industrial and urban centres into closer touch with near-by holiday resorts. Circular, day or week-end tours by road have proved very popular, while longer runs, some indeed over 1,000 miles in length, have been well patronized by the public.

The motor coach or char-a-banc, though practically a post-war development, appears to have secured a marked degree of public favour, though perhaps some part of its popularity must be ascribed to its novelty. Many are attracted by the glamour of the open road, and it must be admitted that the motor coach provides for many persons an agreeable method of exploring their own country.

Though long-distance tours are often undertaken, the special and most favourable field for the activities of motor coaches is that of providing sightseeing tours around the various tourist centres or short-distance runs to pleasure resorts near large towns. Country runs through picturesque scenery or to places of interest inaccessible by rail afford special opportunities to motor coach proprietors, and in many districts full advantage is taken of these possibilities. Road traffic of this nature, it may be noted in passing, often helps to augment rail traffic by adding to the attractions of holiday resorts.

Rail and motor coach facilities may thus be complementary one to the other and not competitive. Railways can bring visitors in great numbers at excursion rates, while motor coaching facilities serve to attract holiday makers. An interesting example of the mutual dependence of the two systems is afforded by a recent experiment at Scarborough where direct co-operation has been effected. The L.N.E.R. and a privately operated motor coach organization have entered into a direct working agreement to their mutual advantage. Routes are so arranged that competition between rail and road is eliminated, while advertising and organization is provided on a combined basis. The railway company advertises the coach tours at its stations, and has leased parking facilities, a taxi-rank and a booking office to the road company. This experiment is important, and no doubt will be followed in other places, since it has been amply demonstrated that the arrangements are of great benefit to both the parties concerned.

For conveying excursion parties for picnics and for bringing enthusiasts to football matches, races, etc., the motor coach has obtained a considerable vogue. It has the advantage over rail in that the party can be transported to meet any special requirements of the members, and further, the individuals are not separated but travel together. The journey can be made direct without any changing or break, while times of departure, etc., can be adjusted to suit the particular needs of the party.

Long-distance coach travel is now of considerable volume, and this will be seen to be the more extraordinary when the keen competition of the railways through cheap excursion facilities, etc., is realized. For instance, trips from London to Harrogate, Devon, Derbyshire, Bath, etc., are frequently run, while even longer tours embracing districts as far apart as Scotland and Devon on the same tour have been inaugurated.

No doubt patronage is obtained for the long tours from among those who regard the journey by road as the main part of the holiday, and by that minority, albeit a considerable one, who wish to revive the romance of the road associated with the old stage coach days, but more in consonance with modern ideas as to speed.

On these longer journeys, however, the railways can compete on more even terms, and with the revival, after the war, of excursion rates, tourist ticket facilities, etc., the competition has become more acute. Rail has great advantages in bad weather, while comfort and speed are greater, a matter of some importance on long journeys, though, on the other hand, the same facilities for viewing the scenery are not afforded. Where the main object is the destination rather than the journey itself, the motor coach cannot compete with the train. If comfort by road were to be increased, as, for example, by providing smaller and faster vehicles (say 14-seater) fitted with pneumatic tyres, higher fares would have to be charged.

The popularity of the motor coach seems to have fallen somewhat short of the previous highwater mark, though this no doubt may be largely due to industrial depression and to the succession of bad weather during recent summers. A number of the smaller concerns have not managed to survive the competition and difficulties of the period, and have had in consequence to give up business. Competition for the available traffic has been very acute, especially on the better recognized routes, such as those between large towns and the coastal resorts.

In many districts, to prevent undue "rate cutting" and to promote co-ordination in the area, various attempts have been made to form associations or combinations among the various coach owners. Meetings have been called for the purpose of stabilizing fares, or to promote co-ordinated effort, as, for example, through combined advertisement or the exchange of passengers. There appear to be considerable opportunities for economies through co-ordination. The exchange of passengers, for instance, would enable one vehicle to be run in place of several with partial loads, such as often occurs when the weather is bad, or when for some other reason demand falls below expectations. Such pooling of passengers would mean a reduction of running costs and the elimination of waste. Likewise combined advertising should help to reduce considerably the expense involved by this item. By means of a co-operative agency, associated coach owners should be enabled to retain a greater part of the profits to themselves instead of as at present a considerable proportion being absorbed by the outside booking agency, which can extort considerable commissions where several coach owners are struggling amongst themselves for traffic.

In certain districts, associations among motor coach proprietors have been formed, either for purposes of general co-ordination or for fixing standard rates, though in practice it has not been found an easy matter to establish such associations either on a national, district or local basis. In most areas no doubt a certain amount of tacit combination to prevent unduly low rates is prevalent, but during seasons of bad weather, or where rail competition is acute, even these understandings may go by the board, and rates may indeed be reduced so low that they can only cover bare running expenses, since for a time owners may be anxious to get some small return rather than allow their vehicles to remain idle.

The great difficulty that faces the motor coach industry is the seasonal nature of the trade, since it is only during the holiday period that good loads can be expected, while bad weather at such times may mean the loss of the year's profits. Conditions are not so bad around the great towns, since proprietors are not so dependent on visitors, while during any spell of fine weather, though it may be brief in duration, short trips may be provided which may attract considerable patronage.

Sometimes coach owners convert their chassis to haulage work during the winter months, or else maybe to motor bus work, and in this way the industry is rendered less seasonal.

Large and Small Coaches.—Since about 1922, when the Ministry of Transport began to close certain roads to the heavier types of vehicle, the smaller coach, fitted with pneumatic tyres and seating from fourteen to twenty persons, has become popular, and for many purposes it is now tending to replace the heavier coach. The smaller vehicles give greater comfort to passengers, since springing is better and pneumatic tyres are generally fitted ; indeed, they often bear more resemblance to private cars than to their earlier prototypes. Further, speed is not so restricted, since the legal maximum is 20 instead of the 12 miles per hour of the larger coach. Hence the mileage run per day can be increased, and upon the mileage run depends the earning capacity of the vehicle. They are valuable also for those trips to places which are inaccessible except by secondary roads, too narrow for the larger coaches.

A considerable field, however, is still left to the larger vehicles seating up to thirty-two passengers. They will continue to be favoured for day or half-day trips at holiday resorts for purposes of sightseeing, for excursions and for work around the larger towns, etc. Often under such conditions the general level of fares is such that little or no profit would be shown by smaller coaches, but for the large vehicles the availability of full loads renders low charges a possibility. Proprietors in a large way of business often find possibilities in the use of a mixed fleet of large and small vehicles, the smaller being used for special work, such as long distance trips, or for better class traffic that will bear higher rates.

So far the differentiation in use between larger and smaller coaches has generally turned upon the nature of the journey, and has been determined by the length of the run and the state of the roads rather than upon differences in comfort, etc., which might be held to justify a higher fare. In time, no doubt, a difference in fares based upon cost of service will become asserted.

To sum up, it may reasonably be concluded that the motor coach has come to stay in the more or less limited fields in which it is now well established, such as have been indicated above.

The motor coach has its special attractions, and it has the advantage of saving some of the incidental expenses of rail travel, such as cab or taxi fares to and from stations. Further, on journeys of a certain distance the large motor coach can often carry passengers at rates even less than the ordinary third class railway fare under suitable conditions.

However, for the majority of passengers who seek a certain destination rather than the pleasure of travel, the railway has the greater advantage. The lowering of railway fares to the pre-war level of a penny per mile would increase this advantage.

The motor coach is not the first road competitor that the railways have had to face. In former years suburban rail traffic has been hard hit by the competition of first the electric tramway and later the motor bus. The railways have not been able to regain all the traffic thus lost, even after resorting to reduced fares and season ticket rates or to the electrification of their systems. It is thus quite possible that outside the suburban area the new motor coach competition may have similar effects on certain rail routes. Lower railway rates to seaside and other resorts may result, and the progress of electrification may be hastened, as, for example between London and the South Coast.

CHAPTER IX

RURAL TRANSPORT

In many rural areas the need for better transport facilities is immediate and urgent, but the amount of traffic available is generally insufficient to justify the construction of a railway or even a light railway or "agrail." For financial success a railway requires a considerable traffic, as otherwise the heavy capital expenditure involved in its construction cannot be adequately remunerated.

Topographical and other reasons usually render the steam tramway—a familiar method of transport in the rural areas of France, Belgium and other Continental countries—an impossible solution in Great Britain, even if the traffic available were sufficient otherwise to justify such an undertaking. Likewise, the extension of electric tramways into country districts is effectively barred owing to the heavy capital outlay that would be required. An electric tramway must have a considerable volume of traffic, so that a fair load will be provided for a fairly frequent service, if financial loss is to be avoided.

But though the limited amount of traffic forthcoming in rural areas may be altogether insufficient for a railway or a tramway, it may suffice for a road motor. "As between railway—including light railway—and mechanical road transport the Committee consider that, as a general rule, development should proceed along the lines of increased and improved mechanical road transport" (Report of the Convener's Committee of Roxburghshire County Council).[1]

[1] Quoted in the Rural Transport (Scotland) Committee, 1919.

The special characteristics of mechanical road haulage make it very suitable for operation in rural districts. So long as there is sufficient traffic for a single motor, a service can be run on a remunerative basis. The capital outlay involved is comparatively small, and there are no heavy overhead charges to be met. In consequence there appear to be great possibilities for motor transport in rural areas.

The flexibility of road transport is of great importance in country districts, for a road vehicle can stop anywhere, and can thus provide better facilities to farms, hamlets and villages not within appreciable distance of a station, than can the railways.

In the more sparsely populated rural districts the flexibility of road transport assumes an even greater importance, because the vehicle may be utilized on several routes. Thus a single vehicle might be operated from a market town, a railway station, or a port to a series of outlying villages or hamlets, each of which could thus obtain a regular service once or twice a week. Such a service might be a remunerative proposition, though any one route by itself could not be able to provide sufficient traffic to keep the vehicle busy during the whole week.

In the country districts the one vehicle can be utilized for the carriage of both passengers and merchandise to and from the market town or the nearest railway station.

Such vehicles might also serve a useful purpose in the conveyance of children to school where the population is scattered. The possibility of carrying a few passengers in addition to goods is a valuable contribution to the income of the carrier. The only difficulty is the higher rate of taxation of passenger vehicles under present regulations.

In some parts of Britain, and more especially in Scotland, road services have been inaugurated to carry passengers and mails along with goods. These have been found to meet the demands of sparsely populated districts, where there would be insufficient traffic to justify separate passenger or mail services.

RURAL MOTOR BUS SERVICES.

Since the war the inauguration of motor bus services in out-of-the-way districts has proceeded apace, and now most places, even where the population is scanty, are linked up by the enterprise of one or another of these motor services. In the linking up of rural districts with their market town or other commercial or industrial centre, the small rural motor bus enterprises have developed a new traffic, and have on the whole done more good than harm to the railways, since in effect they constitute a network of feeders. In former times the inaccessibility of many rural districts was almost unbelievable. Unless a carrier's cart happened to pass near by, a walk of about five miles was not uncommonly necessitated to reach a railway station. Even at the best a journey to market took up a good part of a day's work, since the carrier's cart was a slow method of conveyance.

The new rural motor bus services are doing valuable work in opening up the country districts, in providing better facilities for marketing, and in helping to improve the amenities of rural life by putting the towns within easy reach of the inhabitants of the rural areas.

In connection with this last point the opinion of the author of a recent work on Agricultural Economics may be of interest: "The Census figures of 1921 do not bear out the 'deserted village' theory, and it would seem as if modern improvements in the means of locomotion, combined with the securing of the townsman's half-holiday, have brought the amenities of town life sufficiently near the villages to make the majority of young farm hands think twice before removing themselves and their families into the heart of large cities." [1]

On market days and other special occasions extra services can be provided, and such facilities are found to be of great benefit to buyers and sellers, who are thus enabled

[1] J. A. Venn, *Foundations of Agricultural Economics*, 1923.

to carry their fresh butter, new laid eggs, or other produce to and from the market with the minimum of trouble.

In some rural districts motor bus proprietors in quite a small way of business have found remunerative openings for their enterprise by linking up a series of villages, often going along by-roads, where they have little competition to meet, as they avoid the railway routes or the districts served by larger road transport concerns. Several services of this nature, for instance, connect market towns, such as Guildford, Farnham or Gloucester, with the outlying districts.

The motor bus has also given good service in providing transport facilities to and from those isolated industrial centres that are sometimes met with, in otherwise rural districts. The question of how facilities for workers are to be provided between their homes and the works presents difficulties in such cases, but the motor bus has gone a long way to solve the problem. Again, in the somewhat similar problems presented where isolated districts have rapidly become industrialized, as, for example, by the opening up of new coal-pits in the Dukeries of Northern Nottinghamshire, the motor bus has proved a valuable solution.

In the operation of rural services cheapness is a prime consideration, since traffic is sparse. Consequently the one-man operated bus is greatly favoured. It is especially suited for this type of work, and enables a service to be provided on a remunerative basis, which, if a conductor had to be employed, would not be able to pay its way.

In recent years it is true that the vehicles employed on country services have become more elaborate than the crude type of passenger vehicle which used to be employed in most instances. In many districts, however, the carrier bus of a primitive type—often a Ford fitted with a home-made body—is still to be seen plying between the towns and the outlying district and seating twelve to fourteen passengers, though maybe, on occasion, standing passengers may bring the load up to a higher figure.

In nearly all cases these pioneer services are owner-driven. The hours, however, are often long, and the proprietor is generally handicapped by want of capital, as he may be buying on a " hire purchase " scheme.

With small vehicles, however, labour costs are at a minimum, fuel consumption is low, and the capital outlay is not considerable, though it may be heavy enough for a small business. Running costs are thus low, while overhead charges, except for interest and depreciation, need not be at all heavy, since a garage, for example, may be an old stable, while office and administrative expenses, etc., will be practically nil.

The rural motor bus can thus provide services at a lower cost per passenger-mile than any other form of transport in the circumstances, and it may be said that for quite rural services there exists no practical alternative to the motor bus.

The Carriage of Mails in the Rural Districts of Scotland.

The problem of postal deliveries is one of considerable difficulty in many parts of Scotland owing to the scant population.

Road transport by mechanical vehicles has, however, gone a long way to provide a solution, and is now in general use by the Post Office. The services are provided either by local carriers working under contract, as mentioned above, or, where the work is heavier, by vehicles hired from contractors and utilized for mail services only, or by mail road vans owned and operated by the Post Office. This last method—the policy of State-owned vehicles—is a fairly recent innovation, but it is now being adopted on an extensive scale. Generally in the rural districts either Ford vans or Triumph side-car carriers, driven by postmen, are employed. The vehicles carry the mail from a head office to sub-offices, and in isolated districts they are also employed on house-to-house delivery work. Some of the routes, it is interesting to note, are not exclusively rural services. From about 1911 the Post Office commenced to utilize road motors for parcel carrying owing to the heavy charges exacted by the Railway Companies. During the war years, however, the Post Office where possible reverted to the railways, which were then State controlled.

The following table gives the mileage covered by motor mail transport in Scotland in 1923 and 1911 respectively, but excluding the Glasgow district.[1]

	Number of Routes.		Weekly Mileage.	
	1923.	1911.	1923.	1911.
Motor cycles ridden by postmen	2	—	477	—
Motor vans owned and worked by P.O.	3	—	575	—
Contracts for conveyance of mails only	5	2	2,570	834
Motor passenger services conveying mails	123	19	21,600	4,430
Motor boats	11	7	1,100	1,030

Railways and Rural Road Services.—In the rural districts distinct possibilities appear to lie in the harmonious conjunction of motor and railway services. In outlying country districts road services can be operated where the traffic is not sufficient to warrant the construction of a branch line. Road services, which in effect constitute a "rudimentary form of branch line," can be usefully employed on pioneer or development work.

In this connection it may be recalled that a few railway companies even before the war had adopted such schemes in certain areas where it would not have paid to lay down an extension. To develop tourist traffic, the Great Western Railway has operated such road services in the remoter districts of its area for a considerable number of years.

[1] Taken from *Motor Transport*.

The Great North of Scotland Railway (now incorporated in the L.N.E.R. Group) has also operated several such services, some of them not only during the tourist season but all the year round. As far back as 1904 a motor service was instituted between Braemar and Ballater, while at the present day numerous services by road are run to supplement their rail facilities, principally around Aberdeen, Banff and Elgin. The number of passenger vehicles engaged on these services is over thirty.

The same Company has also instituted a number of road services by "steamers" for the carriage of goods in those districts in their area where the rail does not penetrate. Their road fleet, consisting of eleven "steamers," connects the main stations with the outlying country districts, bringing out loads of coal, manure, etc., while grain and other agricultural produce are brought back for dispatch by rail.

The Company, however, declared in 1919 that while they had found road transport important as a means of improving transport in the districts served, yet they were of opinion that road services did not allow the traffic to be fully developed, and stated that road services had probably only postponed the demand for railways.[1]

In the harmonious conjunction of motor and railway services, where the buses run to a time-table adjusted to the time of arrival and departure of trains, there appear to lie considerable possibilities; but at present, owing to the ambiguous position of the railways in regard to road powers, the companies cannot inaugurate new road services, though they are continuing the old pre-war ventures, for some of which indeed they possess statutory powers.

In consequence, the extension of rural services in connection with the railways is only being undertaken where private individuals have seen fit to provide the requisite facilities.

The Farmer and Road Transport.—In this country, where

[1] Report of Committee (1919 on Rural Transport (Scotland).

farming is undertaken for the market, not for subsistence, transport is an essential requirement of the agricultural community. In many cases road transport can provide in an especial degree the type of facilities required by the nature and conditions of agriculture.

As compared with horse transport, much greater distances can be covered, and several journeys can be made in a day if the distance is short.

By means of road transport the early market can be expeditiously and conveniently reached so long as the distance is not too great, and with early crops this means better selling prices. As was pointed out in connection with the transport of perishable commodities, road transit has certain advantages over rail, since the produce can often be carried to market in fresher and better condition.[1]

To the live-stock farmer mechanical road transport also presents attractions, especially where pedigree or other high-class animals are concerned. When conveyed by motors, they reach the market or the ring in much better condition than they would if sent by rail or other method. Valuable stock can be brought back from shows, etc., the same evening, and thus do not need to remain away overnight. The special advantages of motor road transport in these connections, and the fact that with it the stock can be sent direct from the farm to the destination, more than compensate for any greater expense over rail that may be involved. With expensive live stock it is a *sine qua non* that they should reach the markets or the shows in the best possible condition if the best prices are to be obtained.

For the transport of light but bulky produce, such as hay, straw, cabbages, etc., economical and rapid transit can be effected with motor vehicles if suitable bodies are provided.

The Haulage Contractor and the Farmer.—In many districts, haulage contractors have organized road services to meet the requirements of the agricultural community,

[1] See Chapter IV, pp. 55–57.

and this system appears to work well and to afford a fair return to enterprising carriers. Such rural services find considerable scope for their activities in agricultural districts lying around some market town or railway station. Very often farms are situated at a distance from 5 to 10 miles from the nearest railway station, and there is thus a good field open for the haulier in transporting the farmers' produce to the rail, while return loads are provided by the needs of the agricultural community, such as fodder, manures, feeding stuffs, oil, household goods, implements, etc.

Another type of enterprise very suited to motor transport is the conveyance of milk either to a railway station or direct to the towns. The railway strike of 1919 did a great deal to popularize this method of transporting milk, and during that period an elaborate system of road transport was quickly built up to secure the distribution of that essential commodity. After the strike road transport managed to retain a considerable volume of the milk traffic, and nowadays motor vehicles play an important part in such work in those districts not too far removed from the towns.

The farmer appreciates road services, as they save the expense and delay of carting to and from stations. The churns are generally left by the side of the main road or on a small platform to save delay in loading, and are collected either by a haulage contractor or by some farmer who owns a lorry and is willing to undertake transport work for his fellow agriculturists. A useful return load is provided by the return of empty churns, which are left by the roadside to be collected by the farmer. It is now a common sight in many parts of England to see churns left at the wayside, to be transported to market or the railway station or reclaimed by the owner. Some haulage contractors simplify the business of the farmer by collecting his money from the dealers and retaining out of it the cost of transport. The farmer is thus saved much trouble, and has not to meet transport charges until he has received payment for his products.

In other directions, too, this method of arranging for the collection of produce from farms lying some little distance from the main road has secured a considerable degree of popularity, and contractors engaged in the collection of small loads of varied types of produce from a number of farmers find that the bulking of loads provides remunerative work.

In the U.S.A. somewhat similar schemes have met with a fair degree of success. What are called "Rural Motor Express Services" are now, and have been for some time, in operation in the vicinity of many of the larger towns. In Maryland especially their development has been rapid.

In a Bulletin of the Council of National Defence the services are thus described: "These lines have been developed on a sane practical basis, without any special promotion or encouragement from any State or national organization. The trucks start at a small town, gather the produce of farmers and merchants along the roads to the city, deliver it at the market, secure a return load from city merchants, including orders by farmers, and return to the country terminal, delivering the orders along the routes. . . . Many farmers living a short distance away from the rural express route bring their milk and produce to a point on this route with horse-drawn buggies and wagons, and these constitute feeders to the lines." [1]

Since the publication of this Report, however, the development of these rural services has not been as rapid as might be expected from the importance assumed by road transport in the U.S.A. But this, it is said, has been due largely to agricultural depression, and in part to lack of knowledge in management and operation by some of the lines, rather than to any unsuitability of road transport for such work. The value of the system of rural motor express

[1] Quoted by Sir Evan Jones in his evidence before the Select Committee on Transport, October 1918.

services when properly organized is said to have been fully demonstrated.

The establishment and growth of agricultural motor services, however, may be encouraged by the increasing importance of movements aiming at the better organization of farmers, such as, among others, the American Farm Bureau Federation.

To return from this digression to conditions in Britain. Many farmers have adopted mechanical road vehicles of their own. On the whole, farmers generally prefer to own their vehicles rather than to contract with road hauliers for their transport requirements, and particularly in the northern counties this practice is more generally followed. To own a motor vehicle or several vehicles makes a farmer more independent, since he can then arrange for the transport of his produce or materials at times most suitable to himself and at his own convenience.

As regards the type of vehicle favoured, it would appear that the agrimotor or small tractor, despite the advantage it has of being capable of use as a stationary engine or in various kinds of agricultural operation, has not become so popular as the motor van or lorry. There are no doubt several reasons for this, one perhaps being that higher speeds are practicable with vans or lorries. In general 1-tonners — frequently "Fords" — are employed by farmers, and these have been found well suited for most kinds of work, especially in dairy farming, fruit growing, or vegetable and market gardening. For heavier commodities, such as potatoes, and for longer distance work, the 2- or 3-tonner has been found more suitable.

A difficulty of considerable magnitude, however, may face a farmer desirous of utilizing mechanical transport, for his loads may not always suffice to provide full employment for the vehicle or vehicles, and thus the initial capital outlay may not be justified.

In South-West Lancashire the difficulty is overcome by the hiring out of vehicles, when not otherwise required, to the local councils. Farmers' organizations throughout the country could do a great deal to help farmers to economize in the use of road vehicles if they bestirred themselves in the matter. They could co-ordinate the work and provide loads for the owners of vehicles by organizing transport facilities for other farmers not possessing motors of their own or for those who have a temporary need for more transport.

In some cases the provision of a motor lorry would be a useful venture on the part of certain Agricultural Co-operative Societies, as it would meet an important need of their members. In the difficult times now facing agriculture any organization that might prove of advantage ought not to be neglected. The provision of road transport would do something to secure better markets and to eliminate some of the too numerous middlemen.

The Encouragement of Pioneer Services in Rural Districts.

The small man who launches out on a new service may find that his experiment, if successful, or even if only moderately successful, calls out competitors, with the result that he reaps little reward, and fares or rates may indeed be driven down to such a low level that he can barely make a living. His rivals may of course find themselves in a similar position, but for the time they are unwilling to go out of business, as it might mean a sacrifice of capital. At the present time, when motor transport is in a difficult position owing to trade depression, it is said that such possibilities tend to hinder development. It is urged that pioneers are discouraged because of the fear that competitors may come in after the heat and burden of the day has been borne by the originator and reap where they have not sown. The initiation of a service is most difficult at the outset, before a travel habit has been formed, and often means a considerable period of small profit and hard work to build up an adequate traffic.

Now it is true that the pioneer may suffer unfairly in this way, but it is difficult to devise a method that will secure the field to the man who has built it up, without at the same time hindering further development and without fostering a monopoly that may become undesirable in the public interest.

Perhaps the best safeguard of the pioneer lies in securing the goodwill of the neighbourhood and providing an efficient service.

It has been suggested that the method followed in many other countries might be adopted in Britain. This plan is to grant one proprietor the sole right of providing public transport services in his area for a number of years to ensure that he will be secured in the fruits of his enterprise, subject to adequate safeguards as to the quality and sufficiency of the service he provides.

In France the Government has gone further, and gives subsidies to approved services in rural areas where the traffic forthcoming would not suffice to remunerate private enterprise, e.g. in the Pyrenees district, though in this case the grant of a subsidy does not necessarily imply a monopoly.

There are, however, considerable and obvious difficulties in the way of the adoption of any similar policy in Great Britain. Then again, the grant of a subsidy or the fostering of a monopoly—even if for a limited period and however well deserved in cases—is somewhat alien to British ideas of transport development.

Notes.

Subsidized Motor Services in France.—In the country districts which are not well served by railways, and where the construction of railroads would be financially impossible, the French Government has developed a considerable number of motor bus and motor lorry services by the grant of subsidies. The object of this policy is to provide adequate transport facilities in those districts which offer too sparse a traffic to attract private enterprises.

No subsidies are granted to concerns operating in or near large towns or to those that cater only for tourist and sight-seeing passengers.

It is in the thinly populated regions or in the hilly and mountainous part of the country that the subsidized services are to be found, as, for example, at the foot of the Pyrenees. The Government fixes the fares and determines the minimum requirements as to the service that is to be offered. The speed, capacity, route and number of trips per day are all prescribed.

No monopoly is necessarily granted, but a subsidy is paid according to the capacity of the vehicle and the mileage traversed.

Agriculture and Road Transport.—Since the above chapter was written, two important committees on agriculture have reported, both of which attach considerable importance to road transport. In a report by Sir William Ashley and Professor Adams it is stated that "The economy in the marketing of agricultural produce by means of a system which can pick up goods at the farm and deliver them at the final destination makes road motor and steam transport a factor of very great importance for agriculture; and one of the most effective safeguards against undue railway rates will lie in the extension of competition from road transport. We believe that the organization of services of road transport to meet agricultural requirements deserves special attention." (Agricultural Tribunal of Investigation. Cmd. 2145, p. 80.)

In the Report of a Departmental Committee on Distribution and Prices of Agricultural Produce ("The Linlithgow Committee") a similar conclusion was reached. "Our evidence leads us to attach the greatest importance to the new progressive policy of road development and improvement. It should tend materially to cheapen and quicken the transport of farm produce to consumer or market." (Final Report, 1924, p. 19.)

CHAPTER X

CITY TRANSPORT

ADEQUATE, cheap and efficient passenger transport facilities are an essential requirement of urban life. The problem of how these are to be provided is of pressing importance, though not one easy of solution. In the first place the problem is one of considerable social significance, because lack of transport facilities affects the health and well-being of the citizens, since it may mean congestion of population and overcrowding in certain parts of the city. The problem has also its economic side, since transport costs must be as low as possible, but at the same time the greatest efficiency must be maintained. The problem is an administrative one also, since the local authorities must provide for the construction and maintenance of roads, for the control of traffic, and the prevention of undue congestion of traffic. Often indeed they are further called upon to provide and operate transport services.

Further, it is also a traffic problem, since speed in transit is essential, and sufficient accommodation must be provided to meet the varying traffic requirements throughout the day, and this has to be achieved at the least possible cost per passenger-mile. In London and Greater London it has been calculated that the enormous total of more than eight million passengers have to be carried daily.

In a large city few people live within walking distance of their work, nor is it desirable that they should do so, for that could only mean that housing conditions were unhealthy and the population crowded into some few districts.

The provision of adequate transit facilities means that workers can live at some distance from the places of employment. Good transport also helps to spread industries to outside areas, and thus helps directly to relieve the central crowded areas of a city.

The most important problem to be solved in city transport is that of moving the working population every week-day from their homes in the suburbs or outskirts to the factories, offices or shops in the city and back again in the afternoon or evening. To the vast army of city workers rapid and cheap transit is a great boon, while any unnecessary delay or increased cost is a heavy burden. Slow transport automatically reduces the leisure time of every citizen. But the importance of city transport does not cease at this point, for in addition to conveying the rush hour traffic, cheap and rapid transit is essential for those who require to move from one part of the city to another in the pursuit of business, social, educational or other engagements. Many also require to travel for the purpose of visiting places of interest or of entertainment, or to make their purchases at the shops or stores. The growth of the amusement habit has considerably increased the amount of travelling in cities, especially since the rise of the cinema to popularity.

Well organized, inexpensive and efficient transport facilities are of the first importance in the economic and social life of our cities and towns.

In relation to health, the housing problem, the prevention of overcrowding, and the development of new residential areas, urban transport has an important part to play. Where the means of travelling is brought within the reach of all classes by an efficient and well-planned transport system, the population can be spread over a wide area, with the result that living is at once more pleasant and more healthy. The inhabitants of residential districts are placed within easy and convenient access of the cheaper markets and shopping centres, with the result that retail prices tend to be more equalized. Away from the centre portions of the town rentals are lower, since the area available for building increases much more than in proportion to the radius from the centre of the town. Cheap and rapid transport thus helps to reduce rents—that important item in the family budget.

Heavy transport charges constitute an appreciable pecuniary burden not only on manual workers, but also on the great army of clerks and other workers in receipt of small salaries, and thus cheap fares are of the greatest advantage to the worker.

As a city grows in size the necessity for additional transport facilities increases in a greater ratio, since the population tends to spread out away from the central parts, which become more and more non-residential in character. If this centrifugal distribution of the population does not take place serious evils may result. The central area will become crowded and unhealthy, and may perhaps develop into a slum. It is an impossible proposition to house artisans or labourers in those central parts so that living conditions may be good while rents are moderate, even if there was sufficient room to do so. Congestion must be prevented, and the most effective means to this end is to provide cheap and efficient transport. A celebrated Royal Commission on London traffic declared with reason that "the evils resulting from slow and imperfect means of locomotion appear to us to be quite as serious from a social as from an economic point of view." [1]

Few social problems are more pressing than the clearance of slum areas and the improvement of housing conditions in our large towns. Anything that will help in the solution of this problem is of the first importance. Now, one important aid, though not of course a complete solution in itself, is cheaper transport and more of it. The improvement of transport facilities gives a greater inducement to the town dweller to reside in the outlying areas and the surround-

[1] Cd. 2597, 1905, p. 9, para. 12.

ing country districts. It is not sufficient, however, that transport undertakings should provide only for existing conditions, however well they may do it. New traffic must be built up, and where possible transit facilities should be planned ahead of the actual requirements of the day, so that the further development of outlying residential areas will be encouraged. Transport should thus lead the way in the movement towards decentralization of urban life.

If facilities are provided for going out in all directions, not merely in a few areas, ground rents would be lower, since the demand would be dispersed over a wider area and not concentrated in the one or two accessible districts. " In order to relieve overcrowding means must be provided for taking the population into and out of London not in one or two directions, but in many directions at rapid speed, frequent intervals and cheap rates." [1] This dictum of the Royal Commission on London Traffic applies not only to London, but to many other towns.

In 1919 another Committee declared that the solution of the housing problem largely depends upon the provision of adequate transport facilities.[2]

The chief obstacle to the extension of city transport systems is that of finance. Extension may mean that a large amount of capital has to be sunk, and this cannot be expected to yield a return for a very long period. Development services, however, cannot be expected always to pay their way fully for some years, and such routes have generally to be subsidized by the better paying routes.

Since a progressive policy is essential and since traffic needs to be built up, a strong argument is furnished in favour of single control, if not ownership, of all transport facilities in a district. Routes which, if viewed in isolation, would be unremunerative, can be served, if control is unified and the various essential links in the chain of city transport can be provided for on a systematic plan. Competition,

[1] Cd. 2597 (1905).
[2] Report of Select Committee on Transport (Metropolitan Area), 1919.

on the other hand, might mean that the better paying routes would be over provided with facilities, while other routes would be completely neglected. If the best system of city transport is to be evolved, the problem must be viewed as a whole.

The question of the adjustment between remunerative and non-remunerative or development services is one of particular nicety, for, on the one hand, it would not do to starve the latter routes, but, on the other, if numerous light traffic routes are operated, the result must be that higher fares have to be charged on the better paying routes. The possibility of extension viewed from the economic point of view depends largely on the particular system, or rather method of transportation, that is to be utilized for the purpose.

In Edinburgh, for instance, before the conversion to electric operation in recent years, any new development was practically prevented by the great expense involved in the construction of new cable tramway routes.

By the correct appreciation of the economic characteristics and traffic suitability of the various types of transport, an adequate transport system can be provided in many cities by a combination of the different methods.

The electric or steam operated railway—surface, underground or elevated—is only suitable if traffic be heavy. Likewise a tramway, if it is to be remunerative, requires considerable though not such heavy traffic. But in recent years, and especially since the war, the coming of the motor bus has done much to simplify the problem, and buses are now employed as "feeders" to many municipal tramway concerns, and in some cases the buses penetrate far into the countryside.

On routes where traffic is not dense or in outlying areas the motor bus has marked advantages over all other systems of passenger transport. It is a very flexible mode of transport, and it can thrive on a light traffic.

Road transport, whether bus or tramway, has a great

advantage over the suburban railway in that people are not massed around railway stations in crowded communities that may become "suburban slums." Since passengers can be picked up or set down at any point, the population is spread out along the line of route, as well as laterally to some distance on each side.[1]

There is, however, no finality in the answer to the question as to what constitutes the best type of urban passenger transport. It is impossible to say that any one method is the best, and indeed in a large city the solution can only be found through the co-operation of many forms of transport. The different systems—tram, bus, railway, underground, etc.—have each their own merits, their limitations and their own traffic requirements. In particular the nature of the traffic—its density, the length of journey, and the hourly distribution—must be considered.

"The point where each vehicle becomes the economic instrument cannot be defined in general terms, as with the growth of services, longer hours of operation, larger units of conveyance and lower fares all operating together, the point where each respective system becomes the economic instrument is modified, giving really an overlapping period indeterminate in duration except by reference to a precise route."[2]

As regards traffic density, for instance, the motor bus has not been found to be best suited for coping with heavy rush hour traffic, and in London the trams, tubes and railways carry a far greater proportion of this traffic than do the buses.

The length of the journey is another important factor, and a broad distinction between long and short distance journeys is observable. What have been called "the rapid transit" facilities, as afforded, for example, by tube or rail, cater especially for the longer distance passenger,

[1] See Cd. 2987 (1906), Royal Commission on London Traffic, Appendix G, by Stephen Sellon.

[2] Report by H. Mattinson to the Manchester Corporation Tramways Committee, July 31, 1923.

and the choice between these and tram or bus is determined by the two factors of speed and road congestion. For short distances, say up to 2 miles, the saving of time is not very appreciable, but for greater distances the bus or tram are slower.[1]

Frequency of service is an important consideration, since it may help to build up traffic that otherwise would not be forthcoming. If passengers are to be attracted in urban areas, the service offered must be frequent as well as rapid. It is principally for this reason the suburban railways often find it desirable to electrify their lines. This policy has often been forced upon them by the competition of their rivals, first the tramway and now the motor bus. It is true that the capacity of steam-operated lines can be increased by the construction of shorter block sections and improved signalling, but electrification where conditions are otherwise suitable has proved in general the better alternative. The L.B. & S.C.R. (now incorporated in the Southern Railway) found that its suburban traffic increased greatly after electrification was adopted. When the Manchester–Bury Railway was electrified traffic increased by nearly 60 per cent.

In certain towns any one of the various methods of urban transport may be the most suitable and the most economic, while in other cases it may be an entirely unsuitable method. In the larger cities a combination of various methods has been found to be essential.

The Problem of Traffic Congestion in Cities.—In recent years the problem of traffic congestion has been brought very much to the front as a result of the growth of our large cities and the large increase in the number of journeys per head of the population. In London the problem has become particularly acute, though, of course, the problem of congestion is not confined to London.[2] On the London

[1] On these questions see a valuable paper by H. H. Gordon on " Passenger Transport in Large Cities " (Institute of Transport, N.W. Section).

[2] See Note at end of chapter for statistics of London traffic.

streets the average speed of movement has been greatly reduced as a result of the great increase in motor bus and other vehicular traffic. Before the war London traffic moved as fast as that in any of the world's large cities, but now it is amongst the slowest. In certain parts the average speed is below 5 miles per hour, it is said, and this is to be compared to a pre-war average of 8 or 9 miles per hour. The traffic problem in London bristles with difficulties, and is perhaps more acute than in any other great city, with the exception of New York.[1]

London is the only capital city in the world where no attempt has been made by the Government or city authorities to regulate and control the provision of transport facilities. The matter, however, is now being taken in hand, though for many years past Committee after Committee on the subject of London transport has recommended the setting up of some sort of controlling authority.

In the London area there are a number of distinct types of passenger transport to furnish the facilities required—the tubes, motor omnibuses, tramways, numerous taxi-cabs and private cars, and, especially in suburban and outlying districts, electric and steam operated railways—but so far the only co-ordination has been effected by a private combine which controls the Underground railways, the London General Omnibus Company and certain tramways. This Combine works the various systems under its control in conjunction with each other and provides through facilities, etc., while, on the financial side, each system contributes its profits to a common pool. By means of this

[1] In New York City few motor bus services are run, but immense numbers of taxi cabs and private motor cars utilize the streets, which are thus very congested. The difficulties experienced and the slowness of travel led to the introduction of novel methods of traffic control. A definite scheme was adopted on a basis suitable to the rectangular planning of the streets. The police exercise control by means of high traffic towers set up in the centre of the streets at certain points, and by this means the whole traffic movement of the main centres is synchronized, north- and south-bound traffic having the right of way for a time, then east- and west-bound, and so on in rotation. At night distinctively coloured lights are used to guide the traffic.

common fund the prior charges on each system are met before any dividend is available for the ordinary shares of any of its constituent companies.

The problem in London is a twofold one, for it is both a financial and a traffic problem. Congestion means that the various systems do not pay their way as they should, while it also means that the rate of travel is unduly slowed down.

The Police Authorities in London have no powers to deal with the problem of traffic congestion other than those which require them to regulate the traffic passing along the streets. Vehicles that are utilized for public conveyance, such as motor buses or taxi-cabs, are licensed by the police, but there is no control exerted as to the numbers that are placed on the streets. So long as the vehicle comes up to the requirements of Scotland Yard and is thus passed and licensed, it may be put on the road without any further restrictions.

As regards the causes of traffic congestion, these are numerous. One important source of congestion which applies to many towns and cities as well as London is almost unavoidable, as it is due to the rush hour traffic. During recent years the shortening of the hours of labour has intensified peak hour traffic, for now the exodus from shops, offices and factories more or less synchronizes, and, instead of being spread over two or three hours, is concentrated in a shorter period of time.

Another important factor, especially in London, has been the increase in the number of vehicles on the streets, due to the rise of new motor bus competition. By January of 1924 seventy-four new concerns, owning two hundred and eight vehicles, had grown up in the short space of a few months. Though many of these concerns were operated on a very small scale, yet in the aggregate a considerable number of new buses had been put into commission, and the number, for the present at any rate, is increasing month by month. Moreover, to protect its interests, the Combine has also put a large number of new vehicles on its routes. The result has been to increase traffic congestion very considerably, and to slow down the speed of transit without increasing to any great extent the number of passengers carried. It has also meant that the better paying routes have too many vehicles, while it is probable that the services on poorer traffic routes may be curtailed.

The great increase in the number of vehicles on certain routes may also increase the dangers of the streets, and already several cases have come before the police courts of alleged obstruction, reckless driving, "swinging" or "nursing" to cut in on rivals and the like. In fact, all the old evils of the period of acute competition of the old horse-drawn omnibus days before a Combine was formed have reappeared.

Undue competition, under the circumstances, would destroy any chance of development of traffic facilities along proper lines, increase the danger of the streets, cause nuisance to the public, and would be likely to mean financial loss to all the competitors.

Yet another element in the problem is the competition between omnibuses and the tramways. Competition of this nature, where the same route is served, will generally mean that neither form of transport can be placed on a secure and satisfactory basis, and involves waste and uneconomic operation. It is even said that the Combine has had to put buses in competition with its own tramways to safeguard the route from rival bus concerns.

In London confusion is further increased by competition between various municipal authorities and also between the municipalities and private traders. "The dilemma remains that, however you look at it, successful omnibuses are insufficient compensation for starved tubes and impoverished tramways. London wants all the facilities it now enjoys and more, and wants them healthy, sound and progressive" (Lord Ashfield).

Another factor contributing to the confusion is that no attempt is made to co-ordinate the work of road repair and to provide that the amount of traffic dislocation involved thereby will be kept down to a minimum. As it is, the work is not done on any ordered or systematic basis, and it sometimes even happens that parallel roads or alternative traffic routes are under repair at the same time and partially or completely closed to traffic. Further, no co-ordinating authority exists that can prevent a road being pulled up unnecessarily or too frequently. It would be an easy matter to arrange that the various undertakings, such as gas, water and electricity supply, or telephone, telegraph or sewer authorities, should get all necessary work required performed as much as is possible at the time when the road is already up, and thus the too frequent disturbance of the road surface would be avoided.

Something could also be done to relieve congestion if traffic problems were dealt with on a more systematic basis. It would, for instance, often be a simple matter to arrange for alternative routes which should be clearly sign-posted so as to be known to all road users. Such a policy would do something to relieve congestion on overcrowded thoroughfares by encouraging drivers to take less congested routes. Likewise in the case of narrow streets, a simple expedient would be to limit them to one-way traffic, provided, of course, that parallel or alternative routes were available.

In many cities the traffic problem is accentuated by the amount of through traffic that passes along the streets. Sometimes, indeed, a main road cuts through the centre of a town, and all through traffic has to pass along a virtual bottle-neck, as in many of the older towns the streets are tortuous and narrow. Besides increasing congestion, it has the effect of considerably slowing down the rate of transit between other centres. The remedy for this state of affairs is the construction of new routes that will pass around the outskirts of the town. Clear indications as to the best route should be provided on the main traffic routes outside the towns, so that motor vehicle drivers will be able to avoid passing through the busy centres. This was the policy followed by the military authorities in France and Belgium during the war. "Avoiding Roads," as they were called, were built around the towns, and along these all through traffic was diverted. Unless these alternative routes had been provided mechanical road transport would have been greatly reduced in efficiency, if indeed it could otherwise have coped at all adequately with the work to be done.

Congestion is also frequently caused by vans standing in streets for the purpose of loading or unloading; hence it has been suggested that vehicles should only be allowed to stand in narrow congested streets at certain hours of the day.

The provision of back entrances to warehouses, large shops, etc., would also prove helpful, since loading and unloading could be then carried out without interference to other traffic.

Mechanical road transport, as anyone can observe, is frequently held up by slow horse-drawn transport, and a single-horsed vehicle can often be observed holding up a string of motor vehicles for a considerable time until some opportunity is presented for them to pass it. It has been argued that in the busiest parts of large towns and cities all horse-drawn traffic should be prohibited except during certain hours.

Horsed vehicles, it is asserted, should be diverted to the less busy streets. Lord Montagu of Beaulieu is a well-known advocate of such a reform, and the arguments brought forward in favour of this policy may be best presented by quoting from a letter of his Lordship to *The Times* on this subject. In this letter he stated that "Everywhere horse-drawn carts and vehicles block the faster traffic, despite the praiseworthy, even if not universal, attempts of the police to enforce the rule that slow traffic should keep near the kerb. In the Strand, Regent Street, Oxford Street, Piccadilly, Edgware Road—in fact, in any of the great thoroughfares of London—the horse-drawn vehicle delays 95 per cent. of all the other mechanical traffic, and accentuates and increases the dangers of the streets to pedestrians and road users alike."

"The principal streets of London are, generally speaking, too narrow for the traffic which uses them from 10 a.m.

to 6 p.m. If horse-drawn vehicles could be forbidden in certain crowded thoroughfares between 10 a.m. and 6 p.m., what immediate relief there would be ! "

"Twenty years ago the horse-drawn vehicle was still necessary for commerce, for there were no mechanical vehicles, heavy or light, to take its place. To-day the vehicle propelled by petrol, steam or electricity can do everything that a horse vehicle can do. In many cases the new form of transport is cheaper, and only in a very few special cases does it cost more, and the time saved by mechanical transport more than compensates for any slight extra cost. If all our street traffic moved at a higher and more or less equal speed the relief would be immense. Our working population, using both motor omnibuses and tramway cars, could get to and from their homes more quickly and all citizens would benefit. Incidentally, also, our streets would be more sanitary, for it is chiefly in horse-dung that the pestilential fly breeds, the fly which is more deadly to infant life than any other single cause."

Finally, adequate sign-posting—a thing till recently almost unknown in our cities—would do a great deal to relieve congestion, as nearly all traffic follows certain main routes merely because alternative roads are unknown to strangers. The Ministry of Transport and the various motor associations have, however, taken the matter in hand, and direction signs are now being erected in many towns.

To remedy the chaotic condition of London traffic, it has been suggested time after time that the only course is to institute some authoritative body which would view the problem as a whole and regulate and co-ordinate the numerous factors in the solution of the problem.

The setting up of some such body has been recommended by practically all of the numerous Committees or Commissions appointed to investigate the problem from the time of the Royal Commission on London Traffic of 1903–5.

In 1919 an Advisory Committee was established, but its powers were very limited, and it was only able to apply its energies to the settlement of certain minor traffic problems.

This Committee, which consisted of representatives of the "Underground," the L.C.C. Tramways, the Police and the Transport Workers' Union, did good work in the limited sphere open to it, but its powers were altogether insufficient to enable it to tackle the main problems.

In 1920 a Conference was called between the Minister of Transport and the L.C.C. and the "Combine," where it was agreed that the unified operation of local passenger transport services in London and adjacent districts was a necessity, and that it was desirable that a Traffic Control Authority should be set up.

It is now generally agreed that some supreme traffic authority is required, but there is no unanimity as to the powers that ought to be granted to such an authority or as to its constitution.

As to the composition of such authority, two main but divergent proposals have each their advocates. There are first those who favour the formation of a small body of paid experts who would be attached to the Ministry of Transport. Others, however, favour a body consisting of delegates from the various local authorities and other interested parties.

Further discussion turns on the powers to be granted to the body—some advocate advisory powers only, others hold that legal powers are necessary if its work is to be effective. If the body is merely advisory, it is contended that in practice it would not be effective and that its recommendations would not be carried out. But, on the other hand, it may be argued that if a statutory authority of experts be created, then the difficulty would lie in the question of its finance. The Government could hardly draw upon national funds for the benefit of London, while local authorities would no doubt be unwilling to raise revenue through their rates for the experts to spend as they thought fit.

In favour of an expert body of a few members it is urged that it would be impartial and could develop a continuous policy uninfluenced by changes in the local authorities. It is said it would mean that the rival claims of private transport concerns and municipal enterprises would be balanced more impartially than could possibly be the case if the authority was composed, say, of the representatives of local authorities.

In 1922 an important memorandum was submitted by Sir Henry Maybury, the Director-General of Roads, to the Royal Commission on London Government. Herein it was recommended that a Traffic Committee be appointed to give advice and assistance to the Minister of Transport on all matters connected with London traffic. This Committee, it was suggested, should consist of not less than eleven or more than fifteen members, representing the Ministry of Transport, the L.C.C., the Metropolitan Boroughs, various County Councils, Labour, the "Combine," Railways, Users of Horse and Motor Transport, etc.

The area to be regulated by the Authority was fixed as that within a 25-mile radius from Charing Cross. Among its duties were to be included the co-ordination of all passenger transport agencies, the preparation of a development plan for London traffic, control of town planning and housing schemes from a traffic point of view, traffic regulation, etc.

In March 1924, as a result of a tramway strike, a Bill was introduced in the House of Commons with the object of setting up some supreme traffic authority, the provisions being based largely on the memorandum of Sir Henry Maybury and the Report of the London Government Committee.

By a subsequent Act—the London Traffic Act, 1924—an Advisory Committee, representative of the various interests involved, has been set up to advise the Minister of Transport on matters connected with the means of transit in "Greater London." This Committee, known as the "London and Home Counties Traffic Advisory Committee," has itself no compulsory powers, and the Act is limited to a four years' period (up to December 1, 1928). The duties of the Committee are to consider and report to the Minister on any matters within the scope of the

Act, e.g. limitation of buses on certain streets, the closing of streets for repair or public works, etc.

Note.

London Traffic Figures.—During the last twenty years or so there has been a great increase in the number of passengers in the London area.

In 1903, according to the Reports of the London Traffic Branch of the Board of Trade, the number of passengers carried in London by tramways, omnibuses and local railways (including certain Tube and suburban railway services) was 972,465,682. By 1914 the number had risen to 2,064,612,057.

In the subjoined table the number of passengers carried by the various transport systems is shown for the years 1920, 1921 and 1922, the figures being taken from those compiled by the Valuer of the London County Council Estates and Housing Departments.

	1920.	1921.	1922.
Omnibuses, L.G.O.C. ..	767,953,469	761,251,405	846,682,673
Omnibuses, other companies	167,992,533	170,499,637	147,126,917
Tube railways (Combine)	265,587,941	216,996,197	207,449,968
Tramways	1,062,986,520	1,009,043,113	1,036,176,655
Local railways (excluding Tubes, but including District, Metropolitan, Whitechapel and Bow, G.N. and City, North London) (approximate) ..	424,000,000	371,000,000	365,500,000
Suburban traffic on trunk railways (estimated)	368,000,000	324,000,000	319,000,000
Total (approximate) .	3,056,000,000	2,852,500,000	2,921,500,000

It is to be expected, of course, that the traffic figures of 1921 and 1922 should fall below those of 1920 owing to trade depression.

CHAPTER XI

THE MOTOR BUS

In the commercial utilization of mechanical road transport the motor bus has been the pioneer. As far back as the early years of the nineteenth century, as has been described in an earlier chapter, steam coaches were put into operation on the roads as public vehicles, and for a time it seemed that they might rival the railways. Again, in the early years of the present century the first general application of the new transport to commercial purposes was for the carriage of passengers.

Since the war the motor bus has become increasingly popular, and now motor services are to be found operating in nearly all towns and cities as well as in many rural areas. Regular road passenger services have, indeed, increased to such an extent that the issue of a motor bus "Bradshaw" once a month has been justified. It is now, indeed, possible to travel from the South of England to Scotland, or from London to the West, by utilizing the services of the existing network of regular road passenger carriers without having to travel a single mile by railway.

In urban areas the motor bus is growing in favour as a method of carrying the inhabitants of the suburbs and the surrounding country to the centre of the town or city, and during recent years considerable development has taken place in the promotion and extension of such services.

Outside the urban areas the motor bus has also captured a secure position for itself, and services now penetrate into the remote country districts, connecting hamlets and villages with their market towns. The new transport has served to open up those districts that hitherto have been inadequately served by the railways, and also those parts removed by several miles from a railway station.

Many of the existing passenger-carrying undertakings have sprung from small beginnings. During the last few years the pre-war concerns have generally extended rapidly, while services established even after the war are now in many instances flourishing undertakings.

In brief it may be said that motor bus services are now an indispensable factor in every day life, and the motor bus is secured as an essential type of transport that could not easily be dispensed with.

The Advantages of the Motor Bus.—Where traffic conditions are suitable, the motor bus has many special advantages for the transport of passengers in both urban and rural areas.

The motor bus has proved a severe competitor to the tramways, and also to the railways where distances are not too long, even in the years before the war, while as the result of the great development of this means of transportation that competition has been considerably intensified since the war.

The assets of the motor bus lie in its flexibility and in the low proportion of the overhead charges to running costs.

Passenger transport by rail, tram, river or canal, is confined to a fixed way, but not so the motor bus. It can go almost anywhere, since our roads lead everywhere. This flexibility confers several advantages on the motor bus. Since no capital has to be sunk in providing a specialized permanent way before a service can be inaugurated, motor bus routes can be readily changed without entailing additional expense. Experiments can thus be tried without danger of loss of capital, for if one route does not pay another can be substituted.

The motor bus has greater freedom than the tramcar, which is confined to its track, and thus it can steer in and out of obstacles on the roadway. This mobility is of considerable importance, especially in busy thoroughfares, congested streets, and narrow roads. Motor buses cause less interference with other vehicular traffic, since they can take their place in the main traffic streams, and are not forced to follow a definite path like the tramcar. Motor drivers complain that tramcars cause obstruction and hold up other traffic, especially at corners and cross-roads. The break-down of a single vehicle does not hold up the whole system. Further, motor buses can pass and repass one another, and thus time can be saved and the loading of the vehicles will be more equalized. With a tramway, it often happens that a tram is held up by one in front, and it is not uncommon to see one car overloaded while another immediately behind may be almost empty. The bus has a further advantage in that it can draw up at the kerbside for the purpose of setting down or taking up its passengers. In busy streets this means greater safety, as passengers do not need to cross a line of road traffic, as is generally the case if they have to board or leave a tramcar. With a motor bus system no overhead and often unsightly wires are required, and hence such a method of transport interferes less with the amenities of the streets.

Like the tramway, but unlike the railway, a motor bus can take up or set down its passengers at any point *en route*, and this is of especial importance where journeys are short. Other advantages of the bus as compared with the railway are that it can often take shorter cross-country routes ; that passengers may be saved the time and fatigue of walking to and from stations, since the motor bus runs through the streets ; or it may be that a motor bus service can take passengers right into the market place or the centre of the town, whereas the railway station may be some distance outside, as for example in Oxford.

A motor bus undertaking may also be able to afford more frequent and convenient services than can be provided by the local railway, since the frequency and timing of trains is often determined by other than local needs. Also the motor bus does not require so many passengers to give a paying load, and in this connection it may be mentioned that in certain places the railways have themselves experimented with motor buses fitted with flanged wheels and run over the railway lines, so that a more frequent service can be given without the excessive cost of running a train capable of seating large numbers, but only partially filled because traffic is small.

Passengers by bus are saved the formality of purchasing a ticket at a booking office and the trouble of finding the train, and for short-distance travelling this may suffice to incline some in favour of the bus, though no doubt habit also tends to influence passengers one way or the other.

The second characteristic of the motor bus, i.e. the relatively low ratio of capital on-costs to running expenses, is of great importance where traffic is light. Capital expenditure can be more evenly proportioned to the traffic that is available than it could in the case of railed transport. If the traffic increases, the number of vehicles can be increased to meet the developments as required, and without involving any great jumps in the total capital outlay of the system. For railways or tramways a heavy capital outlay is required whatever the traffic volume that is to be catered for. An expensive and specialized track must be laid down, and for tramways or electrified railways the necessary electric equipment must also be provided. The heavy initial capital outlay necessitated by such systems obviously precludes their construction unless a reasonable volume of traffic is likely to be forthcoming. A motor bus service, on the contrary, can be inaugurated without risk so long as sufficient traffic is likely to be available to remunerate the running of a single vehicle, since the overhead charges are low. The motor bus can thrive on a light traffic, but not so the railway or the tramway, which require to be worked at high pressure to give the best financial or economic results.

On the road the unit is the vehicle, not the system, and

no permanent way, electric equipment or power station is required.

Limitations.—Despite the great improvements made in the technique of motor bus construction during recent years, they still suffer from several defects and limitations. The motor bus is frequently uncomfortable, sometimes, however, unnecessarily so. Continual vibration, bad ventilation and noise tend to make bus journeys unpleasant, and may thus drive away prospective passengers. The motor bus is not suited for long through journeys, though for distances up to, say, 10 miles it forms an indispensable mode of conveyance.

Many types of motor bus outside the Metropolis have only a limited seating capacity, and this means overcrowding, while the task of coping with rush hour traffic is made doubly difficult.

No doubt in time it will be possible to mitigate these disadvantages.[1] Already, despite limitations as to length, etc., imposed by Scotland Yard, the L.G.O.C. buses have been constructed so as to accommodate large numbers of passengers, fifty-four in the case of the "S" type and fifty-two in the "N.S." In many places experiments are being tried with giant pneumatic tyres and improved springing. The advantages of pneumatic tyres are so great that it is a pity that their adoption is not more general, but the difficulty lies in the increased expense as compared with solid tyres. The use of pneumatic tyres would mean far greater comfort to the passenger, less noise on the roads, less wear and tear of the bus body and chassis, with a consequent saving in the cost of repairs, a smaller petrol consumption, and less damage to the roads.

Another difficulty that tends to restrict the development of the motor bus is the legal limitation of speed to 12 miles per hour in the case of the larger vehicles. If buses were allowed to travel at 20 miles per hour they could compete

[1] Recently top-covered buses have been introduced in several cities, e.g. New York, Sheffield and Birmingham.

more easily with local train services as regards journey time, for where there are numerous stations, local trains may take over an hour to cover 20 miles.

There is no doubt that speed and comfort are well worth attention on the part of motor bus proprietors, for these two factors have considerable bearing on receipts.

Large and Small Buses.—The rival merits and disadvantages of the large and the small bus have provoked much discussion, and each has its partisans. The influence of the requirements of London and other large cities has had considerable weight with manufacturers who have devoted their attention to the evolution of a bus with large seating capacity. Undoubtedly in such cases the large bus is best suited for meeting the particular traffic requirements of those areas, since the problem there is to cope with heavy traffic especially during the rush hours. The growth of traffic in urban and suburban areas, and competition by the tramcar with its large seating capacity, have done much to popularize the double-decker. Even in the moderate-sized towns large buses are essential if rush hour traffic is to be catered for at all adequately.

In some towns traffic problems present very considerable difficulty to operating companies, since during a large part of the day traffic may be light, but may increase very greatly at the rush hours. No doubt the best solution would be the employment of both large and small capacity vehicles, but such a course is generally impossible, as it would involve too large a capital outlay.

In small towns, villages and rural areas, as well as on the routes of sparse traffic in the larger towns, the single-deck bus with its more limited seating capacity, but with its lower running costs per bus-mile and its lower licence duty, is the more suitable. Not only are running costs, such as petrol, oil, etc., reduced, the capital outlay is also smaller, while if one-man-operated buses be employed the wages bill is also cut down. In such cases the smaller bus is the best, since operating costs are less. It would indeed be wasteful to employ a larger vehicle, for it would generally have to run with many of the seats vacant.

The Passenger Trailer.—In light traffic areas a difficulty often encountered by bus-operating concerns is that at certain times, for example on Saturday afternoon, market day, etc., the traffic requirements of the district are quite disproportionate to the normal. It is obvious that the conditions do not warrant the employment of more vehicles, since they would only occasionally be required, and yet if they are not available some people may be crowded out and unable to avail themselves of the service. Where no spare vehicles are kept there can be no elasticity in the facilities provided, for there is no margin with which to meet an unusual or occasional increase in traffic. In America such difficulties are often surmounted by employing a trailer. A greater elasticity is thus afforded in the passenger-carrying capacity of the service, since the trailer can be utilized or not, according to the traffic requirements of the time. The use of trailers is thus a possible method of increasing the capacity of the service at a small cost, for naturally a trailer involves a very much smaller capital outlay than would a second power-driven vehicle.

In this country, however, the use of trailers for heavy passenger vehicles is forbidden by law, though in many quarters it is felt that some modification is now desirable. The principal objection lies in the question of safety, and any modification in the legal position could only be made with due regard to this factor. The trailer would have to be solidly built with a low centre of gravity, while special attention would have to be paid to the drawbar and the brakes. The recent successful application of the Westinghouse air brake to six-wheelers could usefully be extended to trailer operation. It should be so fitted that if a coupling broke, the brakes would be automatically applied.

The advantages claimed for passenger trailers are that they would mean a reduction in running costs, that traffic requirements could be more easily met, and that road wear would be reduced, since the load could be spread over a greater number of wheels.

Provided adequate precautions are taken as regards safety, there seems no reason why the use of trailers should not be allowed for passenger-carrying motors in certain areas. Licences could, of course, be refused where conditions were not deemed suitable, e.g. on routes with heavy gradients, through busy towns, etc. Every vehicle before a licence was granted should have passed adequate tests, designed to prove its reliability and safety.

The Six-Wheeler or Tractor Bus.—In Britain the law regards the flexible six-wheeler or tractor bus as a motor vehicle with trailer, and consequently the use of such vehicles for passenger services is prohibited. The six-wheeler has recently secured legal recognition for the carriage of goods and merchandise, and in consequence designers have now turned their attention to the construction of six-wheeler buses, while several firms have got out specifications, and indeed produced experimental buses, as they consider that it may only be a matter of time before the tractor bus obtains a definite status like its commercial goods-carrying brother.

The advocates of the tractor bus argue that if the type is both safe and suitable as a goods carrier, it must also be safe as a passenger carrier, since passenger loads are lighter. Further, the continued development of the type is also stressed, for the safety factor has been greatly increased through the adoption of the Westinghouse air-pressure-operated brakes. In some models at least these brakes are utilized for both the tractor and the trailer wheels. Any tendency for the rear portion to skid round can be prevented by arranging for a greater application of braking power on the trailer wheels, for this would tend to straighten out the vehicle.

For certain purposes six-wheeler buses would have the great advantage of large carrying capacity. It is said that a double-deck six-wheeler could easily accommodate over ninety passengers, while over forty could be carried in a single-decker. These latter would no doubt prove advantageous on routes which at present are only suitable for single-deck four-wheelers, because of such obstructions as low bridges over the road, overhanging trees and overhead wires. As a goods-carrying unit the six-wheeler has demonstrated its superiority where loads are heavy, and likewise where heavy passenger traffic was forthcoming the utilization of six-wheeler buses should result in a reduction in the cost of transport.

If the type, however, is to be adopted for passenger carriage attention would have to be paid, as in the case of the passenger trailer, to the prevention of any possibility of accident, though no doubt the tractor bus would be considered by most people to be on the whole safer than a trailer. A tractor bus should have adequate brakes, should possess accurate control in reverse, should be adequately sprung, and finally the connection between the two portions should be secure.

It is interesting to notice that in other countries the six-wheeled bus has been adopted, and from all accounts it seems to have proved quite satisfactory in daily use. In Paris, for instance, a fleet is being operated on the Madeleine–Bastille route.

Rural Passenger Transport.[1]—The special characteristics of the motor bus give it great advantages for operating in rural districts and other light traffic areas. Thus many municipal authorities utilize motor buses in outlying areas as "feeders" to their tramway systems. The heavy capital expenditure necessitated by a tramway is an effective barrier to their extension into country districts.

Municipal Motor Bus Services.—Nearly all the principal provincial municipalities have secured statutory powers to operate bus services, and actual services are being provided by about fifty cities and towns. About double this number of municipalities have been granted the necessary Parliamentary powers, but since adequate services are being provided by private concerns, many of these local authorities

[1] See Chapter IX.

have not seen fit to exercise their powers. In London immunity from municipal competition has been retained by the L.G.O.C., despite applications for Parliamentary powers on the part of the County Councils of London, Middlesex, and Hertfordshire. It was felt that the established company was providing adequate services, and consequently that the need for municipal enterprise was not apparent.

Since the war municipal motor bus services have developed considerably. These services are utilized for linking up suburban and outlying areas to the centre of towns, for "feeding" municipal tramway systems, and sometimes for carrying out the entire work of city transport. Fresh scope has been given to this form of municipal transport in some cases by the development of new housing schemes.

In coming years we may expect to see considerable extensions in this form of Municipal Trading. It is significant that during the past few years the number of applications by municipalities to secure Parliamentary powers has been steadily increasing. The work of city transport, including the operation of motor bus fleets, is coming to be regarded more and more as especially suited for civic operation. The reasons for this would seem to be various. In the first place it would appear that since city transport is of considerable social and economic significance, it is felt that such public utility services should be provided by the municipality. Secondly, the work is of a nature suited to municipal operation. Again, the monopolistic organization of city transport has certain advantages, and it is felt that the municipal authorities are those in whom such powers should be vested. A single authority could co-ordinate and control the whole transport work of their area, undertake development services and adjust facilities to the needs of the various districts. Poor traffic routes could be supported by the better paying services, and this it is argued could not be secured under competitive private enterprise, while private monopoly is held on the other hand to be undesirable.

It is said also that a municipality can obtain the necessary capital at a lower rate of interest than could a private company. The advocates of municipal trading state that it means that the economies of monopoly are secured, but that the profits of monopoly are eliminated. The advantages of lower establishment charges, a free directorate and lower salaries, are also adduced in favour of municipal operation.

On the other side, the antagonists of municipal trading bring forward strong arguments. Briefly, they base their contentions on the lack of specialized knowledge among members of municipal authorities, and the diversity of the matters with which such bodies have to deal. They argue also that the monopolistic character and unfair competition of municipal enterprises drive out the private individual or company, even if he performs as efficient or more efficient services. It is also said to be undesirable that the ratepayer should have to bear the burden if a loss be incurred. Efficiency and initiative may, it is also said, suffer if competition be eliminated, while special interests may be able to force the provision of transport facilities that are not economically justified, and thus the whole system may be unduly burdened. It is not possible, however, to enter into any detailed exposition of the advantages and disadvantages of municipal trading, and the reader must be referred to the works cited below.[1]

A further development of municipal enterprise has been foreshadowed by the extension of the activities of the Birmingham Corporation bus system to serve areas outside its own boundaries. It is difficult to say how far such action is likely to be followed by other municipalities. The movement, however, may spread, because a town is apt to regard the surrounding districts as natural tributaries to its own traffic system. Contentions and disputes will no doubt arise if such a policy becomes general, as when towns are near to each other the determination

[1] Avebury, *On Municipal and National Trading*; Knoop, *Principles and Methods of Municipal Trading*; Warren, *Municipal Trading*. See also Chapter XII, The Tramway.

of the area to be served by their rival systems will not be easy to adjust.

The Sphere of the Motor Bus in City Transport.—It has already been pointed out that the use of motor bus fleets as "feeders" to municipal tramway systems has become almost universal, for it has been demonstrated in practice that the economic characteristics of the motor bus fit it especially well for such purposes.

In many towns and smaller cities the motor bus provides the only street services, and where traffic is not very heavy it is an ideal instrument of city transportation, since in such circumstances no other type might be able to pay its way.

In most of the larger cities motor bus services are frequently utilized on routes that would not support a local railway or a tramway.

As regards the policy of substituting motor bus services for an existing tramway system, it will be found that in very few towns or cities has such a complete change over been attempted. However, in one or two cases, e.g. Oxford, public transport facilities are now entirely provided by motor buses, the tramways having been "scrapped." Total substitution, however, would mean that the new system would have to carry the whole or part of the capital charges of the older method, for it is not usual to find that the capital is paid off. In general, this fact alone would be sufficient to prevent total substitution. Otherwise the question must be decided on the balance of the rival merits and demerits of the two systems.

The question of partial substitution is of greater interest, and on it varied opinions are held, for this is a policy that could be more easily carried out. Such partial substitution might take one or two forms. A non-remunerative tramway route, especially when expensive renewals and repairs had to be faced, might be "scrapped" and a motor bus service substituted. In the other case, the policy of partial substitution is recommended for the central and congested areas of large towns. There it is said the streets should be closed to tramways, which it is alleged impede other vehicles, and that the entire public transport services should be performed by motor buses. In Britain the only example of this policy is to be found in London. It must be admitted, however, that conditions in the Metropolis are in some respects peculiar, and thus it is not always safe to argue that the policy, if extended to other towns, would be as successful. In London, the central area from which tramways are excluded is extensive, and there is a considerable volume of traffic to be obtained throughout the day, while the rush hour passengers are carried by the "Underground" to a great extent.

A further use of motor buses, though one to which they are seldom put, is to supplement a tramway. The idea is quite simple: motor buses would be utilized to carry excess passengers when what has been called the "saturation point" has been reached on a busy tramway route. The case is somewhat parallel to the doubling of a railway track in heavy traffic areas. In the case of a tramway it is not possible to double the tracks, while to put on additional cars on a crowded line would only have the effect of slowing down the service, so that in a given time actually fewer passengers would be carried than by a less frequent service. The stopping of a tramcar has of course the effect of holding up every car that follows. On a "saturated" tramway route the provision of additional facilities by motor buses would help up to the point where congestion through heavier street traffic reacted upon the efficiency of the tramcars.[1]

In future years it is probable that the sphere of the motor bus will be somewhat extended, especially in those areas where conditions are not best suited to tramway operation. The evolution of the large capacity motor bus fitted with a covered top-deck is already in sight, while the greater attention now being paid to the comfort of passengers should increase the popularity of the bus.

[1] In a Report by Mr. H. Mattinson—the Tramways Manager—to the Manchester Corporation Tramways Committee, a valuable account is given of the rival spheres of bus and tram in city transport. This Report was reprinted in the *Electric Railway and Tramway Journal*, September 14, 1923.

CHAPTER XII

THE TRAMWAY

In its economic characteristics and traffic requirements for successful operation, the tramway is more akin to the railway than any other type of road transport. A tramway requires a fairly dense and a fairly regular traffic if good results are to be obtained, and herein it differs from the motor omnibus which can thrive on light traffic. Where traffic is dense the heavy capital expenditure involved in the permanent way and electric equipment will be spread over a very large number of passengers. Consequently with heavy traffic fares may be low, for the greater the traffic the less does it cost to carry a passenger.

A fairly regular traffic is desirable, for otherwise full use is not made of the expensive equipment. In cities where there is a considerable amount of shopping, sightseeing, business and pleasure traffic, a tramway will find remunerative work between the peak hours. Rush hour traffic, of course, is bound to occur, and indeed, as will be shown later, the tramway is very well suited to cope with such traffic.

The expense per passenger-mile decreases as traffic increases. In the phraseology of economic science, a tramway follows the law of decreasing cost, for with the extension of its activities numerous economies are obtained.

A tramway is to be included among those industries where a considerable amount of fixed capital (i.e. the capital sunk in its permanent way, overhead equipment, etc.) has to be invested before operations can be started, but the investment once made suffices just as well for large-scale operation as for small. That is, practically the same outlay on these overhead charges is required in the case of a tramway for light traffic as for heavy traffic. Now such a type of industry is very susceptible to the law of decreasing cost, though of course this is not the only form of industry where such a law holds good. Such a type of industry where on-costs are large in proportion to the other expenses of production, and where these on-costs need not be increased to any great extent to provide for increasing production, is not uncommon. For instance, the underlying economic principles of production are similar to the tramway in gas production, electricity supply, newspaper, book and medal production, and especially railway enterprise. In the case of the railway, gas and electricity supply, there is a further similarity in that all these are of the nature of monopoly enterprise, though in every case indirect competition will be found to operate. It would be inconceivable to have competitive tramway concerns running along the same street, just as it would be futile to lay competing gas or water pipes or electric cables. From the very nature of the enterprise, due to the high proportion of overhead costs, economic considerations point to monopolistic supply as the most suitable, though in practice public or local intervention may be called for to prevent the monopolist exploiting the consumer by selling a small supply at a high price, though theoretically it might be to the interest of the monopolist to prefer the larger scale of operation at a lower range of prices.

It follows from the nature of the capital investments required that the greater the number of passengers carried the smaller is the share of fixed capital charges that each has to bear.

If we compare the economic principles underlying the operation of a motor omnibus fleet, it will be at once seen that there is a fundamental difference between the two. In the case of the motor bus no such heavy expenditure is required to start operations, and as traffic increases it can be met by gradual investments; there are no jumps as in the case of tramway or railway extensions, since the unit is the self-contained motor bus. Capital costs are more directly proportionable to the scale of operations with a motor bus fleet than with the tramway, but on the other hand the law of decreasing costs does not operate to anything like the same extent.

It is true that economies of a certain order may be effected through large scale operation, as for example those obtained by the bigger motor bus operating concerns such as the London General Omnibus Company. With large-scale working savings may be effected in repair and overhaul work; through improved organization and better administration; in the purchase of materials, fuel, etc.; by the better adjustment of reserve vehicles to traffic needs, and in many other directions.[1]

Yet while it is fully admitted that large-scale working may effect various savings and economies in motor bus operation, it should be quite clear that these are not of the same order as the economies realizable by those transport systems where the "law of decreasing costs" applies with especial force owing to the fact that the proportion of overhead costs to running costs is much greater. The element in the cost of motor bus services that corresponds to the permanent way charges of railed transport is the licence duty paid towards the upkeep of the roads, but this charge, it should be noted, is strictly proportioned to the number of vehicles, for no rebate is given to large users.

Where traffic is heavy, and where it is spread over the day so that a frequent service is necessary, the tramway will in general provide the best and cheapest method of transport in most towns and cities. Under such traffic conditions, with modern equipment and with a capital outlay, not unduly swollen by unnecessary or unjustifiable expenditure, there is no reason why the tramway should not still prove to be an economic system of transport.

[1] See Chapter XV, Monopoly and Competition.

Those who advocate the "scrapping" of our tramways neglect the fact that these represent large investments of capital, which is not yet redeemed, and consequently any new type of transport that was substituted would be saddled with a heavy burden at the outset of its career, since there are few systems that have paid off their capital cost as Glasgow has done. The capital invested in tramways amounts to the immense total of more than 85 million pounds, and the various systems carry over 4,000 million passengers each year.[1]

The Comparative Advantages and Disadvantages of the Tramway.—There is no finality in the development of the means of transport, and thus there is no *a priori* reason why some better system should not be evolved that will supersede the tramway. Many assert that already the tramway, owing to its lack of flexibility and confinement to a fixed track, is out of date. But as has been indicated above, the question cannot be settled by dogmatic statement, and the relative merits of the different systems must be compared.

The most important factor that determines the suitability of a tramway in any particular case is the density of the traffic that is to be carried, for upon this depends the possibility of the heavy capital outlay proving remunerative. In the transport of large numbers of passengers the tramway still holds its own, and as far as can be seen it is not as yet likely to be superseded.

In relation to "peak loads" or rush hour traffic, the tramway is better fitted to cope with such traffic than any other form of street transport, though where journeys are fairly long the railway—electric, steam, elevated or underground—may also in some places, especially where traffic is very heavy, prove a suitable method of dealing with such traffic. But the tram has the advantage over the railway where journeys are short, as it requires less

[1] For the number of passengers carried by tramways from 1899 to 1923, see Note at end of chapter.

capital outlay, it runs through the streets, and has frequent stopping places.

The question of rush hour traffic has proved to be one of the most important and difficult problems of city transport, and of recent years the problem has been intensified by the general shortening of the hours of labour, as that has meant an even greater concentration of the daily traffic during certain hours of the day. No motor bus system attempts to cope completely with this rush hour traffic of our industrial communities, as the standing charges represented by the extra vehicles required and the other incidental expenditure would render it financially impossible. It would not pay to have large numbers of the self-contained, self-propelled motor buses standing idle during the greater part of the day. A motor bus fleet can be proportioned to the traffic, it is true, unlike the tramway, but the very fact that this is possible necessitates that the units that are provided be kept fully employed, for they are expensive pieces of capital. Even in London the tramways take a greater proportion of the rush hour traffic than do the buses, and further it must be remembered that there is an extensive system of underground and other railways. It would be a mistake to consider London traffic as being provided for, in the central area only, by motor buses. The transit facilities must be viewed as a whole, and if this is done the importance of the underground electric railways will be appreciated.

But though it is said that the tramway is well fitted for dealing with rush hour traffic, that is not to say that the problem of providing the necessary facilities is an easy one in the domain of the economies of tramway operation. In reality it means that often about twice the number of vehicles that are normally required have to be provided, and the traffic is only available for about four hours per day. Since, however, the fixed standing charges (e.g. track, overhead equipment, etc.) are not increased by additional traffic, and these form a large part of working expenses, and further, since the number of passengers per car is considerably higher during the peak hours than during the rest of the day, it is possible for a tramway to deal more or less successfully with this extra traffic, and to do so moreover on an economic basis.

Another reason that renders the tram able to cope with the rush hour traffic is its large carrying capacity. The largest tramcar of the modern type will seat 80 passengers all under cover and with 12 standing its full capacity is 92, though in some towns even this figure is exceeded. As compared with this, the largest motor bus seats 26 inside and 28 outside, a total of 54, and with 6 standing its full capacity is but 60 passengers. The "S" type bus of the L.G.O.C. seats 54, but the latest, the "N.S." type, seats 2 less. The modern tramcar has the advantage of carrying all its passengers under cover, and owing to the uncertain climate of our country this is an important factor. So far top-covered buses have not been employed in London, though it would seem that the L.G.O.C. had evolved a suitable vehicle of this type. Since a bus has to operate on cambered roads, the addition of a top-covered deck might tend, it is said, to increase its liability to overturn, and further the cant due to such camber might cause it to strike lamp-posts or other erections when the vehicle draws in to the kerb. In New York City, however, top-covered buses are run successfully on Fifth Avenue. Experiments are being made with this type of vehicle in Sheffield and other towns.

The other advantages of the tramcar over its rival the motor bus must be considered in less detail. A tramcar has a much longer life than a motor bus, for it is impossible to build a road vehicle as robust and substantial as a tramcar. Greater vibration and shock, and the wear and tear of a high speed reciprocating internal combustion engine make for more rapid depreciation.

The acceleration of a tram is much greater than that of a motor bus, as anyone can see who watches both start away together. Quicker loading and unloading is generally possible on a tram, owing to bigger platforms and wider entrances.

In thick fog, motor bus services are quickly dislocated. Sir Henry Maybury writing in *The Times* gave the following facts and figures relating to the London General Omnibus Company during the three years 1920–21–22. "In that period there were about twenty-seven days on which there were ground fogs. The number of omnibus services seriously affected in the twenty-seven foggy days was 696, whilst the number of these vehicles unable to complete their scheduled mileage was 10,202, the number of miles actually lost being 434,457." But as regards tramways he is able to declare that "of the several road transport services in London, the L.C.C. tramways are perhaps the least affected during foggy weather."

A tramcar is able to proceed during a fog because it has a definite position on the road which is known to all, and an experienced driver has a thorough knowledge of every yard of his route, while other traffic are informed of the location of a tram by its gong. The full schedule of cars is invariably provided, though the mileage run is somewhat less owing to the necessity for care in order to avoid accidents, but the lost mileage is not serious. Tramways can thus maintain a regular service, whereas their competitors have to stand idle. In snow a tramway can operate long after the motor bus is held up.

As regards safety, the tramcar cannot skid latterly, and it can be fitted with lifeguards which cannot be fixed so successfully, if at all, to other vehicles.

As regards comfort, the position is not easy to assess. The motor bus, however, is frequently uncomfortable, so noisy that conversation may be rendered almost impossible, and often overcrowded owing to the limited seating accommodation. It is not always well ventilated, or if so may be draughty, while oil and engine fumes sometimes make it unpleasant. On the other hand, tramcars are often very noisy and uncomfortable.

Two points in favour of the tramway are sometimes lost

sight of, in discussions on its relative advantages as compared with other systems of city transport. The first relates to the supply of electric energy. A tramway system may enable the citizens to obtain a cheaper electricity supply for lighting, heating and power purposes. A tramway provides a long continued, a heavy and fairly constant load for the generating station. Thus electricity can be produced in bulk with consequent savings, for it is a well-known fact that large-scale production of electric energy is in general much more economical. In such cases the price per unit could be lowered to the consumer, and thus in economic phraseology he would gain an increased " consumer's surplus " due to the reduction in price. Secondly, in any attempt to arrive at the true position of the tramway as a method of city transportation, it must be remembered that the tramway is burdened by having to maintain roads, pay special local rates, etc.

Many tramways, for instance, have had to bear heavy burdens for street improvements before permission to construct the system could be obtained. In some notorious cases local authorities have exacted considerable sums for street improvements other than those along the proposed route as a price for granting their permission to the laying down of a tramway track.

By the Act of 1870, tramways have to maintain not only their own track, and to pay not only for the disturbance of the road surface, but also have to repair a considerable portion of the road which is worn out not by trams but by other and maybe competitive traffic.[1] No doubt in

[1] This provision is contained in Section 28 of the Act, which lays down that the promoters " shall at their own expense at all times maintain and keep in good condition and repair, with such materials and in such manner as the road authority shall direct and to their satisfaction, so much of any road whereon any tramway belonging to them is laid as lies between the tramway and (where two tramways are laid by the same promoters in any road at a distance of not more than 4 feet from each other) the portion of the road between the tramways and in every case so much of the road as extends 18 inches beyond the rails of and on each side of any such tramway."

Under Section 25 it is provided that " every tramway . . . shall be laid and maintained in such manner that the uppermost surface of the rail shall be on a level with the surface of the road."

1870, when horse-drawn trams were the rule, this provision was more or less justified, since the horses would use the space between the rails. In the meantime, however, a complete change has taken place in the method of traction and also in the character of other road traffic. The claim for some readjustment is obvious. The tramway might, for instance, be made liable only for the difference in cost between maintaining a road along which it runs and a similar road without tramway rails. Practical difficulties, however, are considerable, and it would not be easy to obtain the passing of a new Act. This burden of road maintenance has been one important factor that has induced certain municipalities to scrap their permanent way, and introduce the railless trolley bus on routes where traffic conditions appeared to be suitable.

In addition to the burden of road repair, tramways have to pay rates on their permanent way and overhead equipment to the local authorities, for both of these are rateable property. As regards the use of the streets, other forms of transport escape this burden, for they pay no direct local rates on their activities.

The motor bus and the trackless trolley bus, it is said, pay but a part of the cost of road repair in respect of the damage they do, while the commercial lorry pays still less. Their contributions are levied through the vehicle tax, and go in the first place towards the Road Fund, which later is distributed to local authorities throughout the country ; but of course these grants only suffice to bear part of the expense which local authorities have to meet for the upkeep of roads in their area.

It has been computed for London that the trams pay 1s. 7d. per car-mile for the two items of road maintenance and local rates, while the motor bus contribute only 7d. through the vehicle tax.

In any consideration of the relative merits of tram or bus it is necessary to take these contributions into account, if it is desired to arrive at the true position of affairs. It may be concluded that in many large towns and cities tramways are on the whole the most convenient and most economical method of passenger transport, and that as far as can be seen at present they will continue to provide the best method of dealing with heavy street traffic. At the same time we must be prepared to see the motor bus and railless trolley increase their scope, and take over the work formerly done by tramways where these are not working to the best advantage. Many tramways were built, for instance, in the days before the coming of the motor bus in areas not suited to tramway operation.

Mr. E. S. Rayner, the Tramways Manager of the Hull Corporation system, declared at the 1923 meeting of the Institute of Transport at Sheffield that "Tramways are and will remain a necessity in large towns and cities. There is no form of road transport that can deal with mass passenger transport as cheaply and effectively as tramways. They fill the gap between motor transport and underground railways, as the motor vehicle fills the gap between the tramcar and walking."

On July 31, 1923, at a meeting of the Manchester City Council, when a report was made by the Tramways Manager, Mr. Mattinson,[1] the Tramways Committee declared they were "prepared to adopt any means at once economical, expeditious, comfortable and safe, whatever it may be, for the passenger transportation of the city. Their adherence to the tramway for the public conveyance of industrial communities arises not because it is a tramway, but from an assured knowledge that at the present time no other instrument is available that can supersede it on its essential merits." These conclusions are borne out by recent developments of the tramway, which is now beginning to recover from the ill-effects of the war period. Thus the recent conversion of the cable system to electric operation in Edinburgh has demonstrated the vitality of the electric tramway, and it has proved that a well-organized electric

[1] This important report should be read in full, and is accessible in the *Electric Railway and Tramway Journal*, September 1923.

system can provide cheaper and more efficient transport under suitable conditions than can alternative forms of transport. Is it not also significant that recently new constructions and extensions have been carried out by a number of undertakings? Some of these, it is true, are only for the purpose of linking up dead ends, but several of the projects are of a more ambitious nature. The fall in the cost of construction from the high level of previous years has done not a little to accelerate this progress. Liverpool, Birmingham, Glasgow, Newcastle, South Shields, and other cities have put down several miles of new routes. In several cities extensions of considerable length are being built in the outskirts, especially where housing schemes are in progress, e.g. in Liverpool, 9 miles of route have been laid down.

Improvements in Tramway Technique and the Effect on Their Economic Position.—In recent years considerable improvements have been made in tramway technique. New type motors of lighter weight have been introduced, and in Edinburgh, for instance, light-weight cars have been built that show considerable economies in running costs. In Hull experiments are being carried out on a car of novel design: a differential drive is obtained by means of a double worm drive with motors for each half of the axle, weight has been cut down, while drum brakes have been substituted and ball and roller bearings fitted.

Track construction and maintenance has been greatly improved by the adoption of new methods, e.g. of welding, etc.

Where it is possible to lay tramway tracks in a reserved portion of a wide road, considerable economies can be obtained, both as regards first cost and maintenance, by constructing not with the usual concrete foundation and street surface, but more like the usual type of railway track. Where this method is adopted the tramway rails of the usual grooved type are laid on creosoted cross wooden sleepers embedded in ballast.

This system has many advantages and has been utilized

in Continental cities, e.g. Berlin, in the U.S.A., and several cities of the Midlands and North of England. Hull, for instance, has had a ballasted track for over twenty years, bright coloured gravel put between the rails giving a pleasant appearance to the track. On another line opened in 1914 the first expense on maintenance was incurred in 1923 when the ballast was packed up again.

Open sleeper tracks have also been laid at Southend-on-Sea, Liverpool, Birmingham, Glasgow, Bradford, Newcastle, and South Shields. On new roads of a width greater than 100 feet it is now common practice to reserve a portion for the tramway. Except for crossing-points here and there, the permanent way is separated off from the road proper sometimes by a privet hedge or by a grass border, or maybe by a row of trees. The amenities of the new roads are thus greatly increased. Often, too, grass seed is sown between the rails, and in time this gives a pleasing effect as well as helping to deaden the noise. Opinions differ as to whether the tramways should be alloted the centre portion of the road or one side, or given a track on both sides. The advantage of the centre portion lies in the fact that a greater speed is possible than if the track is on the side of the road, since in the latter case care is required to avoid accidents from traffic entering the main road.

The reservation of a special section of the roadway means a great increase in speed, and 20 miles per hour between stops is usual, though speeds of 30 miles per hour or even over are not unknown, and this is to be compared with the usual 14 or 15 miles per hour on ordinary roads. The sleeper track also means more comfort for the passengers and less noise. High average speeds are maintained by having the stops some distance apart, thus for example in Liverpool they are spaced as nearly as possible a quarter of a mile apart.

The outstanding advantage of the sleeper track is the great reduction in cost of construction and maintenance as compared with the usual type of city track. Where the new method is possible it should do not a little to give the tramway a new lease of life, for in effect it combines the advantages of a tramway with those of an electrified light railway, and moreover these advantages are obtained at a smaller expenditure of capital.

Even if the cost of paving is taken as low as 10s. per superficial yard, it will be obvious that a sleeper track means a very considerable saving under this head alone per mile of route. The cost of construction is put variously at anything between 50 per cent. and 20 per cent. of the orthodox type of track construction. But not only is capital cost greatly reduced, maintenance charges are also much less, especially if the track is well drained. Further, since running is smoother, the cost of car maintenance is reduced. Unfortunately the sleeper track cannot often be introduced into built-up areas, as street widening would be too expensive. However, if even short portions of the track are constructed in such areas with a separate portion of road, considerable relief is given to traffic.

Where the necessary land can be obtained at a fair price, the sleeper track system of construction possesses very great advantages, for it gives freedom both to the tramcar and to other vehicles, and means greater safety to pedestrians as well as making for the better success of the tramway system on its financial side. It means, in short, that the tramway will be able to compete on successful terms with other types of transport—road or rail—in the outskirts of the large towns, not only in cost of transport, but also in speed and convenience and comfort to passengers.

Unification of Tramway Systems.—Though it has been emphasized that a tramway requires a heavy traffic to prove remunerative, and that in general if this traffic be not forthcoming the motor bus is more suitable, this must not be taken to mean that necessary extensions for development services or for public convenience must not be undertaken. It is often necessary in the best interests of the community that temporarily unremunerative extensions should be made and subsidized in part from the richer portions of the system. If such a policy had not been followed, some of the best systems to be found to-day would not exist. The danger is that extensions, which will never prove remunerative, may be made in areas that would be better served by some other system of road transport, and this danger has to be guarded against. Extension of course is a very different matter from new construction, because certain fixed charges will not be increased by extensions, or at any rate not in proportion.

Transport undertakings must be viewed as a whole, and it is not always essential that every route should prove profitable so long as the system itself is on an economic basis. This, indeed, is a strong argument in favour of unity of administration in a natural transport area. Just as pressure of economic considerations has hastened amalgamation and co-ordination of railways, so likewise in city transport grouping and co-ordinated development would help to achieve financial success and to provide better facilities, though it is essential that the economic characteristics of each type or system of transport be appreciated, and each put to that service for which it is best suited.

There are then strong arguments in favour of unified administration over large areas that are contiguous in the traffic sense of the term, and though it is not possible to lay down any exact limits as to area, it may generally be taken that a large city and its suburbs and residential areas, or a group of towns like the Potteries and their outlying suburbs, do form such an area.

Thus, to give some examples, the unification of tramway systems in Dublin, Glasgow and district, and Edinburgh have meant better facilities and more economic working.

In the case of the Potteries, some of the lines could not have been profitably worked under separate management, but worked as a whole they have proved remunerative, and have been able to provide facilities of great importance that otherwise would have been lost. Break of services would cause great and unnecessary inconvenience. Forces making for such amalgamations have been at work continuously for many years past, and no doubt in the future fusions or joint working will continue, since the economic incentives for such co-ordination are strong. It is possible, for example, that the recent extensions of the South Shields tramway system may lead to the interconnection of the various systems in the large industrial districts of the North-east Coast.

A great difficulty in the way is the lack of uniformity of gauge in many districts. About half of the systems in the United Kingdom have been constructed of the standard gauge of 4 feet 8½ inches, but of the remainder the gauge varies between 3 feet and 5 feet 3 inches. Thus in the large contiguous systems of Yorkshire a variety of gauges is to be found : Bradford is 4 feet, Halifax 3 feet 6 inches, Huddersfield 4 feet 7¾ inches, Leeds and other places 4 feet 8½ inches.

Tramways have suffered even more than the railways in their earlier days from lack of this pre-requisite of amalgamation—uniformity of gauge.

Another difficulty that arises is what is to happen if a tramway owned and operated by a municipality penetrates the area of some other authority ? A tramway cannot always stop at the end of an artificial area, and further the amalgamation of two systems may be in the best interest of all the inhabitants of two such areas. No difficulties need arise on this count where tramways are privately owned, but if they are municipal systems some troublesome questions arise. There appear to be three solutions of the problem :—

1. Each authority may work its own system and agree to the linking of the services by giving mutual running powers to each other ;
2. One authority may be allowed to run the entire system, this for example is done by the Glasgow Corporation in a large number of cases ; or
3. A Joint Board may be set up.

The Carriage of Goods and Parcels by Tramways.—On the Continent, in the cities and even sometimes in the country districts, the carriage of merchandise by tramways has been developed to a far greater extent than it has in this country. In France and Belgium, for instance, there is an extensive network of steam tramways, and most of these operate goods traffic as well as passenger, or at least carry a baggage van attached to the train. On many of the electrified systems, as for example the Belgian coast route, steam traction is used for the haulage of goods.

In some German towns, municipal electric tramways also operate goods traffic through their town. In Cologne, for instance, it is a frequent sight to see a tramcar hauling two or three trucks loaded with coke, coal or other merchandise, and sidings are laid down to connect with the railways, railway goods depots, or the yards of coal merchants or other private firms.

In Great Britain legislation does not forbid the transport of goods or parcels, though the extent to which such traffic may be carried is not laid down in the Tramways Act of 1870. Certain sections of that Act—e.g. those which relate to gauge, state that unless otherwise determined the gauge shall be such as to allow railway rolling stock to operate over the system—seem to presuppose that goods traffic was to be carried.

Whatever may have been the intention of the framers of the 1870 Act, it is now the general practice to insert a more or less standard clause in a Tramways Act or Order authorizing the conveyance of "animals, goods, minerals and parcels." Amongst the authorized concerns at present in operation, some systems have obtained complete powers for these purposes, others have only limited permission to carry parcels under certain weights, while yet others, as the L.C.C., can only carry dogs or passengers' luggage. On nearly all tramways, however, the carriage of mails is obligatory, as the provisions of the 1893 "Conveyance of

Mails" Act has generally been applied when powers are sought to construct a tramway.

The carriage of merchandise excepting that of parcels has not been developed to any extent in this country. The Corporation Tramways of Huddersfield have, however, for a number of years undertaken the carriage of coal over their system. For this purpose special trucks are provided, and the coal is carried from the railway depots to the works of three manufacturing firms some miles away. In 1919 the volume of the coal traffic amounted to 11,870 tons.

In the Black Country, also, the carriage of goods has been undertaken by the extensive tramway system of that area. Old tramcars with a capacity of 5 tons are utilized for this purpose, while in addition special vehicles carrying loads of 10 tons and drawing a trailer holding 2 more tons have been constructed.

During the war years some developments in goods traffic working took place, as it was essential that transport of all kinds should be conserved to meet the emergencies of the period. The Road Transport Board[1] encouraged the use of tramway systems for this purpose.

In Leeds an extensive system of goods transport was built up by the Corporation Tramways as the conveyance of the material required by a Fireclay Company from the pits to the company's works, a distance of about 5 miles, was entrusted to the tramway. The traffic was worked over the system during the night and evening when the normal passenger traffic had ceased or was slack.

As regards the possibility of utilizing railway rolling stock on tramways, the idea has sometimes been considered, and in this country at least two systems—Huddersfield and Blackpool—have proposed to connect their lines with the railway.

It was no doubt with this purpose in view that some tramway authorities laid their lines on a gauge of 4 ft. $7\frac{3}{4}$ in., as the narrow grooved tramway rail requires to be

[1] See Chapter III, p. 41.

laid on a slightly contracted gauge if the standard rolling stock of the railways (gauge 4 ft. 8½ in.) is to operate over them. On the Continent, tramway lines are sometimes utilized for goods traffic, by standard railway locomotives and rolling stock, as for instance on the Cologne–Bonn tramway. Goods trains may even be seen in the city streets.

As regards possible development, though the transport of merchandise by tramways has been proved feasible, it is not on the whole likely that goods traffic will ever be operated in bulk over British tramway systems. Development of goods traffic on anything like a large scale would require considerable capital expenditure on sidings, depots and service cars, and any tramway concern seeking powers to operate such traffic would be certain to meet with strong opposition from railway companies, carriers and other vested interests. In 1918, for instance, when Sheffield applied for powers to carry goods and parcels, considerable opposition was raised, and it was only with difficulty that the powers desired were obtained.

In some cases, however, the inauguration of tramway goods services would be attended with advantage, and the locality and certain industries would benefit, while at the same time a new source of revenue would be opened up for the tramways.

Municipalities might also find it advantageous under certain circumstances to utilize their tramways system for transporting refuse to their dumps or destructors, or for carrying coal, etc., to electric generating stations.

Parcels traffic, as distinct from the carriage of merchandise in bulk, has been developed to a much greater extent on British tramways, and now many tramways, municipal or company, undertake the carriage of parcels. Some of the services, it is true, are not very important and yield but little revenue, being performed rather for the sake of public convenience, but some are worked on a large scale and add considerably to receipts. Since the ordinary tramcar services may be utilized, and since nothing is added to overhead charges, a parcels service will generally help to contribute something to the profits of the undertaking, even if not worked on a very extensive scale. In Manchester, Bradford, Huddersfield, Edinburgh, Sheffield and other cities, the tramways parcel services are important, and are largely utilized by shopkeepers and others to carry out their delivery work. In Edinburgh in the year 1922–23 the special expenses incurred on behalf of the parcels service amounted to £2,720, while the revenue obtained was £3,470, giving a balance of £750 that otherwise would not have been earned, and which contributed to bear part of the overhead expenses.

In Manchester a parcels service was instituted in 1905, and the volume of business and the area served are both very considerable. Parcels are collected or delivered in all directions, extending from the centre of the city to distances of 8 or 10 miles, while working agreements have been effected with adjoining systems, so that now parcels can be dispatched from the centre of the city to places at a considerable distance. Parcels can be handed in to the conductor of any city-bound tramcar, or they are called for by van if required, and thus sent to a central or local office. Thence they are dispatched by tramcars, for which purpose a basket is placed in front of the cars, to the sub-office nearest their destination. Delivery to the consignee is effected by vans, if distance is considerable, or if short, by messenger boy. An idea of the scope of the Manchester service may be obtained when it is mentioned that the average number of parcels handled in a year exceeds one million.

NOTE.

The following table, compiled from the Reports of the Board of Trade and the Returns of the Ministry of Transport, gives the total number of passengers carried by tramways from 1899–1900 to 1922–23. The steady and great increase in the total number of passengers carried is very noticeable.

The failure to maintain that increase during the year 1921–22 is probably due in large part to the trade depression.

I. Total Number of Passengers carried by Tramways in Great Britain. 1899–1923.

Year.	England and Wales.	Scotland.	Total.
1899–1900	816,768,639	175,565,530	992,334,169
1900–1901	932,052,219	186,837,823	1,118,890,042
1901–1902	1,082,192,712	230,702,794	1,312,895,506
1902–1903	1,336,543,197	259,886,112	1,596,429,309
1903–1904	1,425,327,430	287,096,768	1,712,424,198
1904–1905	1,665,084,669	311,942,513	1,977,027,182
1905–1906	1,803,927,826	343,078,757	2,147,006,583
1906–1907	1,976,141,862	376,545,521	2,352,687,383
1907–1908	2,126,020,172	388,401,601	2,514,421,773
1908–1909	2,169,237,933	385,502,310	2,554,740,243
1909–1910	2,253,399,207	383,492,627	2,636,891,834
1910–1911	2,388,957,879	406,527,349	2,795,485,228
1911–1912	2,553,194,237	454,999,212	3,008,193,449
1912–1913	2,599,041,905	497,777,056	3,096,818,961
1913–1914	2,766,830,624	534,984,196	3,301,814,820
1914–1915 1915–1916 1916–1917 1917–1918	Not available		
1918–1919	3,668,870,327	735,436,245	4,404,306,572
1919–1920	Not available		
1920–1921	3,943,255,618	726,660,786	4,669,916,404
1921–1922	3,573,764,166	682,504,026	4,256,268,192
1922–1923	3,691,033,179	658,008,062	4,349,041,241

II. Number of Passengers Carried by Tramways in Greater London, 1918–1923.

1918..	991,880,203
1919..	1,052,744,820
1920..	1,062,986,520
1921..	1,009,043,113
1922..	1,036,176,655
1923..	1,032,741,096

CHAPTER XIII

THE RAILLESS TROLLEY OMNIBUS

THE railless trolley omnibus, or, as it is sometimes called, the trackless trolley omnibus, has been evolved as a compromise between the petrol motor omnibus and the ordinary type of electric tram, and this compromise is evident both in its appearance and in the nature of the work generally assigned to it. In appearance it is somewhat of a hybrid, for the body and the chassis look very like the ordinary motor omnibus, single or double deck as the case may be, except that the bonnet is absent, since there is no engine at the front to be covered up. It is fitted with rubber-tyred wheels of motor omnibus pattern, but the power used is electric, and the energy is obtained from overhead wires similar to tramway practice. Two overhead wires, of course, are required for each line of traffic, since there is no metal track to afford a good " earth " or return conductor for the electric current. The trolley booms likewise are doubled, though in other respects they are very similar to those generally adopted in British tramway operation, except that a light spring only is utilized to secure contact with the overhead wires, and that in some of the more recent vehicles refinements in the shape of specially constructed cams have been adopted. In practice little or no trouble occurs through the trolley poles leaving the overhead wires, even when the vehicle has crossed to the other side on a 30- or 40-foot roadway. Indeed, experience in Birmingham, Bradford, Ipswich and other places has proved that the risk of dewiring is negligible.

At the terminus of a route, the overhead wires are generally carried round in a loop for the sake of convenience in changing direction, since by this means the vehicle can simply run round in a circle, and all reversing or other manœuvring of the vehicle is obviated, while only one set of controls need be fitted as in the case of motor bus practice.

In a few systems, it might be mentioned, for the sake of completeness, a special type of current collector has been utilized in place of the ordinary type of trolley boom, though now the latter is becoming the more usual method, and has been employed, as indicated above, on all the newer systems. In Keighley, where one of the earliest systems of railless buses was operated in Britain, the type of current collector employed was a four-wheeled frame running on top of the two overhead wires.[1]

The railless system was first introduced in Westphalia in 1903, but it was not adopted in Britain till 1911, when trolley bus routes were opened to public service in both Bradford and Leeds. Since then a number of other cities have employed this form of traction, for example, York, Halifax, Leeds, Bradford, Keighley, Mexborough, Rotherham, Teeside, Ramsbottom, and, more recently, Birmingham, Wolverhampton and Ipswich; but so far there has been no successful attempt to introduce the system into Scotland. A large number of municipalities in addition have obtained statutory powers to operate railless services, but have not up to the present exercised these powers, while in yet other towns the adoption of the system on certain routes is contemplated. Keighley proposes, in the near future, to scrap its entire tramway system and substitute railless vehicles on all the routes.

The trackless trolley is also growing in favour abroad, and systems are now in operation in Shanghai, Bloemfontein, Boksburg, and on Staten Island, New York, two services are run over hilly country for a distance of about

[1] For an account of this system see Conradi, *Mechanical Road Transport*, pp. 178 *et seq.*

15 miles. Near the Mont Cenis Pass a service is to be inaugurated along 20 miles of mountain highway, and in this case the chief attractions of the railless system seem to be in the low capital cost as compared with that required for a tramway or electric railway, and in the advantage of utilizing cheap electric power that is available from large hydro-electric generating stations already established.

The increasing use and popularity of the railless trolley bus illustrate two important principles in the economy of city transportation. In the first place, it is essential that a proper compromise be made between low first cost and low working expenses. In the second, the suitability of alternative types of transport for particular conditions must be determined by the traffic considerations and the economic characteristics of each type of transport.

The trolley bus naturally partakes of some of the respective advantages and defects of both the tramcar and the motor bus, for, as stated at the outset, it is a compromise between these two. Given sufficient traffic, it can operate more cheaply than the motor bus, but where traffic is heavy, it is not so economical as the tramcar.

In some towns the trolley bus has been introduced on those routes where the traffic density is insufficient to support the capital charges involved in the laying down of the permanent way, but which should suffice to remunerate the capital outlay required for the erection of the overhead equipment. In other towns, railless vehicles have been introduced to avoid expensive reconstruction of tracks, which would involve a capital expenditure not justifiable by the traffic. In these latter cases, the overhead span wires, poles, feeders and conductors would already be in position, and would only require adaptation to the new conditions.

The absence of the permanent way means that the capital cost of a railless system is much less than that of a tramway, while the extra expense involved in erecting a double overhead wire is comparatively not very great. But not only does the trolley bus avoid the heavy permanent way expenditure, it also involves a smaller maintenance expense, because a highway where there is no railed track must be maintained by the appropriate road authority, whereas a tramway has to bear the burden of road repair under the Tramways Act 1870.[1] Again, the local rates imposed on a tramway in respect of its permanent way are avoided. It is true, of course, that the buses contribute through the vehicle tax to the Road Fund, and this Fund in turn is distributed among road authorities, but opinions differ as to whether the amount of the tax paid per vehicle is more, less or equal to the expense of repairing the damage done to the roads by the trolley buses.

The question has also been raised in debates on the policy of substituting railless vehicles for tramcars as to whether it is a justifiable policy, since it may mean that one department of the civic body is transferring a part of the total cost of transport to another department of the same municipality. This question and the connected one, as to whether such a policy means the subsidization of those citizens who utilize the system—supposing it to be run on a non-profit-making basis—by the bulk of the ratepayers, are questions, however, which cannot be again discussed in this chapter. The advocates of the railless system argue that the vehicles do very little damage to the city roads, the more especially as they are well sprung and have a very even drive, since no gear changing or clutch manipulation is necessitated. They hold that the vehicle tax fully covers any damage to the highways that may be caused by the vehicles.

The advantages claimed for the railless trolley bus may be summarized by comparing it on the one hand with the normal type of tramcar, and on the other with the motor bus.

As stated above, the railless trolley bus has the advantage of a lower capital outlay, and of lower maintenance charges as compared with a tramway. This fact is of the first importance where traffic is not very heavy. It has the great advantage of flexibility which is denied to the tramcar

[1] See Chapter XII.

confined to its fixed track. The railless bus can dodge in and out of traffic, avoiding obstacles and thus contributing materially to the relief of traffic congestion. In Ipswich, for instance, it has been proved that the newly introduced railless vehicles can deviate at full speed from one side of a 40-foot road to the other, without any danger of the trolley booms leaving the wires. The vehicles, unlike the tramcar, can draw up at the kerb to take up or discharge their passengers, and the service is not held up if one vehicle breaks down.

One effect of this flexibility is to give the benefit that would result from the doubling of the track in a narrow road. Though there may be but space enough for a single tram line, trolley buses travelling in opposite directions will generally be able to pass each other at any point on the route. Thus it may be possible to give a more frequent and a more rapid service than would be possible for railed transport.

Further important advantages of the railless trolley bus over the tramcar and the motor vehicle are, that vibration and noise are greatly reduced, and from the point of view of the passenger these are considerable attractions. Indeed, for ease and comfort in travelling, no other vehicle in transport service to-day—except the electric battery vehicle—can compete with a well-constructed trolley bus running on a good road.

The main defect of the railless trolley bus system as compared with the tramway is, that it is not so well suited to provide for traffic of heavy density, since with it the cost of carrying extra passengers does not decrease with increased traffic to anything like the extent as is the case with the tramway. The tramcar, with its great seating and overload capacity, still holds the field for heavy traffic. The seating capacity of the trolley bus is necessarily limited to thirty or forty seats in a single decker, and just over fifty in a double decker. Even the rigid six-wheeler—the law does not allow flexible six-wheelers to be utilized for passenger traffic—of Bradford is capable of seating only sixty passengers, though in practice but fifty-nine seats are provided. These figures might be compared with the Manchester and Liverpool tramway systems. In the former, the cars seat eighty-four passengers, and in the latter seventy, and in each case there is a high overload capacity. To take the place of one tramcar two or three trolley buses would be required, with consequent traffic congestion, and it is probable that the cost of transport would not be so low. The rush hour traffic is often a deciding factor, for no other system of street transportation can cope with this as effectively as can the tramcar.

The railless trolley bus is liable to skid, unlike the tramcar, and it can only make much slower progress during fog or snow. The delay caused by fog can, however, be minimized to some extent by the utilization of a simple indicator device that will show the driver the position of his vehicle on the road relative to the trolley wires.

As compared with a motor bus system, it would appear that the railless vehicles have certain advantages. Running costs per passenger-mile are lower than with a petrol bus, provided traffic is sufficient to warrant a service of, roughly speaking, four to six vehicles per hour. This decreased cost of operation appears to be mainly due to the fact that electric energy is utilized. Of course, an infrequent service is not suitable because a certain amount of capital has to be sunk in providing the overhead equipment, and unless a moderate service of at least four vehicles per hour can be operated this will not prove remunerative. The utilization of electric power has, no doubt, been one attraction of the railless trolley bus over motors to those municipal transport authorities who require electric energy for other parts of their system. It should mean that costs of production per unit of energy are decreased, and thus the trolley bus would contribute to the welfare of the whole transport and electricity supply systems, as well as obtaining for itself a supply of cheap power. Railless electric traction would no doubt receive a further stimulus if the projects now under discussion for the bulk production of electricity by tidal or water power, materialize and are carried into execution.

But not only is the running cost lower than with a motor bus, the item of depreciation is also smaller, since in the trolley bus the reciprocating engine, the gear-box and the clutch are all eliminated, and these, it is well known, are responsible for wear and tear to the chassis. Further, the smooth drive and the absence of jerks in "getting away" and in acceleration should mean less wear on tyres. Other advantages of the railless vehicle are that there is a greater space available through the absence of the engine; they have a high overload capacity and the dead weight per passenger is low.

The savings thus effected in running costs under their several headings may serve to more than offset the greater interest charges due to the fixed capital invested in the electric equipment.

The disadvantages of railless as compared with motor bus services next require to be considered. First, there is the greater capital cost required to install a trolley bus system. Overhead electric equipment as indicated above requires to be provided, and this means a capital outlay that is determined irrespective of the probable or actual traffic. Hence for infrequent services the motor bus has a considerable advantage, since each vehicle is an independent power unit. Further, the trolley bus is less flexible than the independent motor. The motor bus has the last word where flexibility is concerned, for it can go anywhere the road leads, and in this country the road leads everywhere. The trolley bus does not carry its own source of power, and in consequence it is confined to those routes where overhead wires have been erected. Further, the motor bus has another advantage in city streets in that any bus can pass or repass another, and thus the vehicles can be better filled and overcrowding prevented, along with a reduction in congestion due to a vehicle having to wait till passengers have boarded or dismounted from a preceding one. Trolley buses going in the same direction cannot pass each other, since they are utilizing the same pair of overhead wires. Even if the railless system be utilized for routes where a service is only run every few minutes, this disadvantage may still operate, if several routes happen to converge for a short distance on one street.

On the whole, the place of the trackless trolley bus is an intermediate one between the tramway and the motor bus; the former, as we have seen, best suited for heavy traffic, and the latter having no rival on lighter traffic routes. The successful utilization of the new system in any urban transport scheme depends on a nice appreciation of its characteristics.[1]

Railless buses have been utilized in several towns to act as feeders to the ordinary tramway system, since extensions can be promoted by their aid at a smaller expenditure of capital than otherwise would be required. In Bradford the trolley buses are utilized on routes of light traffic, radiating from the centre of the town and cutting across the tram routes. In York, one-man-operated trolley buses are run on a route that could not support a tramway. The railless system has also been advocated as the best means of promoting extensions of tramway routes in those areas where it is reasonably probable that tramways will be required in the near future, when traffic has grown. All that would be required would be to erect poles and fit up the overhead wires, and these could afterwards be used for the normal type of tramway. It is said that the erection of the overhead equipment gives an air of permanency to the service and thus encourages house building in the area.

In those districts where there is no likelihood of trams being required, the petrol bus would probably prove more

[1] The reader is referred to an excellent paper by Mr. Alfred Baker General Manager of the Birmingham City Tramways, entitled "Birmingham's Experiment with Trolley Omnibuses," reprinted in the *Proceedings of the Municipal Tramways Association*, 1922-23.

suitable, as it certainly would on cross-country routes and those connecting up the outer termini of tramways.

During recent years important developments have taken place in the utilization of railless traction, and it has proved a helpful solution of the rather difficult transit problem of providing an adequate service on a narrow and congested road. The lead in the substitution of trolley buses for a single-line tramway with crossing loops was taken by Birmingham in November 1922, while not long afterwards Wolverhampton followed this example, as also did Ipswich under slightly different circumstances. In Birmingham the route was not a light traffic route, but one passing through and serving a densely populated region, where now a four-minute service is run. It was not possible to double the track on a congested highway when reconstruction was necessitated and street widening was out of the question. No doubt the increased cost of track renewals at a period of high prices was one factor in the decision to abandon the tramway, but it was not the only factor. It had been found difficult to operate an adequate service on the single line, and the utmost capacity of the line was a five-minute service. The route, which is 2 miles in length, passes along narrow streets with varying gradients.

This experiment and the success achieved mark an important development, for it is the first example of the utilization of railless trolley buses on a thickly populated route requiring a frequent service. The results achieved have been fully up to expectations and have amply justified the experiment. A capital saving of £54,000 was effected and very favourable working costs have been obtained. A more frequent service can be given, and the traffic has increased, while the journey is more comfortable for the passengers. Other road traffic is less disturbed, with consequent greater mobility to all users of the road.

It is evident that the railless trolley bus has important advantages where traffic and other conditions are suitable, and in future years there will probably be a considerable expansion in the use of this type of passenger traction.

CHAPTER XIV

ROAD TRANSPORT RATES AND FARES

Capital, Expenditure and Revenue of a Road Transport Concern.—It is at once evident that there is a striking difference in the amount of capital required to float a road transport concern as compared with the outlay necessitated for even the most lightly constructed railway. Compare the ease with which a road transport service can be inaugurated to the expensive permanent way, the cuttings, tunnellings and embankments, the elaborate signalling, and the numerous other items that have to be provided before a single train can be run. The King's highway penetrates to the most remote parts of the realm, and thus the road user finds his specialized way already provided, and this roadway is open to all to use for their mechanical haulage, provided they pay the necessary tax and comply with certain conditions. To establish a road transport service the capital outlay required is small, and is indeed but little more than the first cost of the vehicle, which may be as low as a hundred pounds or so. The first distinguishing feature, then, of a road transport undertaking is the relatively small capital outlay that is necessitated.

To analyse the capital expenditure involved in road transport working we may group the charges under three headings :—

(1) The capital cost of the vehicle or vehicles required.
(2) Capital cost of buildings such as garages, office, etc.
(3) Miscellaneous property.

It is obvious that if a revenue is to be earned the capital goods enumerated above must be worked and kept in an efficient condition. This involves an annual expenditure.

and thus it is next necessary to analyse and describe the nature of this expenditure.

The expenses of operating may be best considered under the two headings: (*a*) standing charges, and (*b*) running expenses. The first corresponds to the capital outlay, and the difference between it and the second item is simple and obvious. The standing charges, since they are fixed in amount, go on week by week whatever the amount of traffic. The running expenses depend on the amount of work carried out, or at the least they bear a close relation to that factor.

It should be noticed, however, that in the case of mechanical road haulage, it is often possible to vary the standing charges with changes in traffic over fairly long periods of time. For example, if in one year the traffic proved less than was anticipated, the number of vehicles might be reduced, the garage accommodation curtailed, etc., in the next year. This, then, is another point of difference as compared with a railway company, the capital expenses of which cannot be so varied to any great extent. The capital invested in a railway, if useless for that specific purpose, cannot very easily be used for anything else. Nor is it easy to reduce this capital outlay if traffic on the railway declines.

Standing charges are, then, those items of expenditure which are incurred whatever the mileage run.

In attempting to classify the items of this expenditure some difficulties are encountered, and further, if the period considered is short, some things properly to be regarded as running expenses have to be included under standing charges. However, it is general to group the following items under this head:—

(1) Interest on capital.
(2) Depreciation.[1]
(3) Insurance: vehicle, third party, fire, employer's liability, etc.

[1] Strictly speaking, depreciation will be found to vary with the actual mileage run, but in business it is a usual practice to calculate depreciation per year on the basis of alloting a "life" of so many years to the vehicle.

(4) Office and other administrative expenses.
(5) Rents and rates of garages, offices, repair shops, etc.
(6) Licences for vehicles under the present system of taxation.

If, however, part-year licences only are taken out, this item of expenditure could be partially adjusted to traffic variations, and in this case it would not be easy definitely to allot the expenditure to either overhead charges or running expenses, though probably in general it would still be retained in the category of standing charges. Were a fuel tax to be imposed in place of the vehicle tax, the outlay involved would no longer be assigned to overhead charges but to running expenses.

A last item, that of wages, involves further difficulties in an attempt at classification. In the case of a man in a small way of business who acts as his own driver, this item may partake of the nature of a standing charge. Again, where employment of drivers, their mates and conductors is practically permanent, the cost has some resemblance to a standing charge. In the case of a large company the salaries of the managerial staff would be put under this heading, but the wages of employees could hardly be so grouped, since it might be possible to adjust the number of workers to the probable variations in traffic.

The noticeable feature of the standing charges is that, as compared with a railway or a canal company acting as a carrier, they are relatively very light.

Turning next to consider the nature of running costs, they are those costs which increase or decrease in accordance with the mileage run. The principal items under this head are :—

(1) Fuel : for internal combustion engines, petrol, benzol, or some other liquid fuel is required ; for "steamers," coke or coal ; while in the case of the "electric battery vehicle," the corresponding item of expenditure is that involved in recharging or "boosting" the accumulators.

(2) Lubricants, e.g. oil, grease, etc.
(3) Tyres.
(4) Sundries such as lighting expenses, paraffin, sparking plugs, etc.
(5) Repairs, overhaul and maintenance of vehicle.

Three important features emerge regarding the capital outlay, standing charges and running costs of road transport when a comparison is made with rail transport.

These are as follows :—

(1) It is possible to adjust, though it may be only roughly, the capital outlay to the amount of the traffic.
(2) The ratio of running expenses to standing charges is much greater for a road transport concern. In other words, running expenses are a far greater portion of the total cost of transport than in the case of a railway.
(3) Following as a result of this second characteristic, it is possible to allocate costs against particular traffic to a far greater extent than is possible for railway transport.

The particular expenses of carrying certain traffic can be fairly easily computed, since the greater portion of the total cost consists of wages, fuel and other running costs which are incurred specially for this traffic, while certain standing charges, such as depreciation, etc., can be roughly allocated.[1]

From our analysis of the capital and expenditure of a road transport concern, it will be evident that the rates and fares charged for the service provided can be divided into two elements. These are :—

(1) The special costs incurred for the particular traffic—i.e. running expenses, such as fuel, oil, wear of tyres, etc.—and generally, since the cost can be

[1] In Appendix A specimen cost sheets of a motor transport fleet are given.

allocated to the traffic, the wages of the driver and mate and conductor (if any).

(2) The correct share of standing charges, including interest on capital.

Now it is obvious that unless the special costs, i.e. the running expenses, are met, a road transport concern cannot long remain in business. Some of the standing charges, e.g. the amounts set against depreciation, might be postponed for a time if it be a matter of getting some return rather than none at all, but of course such a policy cannot be long continued.

Interest on capital can be postponed without affecting the running of the vehicles, that is, provided the vehicles are not being paid for on a hire-purchase system. If, again, the money be borrowed from a bank, interest cannot be postponed for any length of time. In the case of a company, non-payment of interest would make it difficult to raise fresh capital when required, though it might also tend to prevent new-comers entering the business of road haulage.

In road transport rates the main element is the cost of the particular service. In a railway rate, on the contrary, it is not generally possible to compute with any accuracy the actual cost of providing the particular service, since overhead charges represent a very high proportion of the total cost of carriage. In this respect, the railway industry differs from most other businesses, though not from all, as witness similar types of enterprise, such as waterworks, electricity supply stations, tramways, etc. The amount of capital sunk in the railways is enormous, and this, as well as a considerable portion of the annual expenditure, is incurred for the sake of the traffic as a whole, not for any particular service.

The Theoretical Basis of Road Transport Rates and Fares.—In road haulage, cost of service is in general the determining factor. Competition tends to fix rates and fares for road transport at such a level that the receipts, after all working expenses have been paid and an allowance made for depreciation, etc., afford ordinary profits and a normal return on the capital invested. Hence it may be said that the economic principle underlying the fixation of road rates and fares is quite different to that which is the basis of railway charging.

In theoretical discussion a railway is considered to be a monopoly which is able to charge differential prices. On such a monopoly basis, railway rates would be so adjusted that a maximum aggregate monopoly net revenue would be obtained. In other words, the rates for the different kinds of traffic (e.g. coal, musical instruments, raw cotton, etc.) would be so fixed that in each case the net receipts (i.e. the number of units carried, multiplied by the rate charged, less any special costs incurred for that traffic) would be a maximum. The aggregate of these maxima would give the greatest profit. To obtain the maximum net revenue all classes of traffic would be accepted so long as they sufficed to cover at least the additional net cost of their transport. But any traffic that can bear a higher rate would theoretically be charged up to that limit. As regards passenger traffic, the principle of differential charging is not so clearly marked on British railways, though it is partially operative as regards first and third class. On Continental railways the principle is applied to a greater degree, as four classes of accommodation are sometimes provided, and different rates charged for fast and slow trains.

Under theoretical conditions, that bear some approximation to actual conditions, the difference between road transport and railway charges is thus seen to be the difference between competitive and differential monopoly charging.

In practice, however, the railways have not got a complete monopoly, and their charging powers are modified by statute and custom ; by direct competition between themselves or by indirect competition between them and coasting vessels, canals or road transport. In this country railway charges are regulated under present conditions by the Railway Rates Tribunal, and formerly by statutory maximum rates. On the other hand, in road transport a monopoly may be gained in certain districts, and if this be the case, charges would tend to approximate not to cost of service, but to a level that would yield a monopoly profit to the operating concern.

The essential points of difference brought out by theoretical discussion are of the greatest practical importance.

That in practice railway rates are differential charges, though tempered by other considerations such as custom, legislation, cost of service, etc., is seen by the existence of the various classifications. Commodities are put into different classes, and the rate charged per ton per mile varies as between these classes. In general higher rates are charged for the more valuable commodities, or, if preferred, it might be said that the less valuable the article the less the rate.[1] Canal companies, since they also have a monopoly of their type of transport, are accustomed to charge differential tolls, and for this purpose a system of classifications is put into practice.[2]

On the road, competition generally prevails in practice, and charges tend to approximate to cost of service. Where the nature of the route imposes limitations on the capacity of vehicles, as, for example, through low bridges, narrow roads, etc., this is sometimes exemplified, for higher rates are generally charged in these cases.

At times, indeed, competition may become acute and complaints are heard of "rate cutting," that is, the forcing of charges below an economic level which does not allow for interest charges or depreciation. Sometimes during recent years this has been due to the fact that newcomers have not always attempted to keep accurate costs, and for a time losses have been squared out of depreciation. It is evident, however, that no firm can continue for any

[1] On the whole question see Acworth, *The Elements of Railway Economics* and *The Railways and the Traders*

[2] See Kirkaldy and Evans, *History and Economics of Transport*, ch. x.

length of time working below an economic level. "Rate cutting" generally leads eventually to promote attempts at combination or monopoly, Thus the London "Combine" or "Pool" was formed in the old horse omnibus days as a result of acute competition between the various companies.

Where a monopoly is obtained, either by a big company or a municipality, the effect is in general to raise rates or fares above the competitive level. It may be, however, that the economies of large-scale working offset, at least in part, the rise in charges, so that fares are not unduly raised. In any case the powers of such a monopoly are tempered by indirect competition or by the fear of encouraging rivals if profits are considerable.

The Fixation of Passenger Fares in Practice.—It is essential that road transport fares should be so arranged in practice that the method of charging is simple and clear. The rates and stages should be easily intelligible to passengers, and should be constructed on a definite plan that will facilitate the work of the conductor. Of the various systems utilized in practice, the two most frequent and popular are the "flat rate" and the "zone system."

The flat rate system is the simplest, but it is only practicable in certain cases, for it is unsuited to those transport concerns where journeys are of any length and where passengers travel for varied distances. The same fare is charged whatever the distance travelled, and thus this system has the great advantage of simplicity. It errs, however, in making the short-distance passenger pay for the long-distance traveller, since obviously the rate charged must be an average rate somewhere between the charges for the two. The system of flat rates has, however, been adopted in many American cities, and in London the L.C.C. tramways apply it partially during the mid-day hours, when a flat rate of twopence is charged for any distance.

Zone systems are more general, and the system has been applied in varied forms. In some cases, definite stages are fixed, and for travel within this stage to any point a fixed sum is charged. The zones are usually penny stages, but generally the long-distance passenger is charged less; for instance, a threepenny stage would carry him over more than three separate penny zones. Obviously this system is a partial adoption of a charge based on distance travelled, in so far as short-distance travel is compatible with charging in proportion to mileage. The modifications in favour of the long-distance traveller, however, partake of the nature of a "tapering rate."

A greater approximation to mileage rates is obtained if several overlapping zones are introduced, but there are limits to the number of zones, since it is impossible for a conductor to check the entrance and exit of passengers at every stop. The provision of overlapping zones is much appreciated by passengers, who might otherwise feel a sense of grievance if they were charged the full fare on boarding a vehicle just before it entered a new zone. In one or another of its forms the zone system is the method followed by nearly all motor bus operating companies in this country.

Tramway Fares.—A tramway is by its nature a monopoly, since it is unthinkable that two lines could be laid so as to compete with each other in the same street. The power of a tramway undertaking to charge monopoly rates is generally tempered by indirect competition from motor buses, suburban railways, or other forms of transport, or by the fear of provoking competition, if charges be placed too high. Cost of service, however, is rather indeterminate in this case owing to the heavy capital charges involved in the permanent way, electric equipment, etc., and to the difficulty of apportioning the cost. A comparison with the principles underlying railway charges rather than with those relating to other types of road transport would consequently be more apposite.

One factor that makes for low charges in an enterprising tramway undertaking requires to be noted. The economies of large-scale working are considerable in this type of transport because it does not cost anything like twice the amount to carry, say, 200,000 passengers per week as it would to carry 100,000. Further, if the demand for transport is elastic, then a lowering of fares will attract a considerable number of additional passengers, and thus a compensation will be obtained that may make up for the reduction in fares. To attempt to maximize the profit per unit is useless; what is required is to maximize the profit per unit multiplied by the number of passengers carried.

Municipal Undertakings and Their Charges.—The particular case of municipal transport undertakings, whether bus or tram, is more involved. Municipal officials may think that fares should be so fixed as to just cover the expenses—i.e. on a no-profit basis—so that users will have the full benefit of cheap transport.

In Scotland it has been laid down that tramways should be excluded from rate aid, and the fares charged are fixed with this end in view. On the other hand, it may be considered that the transport concern should help the rates; or contrariwise, that it is expedient in the interests of the community that transport should be cheap so that the development of surrounding areas may take place; that overcrowding in the central parts be avoided; or for some other reason. In this latter case the municipal authorities might think that the transport system ought to be aided from the rates if they considered that the advantages to the community were greater than the disadvantage of increasing the burden on ratepayers.[1]

It has been a disputed question for a long time as to whether tramways should or should not contribute to the rates, though very frequently the matter has been settled by the absence of a surplus.

As regards the facts of the situation, in the year 1913–14 tramway undertakings received £62,600 from local rates in certain districts, but in others contributed in relief of rates the far larger sum of £578,019. In 1921–22 they received £371,303, but only contributed £174,738. Since then the

[1] This is the policy followed in New York City.

position has improved somewhat, and now fewer tramways are on the rates. The difficulties of the war period and the years immediately following were largely responsible for this unsatisfactory state of affairs in many districts. The war years, indeed, had more serious effects on tramways than on any other form of transport, with the exception of canal and inland water transit.

Transport systems ought, however, to be self-supporting, and it would not be an easy matter to sustain an argument in favour of rate subsidization. Clearly the better opinion is that a municipal system should neither be supported from the rates nor should it contribute a surplus in relief of rates, though it may be thought good policy to build up a small reserve fund to meet any emergencies.

Questions of municipal trading, however, are of a difficult and thorny nature, while, moreover, they involve matters of principle that lie outside the scope of this book. The reader must be referred to works on municipal trading for a more complete discussion of the subject.

CHAPTER XV

COMPETITION AND MONOPOLY IN ROAD TRANSPORT

IN road transport, monopoly is not perhaps so easily attained as in many other branches of industry. Nevertheless, tacit agreements, combination, association, fusion or other monopolistic tendencies are to be found in many areas. In rural districts where there is only scope for a single vehicle, owing to insufficient traffic, the road carrier may be without competitors, and hence able to charge monopoly rates. Further, such a carrier may be able to vary his charges, to some extent, on a basis of "what the traffic will bear," since he can exact a higher price from those people able to pay a higher rate and without any convenient alternative means of transport. Such a monopoly, however, is only a partial monopoly, for the carrier must take care not to set his rates so high that competition is invited. It is found also that road transport firms, in certain areas, where services are run to a regular schedule and where the amount of traffic fluctuates from time to time, can sometimes make adjustments in the rates charged for different types of commodities carried; that is, the charges may bear some resemblance to the railway principle of charging according to value. Indeed, classifications are not unknown, and these are not alone based on the cost of insurance and cost of carriage, but also sometimes take account of the value of the commodity.

In certain areas, large transport concerns either providing goods haulage or passenger services have attained a practical monopoly as a result of the large scale of their operations, their large capital resources and the moderate use of their monopoly power. A well-established company working on a large scale may obtain certain economies in operating which would be absent in the case of several competitive but smaller firms catering for the same traffic. Thus it may be that though rates and fares are fixed above the cost of service and afford a monopoly revenue to the proprietors, yet the level of charges may be no higher than they would be under a competitive regime. Where a large fleet is operated economies may be obtained in repair and overhaul work, in garage expenses, in the purchase of materials and in administrative expenses. In goods haulage, the large firm can run regular services, can better arrange for return loads, while office and warehousing expenses do not generally increase in proportion to the size of the undertaking.

The larger capital of an old-established company may give it some advantages over any actual or potential rivals. Thus the possession of a fleet of reserve vehicles may enable it to meet any threatened competition, and the size and amount of its capital would put it in a better position to hold out if rate cutting were indulged in. The very fact that a firm is well established in its area gives it a certain advantage and renders competition by a new-comer with smaller resources more difficult. The established firm may have provided bus or motor coach stations or goods depots, while it may have adopted route numbers that have become familiar to the public, and all of these are factors that would count in any competitive struggle, helping the older firm to retain the patronage of the public. Finally, the scale of its operations may enable it to provide services that would be impossible to smaller rivals.

It would appear to be from reasons such as these that certain road transport firms have obtained a practical though partial monopoly in certain areas. They may thus be able to keep their rates and fares somewhat above the competitive level, provided they take care not to attract rivals by unduly exploiting their monopolistic advantages. Their retention of the position attained, however, depends on the continued provision of adequate facilities, cheap rates and fares and regular services. Such monopolies are rare, however, on the whole, except in the case of certain city transport undertakings discussed below. Indeed, in many areas, competition has been so severe that numerous attempts have been made, and continue to be made, to form associations of road transport proprietors with the avowed object of curtailing competition, despite the fact that combinations among a number of rival enterprises operating in the same district are not easy either to initiate or to maintain. In Chapter VIII it was seen that the difficulties of combined action among motor coach proprietors were very considerable, and that during seasons of bad weather the association was likely to break up. In other types of road transport, agreements to prevent rate cutting are not likewise easy to enforce, though in some areas standard charges and other agreements have been arrived at. The monopolistic power of any such combination is very limited, because if rates are fixed too high, outside competition may easily arise. If profits appear to be considerable, it would be almost impossible to keep newcomers out. Road transport differs from most other types of transport in that the highways are open to all comers, and but a small capital is required to put a motor lorry, motor bus or motor coach on the road. Tacit combination, no doubt frequently exists, and the competing firms hesitate to reduce their charges below the customary rate that is supposed to allow an adequate return. In most areas fares and rates partake of the nature of a customary charge, and this may frequently prevent too keen competition.

The London Combine.—In the case of passenger omnibus services in and around large cities a considerable degree of monopoly is frequently found to exist. In this country the best known example is that of the London Combine. At an early date the bus services passed out of the hands of small competitive firms and were conducted by several large companies. The London General Omnibus Company began its operations in 1856 with a fleet of horse-drawn buses. It gradually grew in size, displacing some of its smaller rivals, though from 1880 competition between it and the Road Car Company was severe. After a period of sharp competition, the several larger firms of bus proprietors came to an agreement among themselves and arranged for the sharing out of the available traffic between them. Occasionally, however, the agreement broke down, and during a period violent fights for traffic were witnessed, before they came together again to form a new understanding. The "pool" made common cause against any interlopers in what they regarded as their territory, and would "nurse" any rival vehicle that appeared on the streets without their permission. For this purpose they would detail one of their vehicles to precede the rival and another to follow immediately behind, with orders to cut in between the new-comer and passengers waiting to board a vehicle. Gradually, however, the London General Omnibus Company absorbed its rivals and came to dominate the bus services of London. The introduction of mechanical vehicles, at the beginning of the present century, has helped on the progress of combination in the Metropolis, because a considerable advantage appertains to large-scale operation. In 1904 the "General" introduced its first mechanically propelled bus—"a steamer"—and from that date there has been a rapid and continued expansion of its fleet, till at December 1923 a fleet of 3,869 vehicles were on the roads, while the Company was adding to it at the rate of twenty-five buses per week in preparation for the following summer.

From about 1912 the "General" was left to itself, for a period of years, and little competition had to be feared, and where the few companies of the earlier years still carried on, working agreements were made for certain routes. The financial position of the bus company was not, however, very satisfactory, owing to the competition of other systems of transport—tram, tube, etc. To avoid such losses, to co-ordinate the work of the various systems and to eliminate unnecessary and sometimes wasteful competition, the "Combine" of tubes, buses and trams (excluding, of course, the L.C.C. and municipal tramways) was eventually formed.

In 1915 the Combine established a common fund into which all the profits from the associated companies were paid, and out of which the various concerns received a share in a proportion agreed upon. Lord Ashfield, the Chairman of the Combine, speaking of the common fund, declared on February 21, 1924, that, "short of a complete fusion of interests, this proved a valuable provision. It enabled the separate companies to sustain wage agreements with their employees which unaided and alone they often could not have borne. It enabled the companies to offer a more generous system of fares and to allow a freer use of the different forms of transport than might otherwise have been feasible. It enabled the companies to embark upon developments because the burden of those which were unremunerative at the first was spread upon a wider foundation. It enabled the companies to pursue a steady dividend policy towards their shareholders, for the fluctuations in net income among the several companies tended to average out. The common fund automatically adjusted the total net income to the needs of the companies, and for the eight years of its operation to date, the summary figures show that it worked out with an amazing fairness when you reflect upon the changes that have happened since it was established in 1915. The key to its success has been the careful and calculated adjustment of the travel facilities afforded by all, so that each found its proper place and fulfilled its proper function undisturbed." [1]

From 1912 to 1921 the London General Omnibus Company had not to meet much competition from other buses, though

[1] Quoted from *The Times'* Report, February 22, 1924.

till 1915 other types of transport had been keen rivals. Profits, however, were small or non-existent till 1921, but in that year a profit of £595,568 shown on the bus activities led to the introduction of numerous competitive buses on the London streets.[1] These new concerns were all run by men in a small way of business, most of them running but one or two buses. The number of competitors increased slowly month by month, and in January 1924 there were 74 such enterprises, running between them 208 buses.

Competition v. Monopoly.—The question of the relative advantages of monopoly and competition in London street transport has thus been brought to the front and has evoked considerable discussion. On behalf of competition it is urged that competition is healthy, that the public gets the advantage of competitive fares, whereas a monopoly may raise fares above the level required to pay expenses and to furnish a small return on capital. It is further urged that competition would mean the opening up of new services, while greater attention would be paid to passengers and their requirements, whereas a monopoly might tend to regard only its own interests and neglect public requirements; that no concern has a prescriptive right to the use of the streets, but that anyone who can provide adequate services with vehicles up to the standard of the licensing authorities ought to be free to do so; that competition is stimulating, and by it new inventions and improvements are encouraged and introduced. In Britain monopoly is distrust, because exploitation of the public is feared, through higher fares and inadequate services.

On the other side, on behalf of monopoly, or rather limited monopoly, strong arguments are also adduced. It is urged that competition in transport is often wasteful, so that while fares may not be above the competitive level—

[1] In 1919 there had been an adverse balance of £424,003, and in 1920 a further loss of £286,942, both of which had to be met out of the common fund.

i.e. that they tend to correspond to the cost of providing the service—yet they may be higher than they need be under monopoly, even though the monopoly rate would be above the actual cost of service, because the monopoly cost of providing the service is lower than the competitive cost. Under combination, numerous economies in running expenses and in overhead charges may be effected, such as through the provision of an adequate reserve of vehicles; reduction in overhauling delays; building of outlying garages; purchases in bulk; saving on advertisement, etc. It is maintained that a combine can afford to build up and foster the traffic on routes which do not pay their way in the initial stages, though the transit facilities afforded may be a great convenience to the public and may later be developed into paying routes. Competition, it is said, would, on the other hand, lead to congestion on the more remunerative routes, while services would be curtailed on the unremunerative routes. The L.G.O.C., for instance, has complained bitterly against what they call the "pirate buses," which they say run just ahead of the scheduled services on an established route and take the pick of the traffic at the rush hours, but do not operate during the slack hours when the service could not be run at a profit. In 1923 Lord Ashfield stated the case for the "General" as follows: "It realizes its responsibility for the efficient conduct of a large portion of the passenger transport of the Metropolis, that it is doing everything possible to fulfil its obligations, that in this regard it must operate a number of services, unremunerative in themselves, but subsidized from the revenue obtained from other and more profitable services, and that therefore it is unfair, and in the long run will be detrimental to the public interest if it has to submit to competition on the better paying routes."

No one maintains that the L.G.O.C. has abused its virtual monopoly, and except for the assertions made some time ago that the company resorted to "nursing" or "swinging" rival vehicles, for a time, shortly after their first appearance on the streets, few complaints have been levelled against it. On the contrary, fares appear to be lower, taking all considerations into account, than they are in most other cities; a greater degree of comfort is provided for the passengers; whilst, on Mr. Bevin's admission, the Company has been able to provide favourable conditions for its employees. It has been efficient and progressive, witness the introduction of the "S" and the "N.S." type vehicles, while at the same time it runs many unremunerative routes for development purposes. In this connection Dr. Marshall's observations on the London Traffic Combine may be quoted. He states that "the recent amalgamation of London's underground railway, tramway and omnibus companies gives scope for great economies and enlarged conveniences for travellers. It may prove a great public benefit so long as those in control are able, energetic, alert to seek improvements in technique, and to promote subordinates with true insight into their qualities of mind and character. But should any slackness intervene the monopolistic power of the amalgamation may raise demands for authoritative intervention, and thus increase the burdens that tend to impair the efficiency of government in that work, which it alone can do." [1] As Dr. Marshall points out, if a monopolistic organization in city transport becomes less alert to seek improvements and comes to follow routine and stereotyped methods, then the public interests would not be served and demands would be raised for interference. Even already, and without any grievance against the Combine on the score of an abuse of its powers, it has frequently been urged that some responsible authority should be set up to regulate London traffic, for the purpose of preventing any such evils from arising, and to secure proper services and co-ordinated development. The formation of such an authority has been supported by the officials of the Combine itself, and it is proposed that this authority should determine what developments were required and would secure the

[1] Marshall, *Industry and Trade*, p. 428, 2nd Edition, 1919.

required services, if those already in the business failed to provide them, from others who were willing to do so.

In most of the capital cities of the world, e.g. New York, Paris, Berlin, etc., the various traffic undertakings have been co-ordinated in some such manner. Thus in Paris, for example, the omnibus companies are deliberately granted a monopoly for a number of years on their route, subject to the necessary safeguards as to the type of vehicle to be used, the fares to be charged, the frequency of service, conditions of employment, etc. In return for its monopoly, the operating company makes an agreed annual payment to national or municipal funds. In effect, this is a compromise between municipal and private enterprise and is a modified species of a leased municipal undertaking.

CHAPTER XVI

THE RAILWAYS AND ROAD POWERS

THE rapid development of road transport since the Great War has established it as an economic system of transportation in this country. In some areas it has become a keen rival of the railways, which find it difficult to cope adequately with certain phases of the new competition. The railways feel that the only effective reply to the challenge is to be furnished by the provision of road services in conjunction with their railway system. But since many traders view with considerable suspicion any new developments of rail enterprise along these lines, fearing the attainment of monopoly by those giant concerns, the question whether railways should be granted powers to run road vehicle services, for merchandise or passenger traffic, has become acute and contentious. No discussion, of course, centres around railway cartage for delivery and collection purposes to and from stations or depots within the usual radius ; it is on the question of providing direct road haulage between definite centres that the debate has turned.

Before the war, it is true, though the fact is sometimes forgotten, some few railway companies had utilized road services, though not on any very extensive scale. Since about 1904 the Great Western Railway has run road vehicles in certain parts of the area tapped by their system. These were mainly of the nature of "development services" in sparsely populated districts, and were originated for the purpose of encouraging tourist traffic. During the years 1904 to 1906, on application to Parliament, statutory powers were obtained by the Great Eastern, the North-Eastern, the North Staffordshire, and the Great North of Scotland Railway Companies for the purpose of running road vehicle services in certain areas. Before the war, however, Parliamentary action in the matter cannot be said to have been uniform, since similar applications were rejected in the case of the Great Northern, the London and South-Western, and the London, Brighton and South Coast Railway Companies.

Certain other railway companies inaugurated road services without any Parliamentary sanction, but no objection appears to have been raised at the time. The Lancashire and Yorkshire, the London and North-Western, the Midland, the London and South-Western, and the South-Eastern and Chatham Railway Companies, for instance, all utilized road vehicles to relieve congestion ; to secure rapid transport of goods and merchandise between terminals and various railway depots ; or even for regular transport work between certain places where circumstances made road transportation more economical than rail haulage.

But on the whole, in the pre-war days such road services were not of great importance, with the exception of those in certain districts. Post-war developments in road transport, however, soon led the various railway companies to view mechanical road haulage, both passenger and goods, in a new light. They became anxious lest they should be debarred from utilizing this now important type of transport. When the Railways Act of 1921 was being drafted, they sought the insertion of a clause that would give them the necessary powers to operate road vehicle services where they desired. When the Bill was under discussion strong objection was taken to this clause on the ground that the title of the Bill did not contain anything that referred to the running of road vehicles, and that therefore the matter was one outside the scope of the Bill. Some members, however, argued as against this that railway companies already carried on such undertakings as hotels, docks, etc., which are ancillary to their main work, and that in fact some companies had in former years been granted legal powers to run certain road services. The Speaker ruled, however, that the clause was out of order, since the Bill was not one for conferring "great new powers on railways." The Bill and the subsequent Act, it will be remembered, related to the basis of railway charging, the "grouping" of the various companies and the relation of the railways to their employees. The clause regarding road powers, the Speaker decided, was one that would require separate legislation.

In 1922 certain constituent companies of the new London, Midland and Scottish Group—the Caledonian, the Glasgow and South-Western and the Highland Railways—promoted a special Bill for the purpose of obtaining road powers. A Select Committee was appointed to consider the application, but after a ten-days' sitting the Bill was withdrawn by the promoters. The cause of this withdrawal was stated to be the unexpected opposition of the Ministry of Transport to certain clauses of a vital nature. The evidence tendered on behalf of the Ministry made it impossible, said the railway representatives, for them to proceed with the inquiry. The stumbling-block was the question of charges. The Ministry, as represented by their witness, held that the railway companies should only be permitted to charge for conveyance by road the same rates as are fixed for the equivalent services by rail (including terminal charges), and neither more nor less. The railways had proposed—and it was to this proposal that the Ministry objected—that the railway rate should be taken as the basis, but that the charges should be modified for road services so that in certain cases door-to-door road transport would be charged at the direct rail rate, applicable to the mileage covered. The view of the Ministry was that charges should be identical for identical services, whether the goods were carried by road, by rail, or by both. One objection, it would appear, was that the Ministry considered that the proposed Bill might, if passed, tend to promote competition between the railways, and thus nullify the intention of the Railways Act, 1921, that wasteful competition should be eliminated. The Ministry of Transport witness also pointed out that a main provision of the Railways Act was designed to secure a " standard revenue " for the railway companies, and to achieve this purpose " standard rates " were to be determined by the Railway Rates Tribunal. If, however, the companies were to carry a large volume of traffic on the roads at rates lower than those applicable to rail services, traffic in considerable bulk might be diverted from the rail, and thus there would be a smaller quantity on which the " standard revenue " had to be raised. Up to the time of writing the matter has been in abeyance, since the withdrawal of this Bill by the Scottish Railway Companies. It is probable, however, that when the " grouping " arrangements and the reorganization of the railways under the 1921 Act have been completed, the matter of road powers will be again brought up. In the future the question is likely to become prominent, especially if the development of the road vehicle continues.

The Arguments for and against granting Road Powers to Railways.—Though railway companies prefer a long haul, and though on the long haul the railway has greater opportunities for economical carriage, owing to the expense of terminal operations, the railways cannot in this country, where transport distances are relatively short, afford to lose short-distance traffic. In a small but densely populated country like our own the bulk of the traffic is for short hauls. Consequently the railways consider that road transport powers would be a great asset to them, since road transit has special advantages for short-distance transport. In this connection an interesting comparison might be made *between* railway development, with its effects on canals, *and* the new road competition, with its probable but more limited effects on railway transport. E. A. Pratt, writing on " The Transition in Trade," states : " The tendency in almost every branch of business is for the trader to have small or comparatively small stocks of any particular commodity, which he can replenish speedily at frequent intervals as occasion requires. The advantages are obvious." [1] A little later on he states: "For trades and businesses conducted on these lines, the railway—taking and delivering promptly consignments great or small, penetrating to every part of the country, and supplemented by its own commodious warehouses, in which goods can be stored as desired by the trader pending delivery or shipment—is a far more convenient mode of transport than the canal boat; and to the railway the perfect revolution that has been brought about in the general trade of this country is mainly due." [2]

Endorsing this verdict, Professor Lilian Knowles writes: "In no other country has the railway so completely superseded the system of inland waterways, but English commerce became so organized that speed, punctuality, warehousing facilities and ease of handling became the important factors, and in this respect the railways far out-distanced the system of inland navigations that seemed so wonderful to the men who remembered the old pack-horse and the earthen unmetalled road." [3]

In brief, then, it is generally held that one cause of canal decadence is due to the superior facilities of the railways, which are better suited to modern commerce than the ill-organized and unenterprising canal systems, with their natural disadvantages and intrinsic unsuitability for certain kinds of transport work.

Now the railways are finding that their new road competitors are reversing the situation, though on a much smaller scale, since even better facilities, such as door-to-door services, rapid dispatch, etc., are provided by road services. It is not meant, of course, to suggest that in the future road transport will necessarily supersede the railways, as

[1] E. A. Pratt, *British Canals*, ch. vi, p. 74. [2] *Ibid.*, p. 79.
[3] L. C. A. Knowles, *Industrial and Commercial Revolutions*, p. 253.

the latter have our inland waterways, but in certain cases the railways are bound to feel the effects of the new competition. Hence from the point of view of the railways the grant of road powers would be of great utility in that it would put them in a better position to retain their traffic. Road transport would offer an alternative to the "pick up" goods train, and would thus in certain cases eliminate the need of a duplicate service. Time lost in loading and unloading or in transhipment would be saved in certain cases. Road transport would enable the railway companies to extend their collection and delivery services. At the present time the railways deliver and collect a considerable amount of goods within a radius of about 10 miles, but they do not possess the necessary powers required to extend this work up to the 40 or 50-mile limit of an independent road haulier. The companies believe that considerable economies could be effected by utilizing road transport between central termini and outlying goods yards or depots. At the larger goods stations, the number of small packages that have to be handled in a day's work frequently amounts to several tens of thousands. In these cases the co-ordination of road and rail services would often promote economies, since fewer handlings would be required; a saving would be effected in locomotive power and in rolling stock; the amount of shunting required would be less, while other operating expenses might also be reduced. In consequence it might be found possible to close many of the smaller goods depots required for the present system of working. Further, services would be improved and quicker deliveries could be given, since terminal and transhipment delays would be avoided. The railway companies point out that they pay local rates, part of which go to the upkeep of the roads, and in certain parts of the country, they state, that they are in fact the largest ratepayer in the district. It is unfair, they declare, that they should be excluded from utilizing the roads, to the upkeep of which they are forced to contribute.[1]

[1] See Chapter XVII, The Road, p. 217.

Strong opposition, however, has been raised against this claim of the railway companies to utilize road transport. It has been argued that the railways with their large capital resources and their efficient and extensive organization might obtain a monopoly, since they might be able to force their less powerful road competitors out of business by resorting to "rate cutting" or other means. Eventually, on this reasoning, the railways could force up freight rates, having destroyed competition, and thus sacrifice the interests of traders and the general public to the benefit of the Combine.

To meet these objections, safeguards against such a monopolizing policy were introduced into the proposed Private Bill of 1922. It was agreed that the rates charged for road services should be such as would produce a net revenue sufficient to remunerate the capital invested by the railway in its road transport department. Provisions were also inserted that the road accounts of the companies should be separated from those of their other undertakings. The aim of this clause was to prevent the possibility of road services being run at a loss for the purpose of squeezing out smaller road rivals, the company for the time recouping itself from purely railway revenue.

Some traders—though not all—are further of the opinion that railways should not be allowed to carry goods by road at all, except for the collection or delivery of consignments in limited areas, since they fear "undue preferences" might be granted to certain firms, as, for instance, by the provision of better facilities, through the arrangement of times of departure or by the more prompt dispatch of goods where the traffic was to pass over other portions of the railway company's system, etc.

Road hauliers fear the powerful competition of the railways, if they be allowed to engage in road transport. Such a development, it is argued, would tend to stifle private enterprise and would be likely to restrict the improvement and progress of commercial road transport.

The established road haulage contractors, as is natural, view such an extension of railway activities with apprehension.

Numerous other antagonists to the railway companies' claims are also very vocal. Local authorities, for instance, complain of the probable competition with their tramways or motor buses. Manufacturers of motor vehicles, motor accessories, etc., fear that the railway companies might proceed to set up workshops for the purpose of building their own vehicles.

In view of the numerous and divergent interests involved, and since it was obvious that the question is one of considerable complexity, a Departmental Committee was set up by the Ministry of Transport as early as January 1921. This Committee, under the chairmanship of the late Mr. J. H. Balfour Browne, was required to advise and inquire on the question of road conveyance of goods by railway companies, the exact terms of reference being as follows: "To inquire and report whether it is desirable that the railway companies should have general or limited power to carry goods by road, and if so, what, if any, conditions should be attached to the exercise of this power." [1]

The Committee, however, failed to reach anything like a unanimous conclusion, and three separate and divergent reports were issued. The Chairman—an impartial member—and two railway representatives advocated the granting of restricted powers to the railway companies. In their report they stated: "Road traction has considerable advantages, for certain distances, over transport by rail. If the process of abstraction of traffic went on, there might in the end be such serious difficulty in carrying on railway traffic at reasonable rates that it might lead to great increases of the charges which the railways would have to make. We have come to the conclusion that railway companies cannot expect to recover the traffic which has been diverted (or keep the traffic which in our view might be diverted in the future) by giving greater facilities on

[1] Reported in 1921, Cmd. 1228.

the railway, or by reducing railway rates ; and under these circumstances we have come to the conclusion that railway companies ought, under certain stringent conditions, to be allowed to carry goods by road."

They considered that it would be altogether undesirable that the railways should obtain a practical monopoly of road transport in this country, but they were not convinced that it was beyond the capacity of Parliament to devise restrictions that would prevent such a happening.

"We have come to the conclusion, notwithstanding the great weight of the evidence we have heard as to the danger of such a course, that the resources of legislation are capable of securing a fair competition between road and railway carriers by road without permitting a combination which would result in injury to the public or a monopoly which would be injurious to the trades which carry or are connected with the service of road transport."

As safeguards they recommended :—

(1) That the existing provisions as to "undue preference," the provision of "reasonable facilities," and compulsory publication of rates should apply to railway companies' road traffic ;

(2) That the Ministry of Transport should have power to establish road services and to cause accounts to be kept and audited ; and

(3) That charges should be controlled in the interest of the public by the Minister of Transport responsible to Parliament.

They were not convinced, however, that the railways should be compelled to fix road rates between two points not less than by rail, since it might be that the distance by road in some cases would be less than a circuitous rail route.

Road powers, it was suggested by these members of the Committee, would enable railways to undertake useful and necessary development services in sparsely populated districts and to build up feeders to their existing lines. "If that were done, it would, in our view, be an advantage to the public, and in many cases that advantage can only be given by the railway company, which in addition to the receipts from the haulage upon the roads was to have a further advantage of a long haul on their railway to which the motor lorry would prove a useful feeder."

They recommended that under such circumstances road powers should be granted for development purposes, and that the railway companies should not be restricted to the carriage of goods along such routes that were ultimately destined for further carriage on the railway, but should be entitled to transport commodities between any points on that route. "We think," they declared, "for the purpose of developing a district in which no transport by independent road carriers existed, railway companies might, with the sanction of the Minister of Transport, be allowed to establish and work a service for, say, three years, even if in these years the receipts from the service were not equal to meet the expenses."

They were of opinion, however, that the powers exercised by railway companies for such purposes should be restricted and controlled. The Minister of Transport should control changes in the interests of the public, while other restrictions should be also imposed, such as the extension to the new services of the clauses of the Traffic Acts relating to "undue preferences."

In a second report, presented by four members representing Road Carriers, the Federation of British Industries, and the Association of British Chambers of Commerce, quite different conclusions were reached, and it was recommended that any extension of the powers of railway companies in the direction of road transport should be refused. They were not of the opinion that any further concentration of transit facilities would serve the public interest.

They declared that "Most witnesses regarded the granting

of road transport powers to railway companies as certain to lead to the securing of a monopoly of the road haulage by railway companies and the extinction of the independent road carriers. Of course, at the present time any carrier by road is liable to competition, but what the present carriers seem to object to is what they call unfair competition by railway companies, which with their large capital and great revenues might charge such rates for conveyance by road and give such preferential facilities to their own road motors as would make it impossible for the independent carrier to continue in the business. Of course, this preference, if it took place, while for a time at least it might seem to benefit the trading community, might in the end result in the discontinuance of the independent carrying trade, and the creation of a monopoly of road carriage in the hands of the railway companies which would be detrimental to the public."

They considered that unfair competition would result if road powers were granted to the railways; that ultimately the railways might gain a monopoly of road transport; that competition between road and rail traffic is healthy and in the public interest; that railway companies if prohibited from utilizing road haulage would, through the competition of independent road carriers, be induced to provide better rail facilities and to fix rates at reasonable levels. In their view, "although to some extent traffic has been diverted from the railway lines to the roads by means of independent carriers by road, that traffic in no sense belonged to the railway companies, but is the legitimate extension of the business of the old road haulage contractor.

They concluded that "it is not desirable that railway companies should have general or limited power to carry goods by direct road services, and that their present powers are sufficient for all the legitimate purposes of a railway company, namely, the carriage of goods by rail and the collection and delivery of goods in connection with transit by rail."

In the third report, signed by the representative of Transport and Vehicle Workers' Organizations, it was stated that a complete solution of the traffic problem is only possible by National Ownership of all means of transport, but that the grant of road powers to railways under present conditions would ultimately result in a private monopoly dangerous to the public interest. He recommended that road powers should not be granted, though for purely development purposes in agricultural or other sparsely populated area permission might be granted for the purpose of the railways inaugurating "test services."

From the conflicting nature of the recommendations of these three reports, it will be obvious that it is not easy to arrive at a clear-cut and impartial solution of the problem.

It will, however, be generally agreed that it is undesirable that full and unlimited powers should be given to the railways, but on the question of the grant of limited powers opinions differ to a considerable extent.

On the one hand, many traders, road hauliers, and the general public fear that monopoly in transport may be obtained, at least in certain areas, even if partial powers only are granted to the railways. On the other hand, however, the advantages to the community that would result from the elimination of terminal delays, the saving of too frequent transhipments and the development of rural areas by road vehicles running in conjunction with the railways when not provided by individuals, are considerable.

If it were possible to devise an adequate method of control and regulation, many impartial persons might be inclined to agree that the claim for limited powers in certain cases, where road transit would result in more economic working, was one that would be reasonable and in the interests of the majority of the community. But since it is denied that such control would prove adequate, the question must remain one on which complete agreement of opinion is impossible.

STATISTICS OF ROAD MOTOR VEHICLES OWNED BY THE PRINCIPAL RAILWAY COMPANIES[1] 1922 AND 1923.

Name of Railway.	1922.	Passenger, 1923.	Goods and Parcels. 1922.	Goods and Parcels. 1923.
Caledonian	—	—	3	3
Furness	1	—	8	8
Glasgow & S.W.	—	—	6	6
Great Central	—	—	22	24
Great Eastern	3	—	13	53
Great Northern	4	4	14	35
Great North of Scotland ..	38	33	11	11
Great Western	66	77(*a*)	257	307(*a*)
London & North-Western ..	5	6(*b*)	964	1,054(*b*)
L. & S.W.	1	1	73	80
L.B. & S.C.	—	—	11	20
Midland	3	3	172	195
North-Eastern	24	25(*c*)	78	79(*c*)
North Staffordshire.. ..	—	—	20	32
S.E. & Chatham	—	—	30	31

(*a*) Includes railways amalgamated during 1922.
(*b*) Includes L. & Y. and North London Railways.
(*c*) Includes Hull & Barnsley Railway.

[1] Abstracted from the *Railway Year Book*, 1922 and 1923.

CHAPTER XVII

THE ROAD

To the economic problems of road transportation there is a double aspect. So far it has been the transport side of these questions that has been discussed, but now it is time to consider the other side—the road problem—which is, indeed, of great importance and which raises many difficult financial, administrative and technical problems, not easy of solution, though pressing and urgent in their nature.

Any adequate treatment of these difficulties and problems would, however, require a volume of itself, and the scope of the present work prevents any more than a brief account being given of the main problems of the economics of the roadway.

Undoubtedly the best approach to present-day road problems would be by means of a historical sketch, for many of our highway problems, such as those relating to local administration, have their roots deep in the past. The limits of space and proportion, however, do not admit of such a task, and it must suffice to remark that while the past has given us a great heritage of roads, it has also bequeathed to us an unsuitable system of road administration.

In Great Britain there are approximately 177,000 miles of road, there being over 152,000 in England and Wales and about 25,000 in Scotland. In Ireland there are in addition 59,000 miles, which makes a grand total of 236,000 miles of highways for the United Kingdom of Great Britain and the Free State of Ireland.

As compared with these 236,000 miles, the railways of Great Britain and Ireland had in 1921, according to the 1923 *Railway Year Book*, 23,724 miles of line open for traffic. In other words, there are practically ten times as many miles of roads as of railways.

The extent of the road mileage will be realized when it is remembered that the area of England and Wales is about 58¼ thousand square miles, of Ireland about 31¾ thousand square miles, and of Scotland just under 30 thousand square miles. This gives for England and Wales approximately 2·6 miles of road per square mile of area, for Scotland 0·8 of a mile, and for Ireland nearly 1·9 miles of road per square mile.

Scotland and Ireland are thus in proportion to area very much less well equipped with roads, though in Scotland that is due largely to the mountainous and difficult nature of a great part of its area.

As compared with Continental countries, the roadways of France are approximately in the ratio of 2 miles per square mile of territory, of Italy 1·2, and of Germany 0·8 of a mile.

Road Administration.—Though the proportion of roads to area is high in the British Isles, our road administration is hardly up to the standard that might be expected even in spite of the improvements recently made. The parochial origins of that administration have left their mark to the present day, and there is in consequence little uniformity to be discovered. In one area it may be the duty of a parish to administer the functions of road repair and maintenance, in another part a County Council may be entrusted with the task, elsewhere Urban Authorities, and so on.

In 1846 it is stated that in England alone 16,000 different local authorities had charge of the highways.[1] Consolidation

[1] On the history of road administration see Webb, *Story of the King's Highway*, and Cannan, *History of Local Rates in England*.

had been urged by several Committees and by numerous individuals, notably Sir Henry Parnell and Davies Gilbert, while Peel proposed to group parishes into districts for the purposes of road administration, so that the number of authorities would be reduced to 600.

This plan, however, was not carried out, and little was achieved as a result of any of the other agitations, so that even to-day, despite a certain amount of gradual consolidation, the number of our highway authorities still exceeds 2,000, and this despite the fact that road transport has become and is continuing to become more national than local. Where traffic was purely local, the small units of administration may have sufficed, though even then the smallness of the unit had many disadvantages ; but with the growth of through traffic and the necessity for more economic administration and the demand for better standards of road upkeep, the small local unit of road administration is somewhat of an anachronism. In all other branches of transport, grouping, consolidation and co-ordination have been shown to be necessary for successful development, yet highway administration in Britain has made little progress in this direction.

For instance, Mr. Rees Jeffreys, of the Roads Improvement Association, has shown that the first 18 miles of the main road out of London to the west was looked after by no less than twelve separate authorities. From London to Carlisle the Great North Road is administered by seventy-two distinct authorities, ranging from small Rural District Councils to one of the most important Borough Councils in England.

In France and Belgium the roads have been the especial care of the State. In Britain the "tardy and imperfect recognition of the necessity for central control of, and financial contribution to, the service of the roads is in strong contrast to the policy of France and Belgium." [1]

From 1743 the main roads of France have been con-

[1] Watson Grice, *National and Local Finance*, p. 107.

structed, improved and maintained by the Central Government in many parts, and engineers have been trained in a special school established for the purpose. In both France and Belgium a definite classification of roads has been adopted, based on the nature of the routes according as they are national, regional, or merely local highways, and to the corresponding authority the duty of upkeep, the administration and financial responsibility has been delegated.

"In France," declares Professor Knowles, "the unity and welfare of the State was held to depend on smooth and rapid communication, and transport has been under the peculiar care of the State during the eighteenth and nineteenth centuries, no matter how *laissez-faire* France might be in other matters. In France, transport developments came from above and were planned on a uniform system; in England, they came from below, and grew up in a patchy, haphazard, piecemeal fashion, with a tendency to amalgamate into bigger areas, but always retaining traces of the want of uniformity with which they started." [1]

In Great Britain there is still somewhat of a chaos in administration; there is little uniformity, and there is much duplication of effort, with consequent waste. Many of the lesser authorities are too poor on account of their small size and mainly rural character even to pay an adequate salary that would attract the best engineers. "The first requisite," declared Sir Henry Maybury, Director-General of Roads, "of the Highway Authority is a competent highway engineer, and the meagre salaries which some of the minor authorities are in a position to pay are not such as to attract well-qualified men."

Again, where road administration is on a local basis, inequitable burdens may be placed on some rural authorities, where roads bear the heavy traffic passing between larger and wealthier urban districts. As far back as 1901, in their

[1] L. C. A. Knowles, *Industrial and Commercial Revolutions*, p. 240.

Final Report, the Royal Commissioners on Local Taxation declared that "the maintenance of main roads is, on the whole, to some extent a national service, and likely to become more so, owing to the increasing mobility of the population and the development of new means of locomotion." [1] Since then the rapid development of mechanical road transport has intensified the problem and has rendered the position of rural authorities on through traffic routes more difficult. Under our chaotic system these burdens are only partially alleviated by the system of grants-in-aid. As will be shown later, the proceeds of motor taxation are distributed among local authorities for the upkeep of main roads, but it is frequently claimed that even third-class roads which are not supposed to receive any grants often bear considerable foreign traffic as a result of the continued development of road transport. Just recently, however, the Road Fund has been "raided" to provide a grant to certain rural third-class roads. The heavy wear and tear on the road surface in rural districts caused by the increased motor coach and commercial motor traffic has been responsible for heavy burdens owing to the low rateability. These roads have not been constructed to carry heavy traffic and rapidly deteriorate under such conditions, and this has meant that the expense of upkeep has become too heavy for those sparsely populated districts. In Essex, for instance, the cost of maintenance of roads and bridges increased from £147,677 in 1910 to £487,358 in 1922, and the corresponding rate rose from 7½d. to 2s. 1½d. in the pound. Comparing the year 1913 with the year 1921–22, when costs were at their highest, in Surrey the rates rose from 5¼d. to 9½d., in Somerset from 10½d. to 1s. 11d., in Herefordshire from 1s. 2d. to 3s. 1d., and in Gloucestershire from 10¼d. to 1s. 11½d.

Complaints by rural authorities have in consequence been frequent. For instance, to take but one example out of many, over one hundred Rural Councils have forwarded

[1] Final Report, p. 12.

resolutions to a quarterly meeting of the Rural District Councils Association, expressing their opinion that the ever-increasing through traffic on their highways had created an intolerable and unjust burden on local rates, and that as the incomes of rural taxpayers had fallen to such a serious extent, it was extremely urgent that increased assistance should be granted to rural authorities for road maintenance and improvement.

Some years before the war a Road Board—not to be confused with the Road Transport Board of 1918—was set up, which later became merged in the Ministry of Transport. In 1909 the increasing cost of road maintenance and the growth of mechanical road transport brought the road question to the front, and in that year the Road Board was established under a clause of the Development and Road Improvements Fund Act (1909). At the same time increased licence duties were placed on motor cars, and a special motor tax was also imposed for the first time, taking the form of a tax of 3d. per gallon on petrol. The proceeds of this motor taxation were to constitute the Roads Improvement Fund, and were to be handed over to the Road Board. These moneys the Board distributed among certain local authorities—in nearly all cases County Councils only—to enable them to *improve* specified roads, but not for purposes of road maintenance. The expectations formed when the Board was established were, however, never fully realized. As a result of its activities, it is true, a considerable improvement was made in the condition of the main roads, but the Board never fulfilled the function of a central and co-ordinating Road Department, for this was a duty beyond its scope, and one indeed for which it was never really created to perform.

In 1920, under the Roads Act (Sections 2 and 3), the old Roads Improvement Fund was superseded by the Road Fund then established. This fund is under the control and management of the Ministry of Transport, and its revenue is obtained from the proceeds of the new motor taxation exigible since January 1, 1921, together with the proceeds of the duties on licences for horse-drawn carriages and drivers' licences. The money thus obtained is allocated to various local authorities as grants or loans for road improvement or maintenance after payments have been made to the appropriate authorities for their expenses in connection with the levying of licence duties, etc.

But though the local authorities are thus given partial aid to meet the expense of improving roads—only a percentage of this expense is paid, the remainder being obtained from local rates—the problem of our unco-ordinated road administration has not yet been resolutely faced. The local nature of road administration which still persists has been one cause of the conflict between user and maintainer, for the interests of the two parties are often opposed, or at the least they appear to be so opposed. It is only of recent years that we are coming to see that the upkeep of our roads is a national problem that requires to be undertaken by national effort, or at any rate by a much more closely co-ordinated and consolidated system of local efforts based on a systematic plan.

At the present time considerable attention is being paid to the road problem, and endeavours are being made to bring our highways up to the new standard required by mechanical traction. During the post-war trade depression the unfortunate prevalence and intensity of unemployment has helped to accelerate considerably the work of road building and improvement, as it has been considered that this type of work is suitable for relief work, since a large percentage of "unskilled" labour is generally employed. In 1920 the Government set aside a special fund of £10,400,000 to aid local authorities to undertake road works as unemployment relief on a basis of a 50 per cent. contribution by local authorities and 50 per cent. by the Government, though the local authority might borrow its share from the fund in certain cases. This special fund was made up of £4,000,000 from the Road Fund, £1,200,000 as a special Treasury contribution, and £5,200,000 available as loans to local authorities from the Treasury. The building of arterial roads, of by-pass and avoiding routes, has gone on apace, and where constructed these have been planned and built to suit modern requirements with good foundations, fine surfaces, and often with a minimum width as great as 100 to 120 feet.

A Committee, known as the Roads Advisory Committee, was set up under the Ministry of Transport Act, 1919, and among the important matters that have engaged its attention since its establishment have been the following: The classification of roads, standardization of road direction posts and warning signs, and the expedition of road works for the purpose of relieving unemployment.

The Classification of Roads.—In 1914 the important work of road classification was begun, but the outbreak of war interrupted its progress. It has, however, now been completed by the Roads Department of the Ministry of Transport, with the aid of the local authorities concerned. The scheme of classification adopted is as follows :—

The roads of the Kingdom are divided into three classes. Those placed in Class I consist of (*a*) the main trunk routes connecting London with the principal towns and ports, (*b*) routes between important towns, (*c*) links between the roads above mentioned, (*d*) routes connecting routes (*a*) or (*b*) with important centres that carry heavy traffic. In a sentence, roads in Class I are those that form the main traffic arteries.

In Class II are scheduled those routes that connect urban areas of less importance or important rural areas, and also the connecting links of less importance.

In Class III are placed the roads of minor importance.

The appended schedule of road mileage for Great Britain, abstracted from the figures given in the Report of the Traffic Census, 1922 (published 1924), shows the details of classification :—

CLASSIFICATION OF ROADS.

Schedule of Mileage.

	Mileage of all Roads.	Mileage, Class I.	Mileage, Class II.
ENGLAND AND WALES.			
Administrative Counties (excluding County Boroughs and London) :—			
Main	28,764·49	15,491·21	6,855·15
District	110,927·89	1,358·33	3,960·91
Total	139,692·38	16,849·54	10,816·06
County Boroughs	10,559·62	1,166·58	544·16
Metropolitan Boroughs and L.C.C...	2,157·61	246·23	119·75
Total (England and Wales) ..	152,409·61	18,262·35	11,479·97
SCOTLAND.			
Counties	23,948·40	4,803·03	3,209·25
Burghs	963·20	164·48	50·19
Total (Scotland)	24,911·60	4,967·51	3,259·44
GRAND TOTAL	177,321·21	23,229·86	14,739·41

These figures show that in England and Wales 12 per cent. of the highways are Class I roads ; in Scotland, 19·9 per cent. ; while in England and Wales 7·5 per cent. are Class II, and in Scotland 13·1 per cent. are of this classification.

There is, of course, nothing to prevent further routes being included in these two classes if traffic grows so as to justify a re-classification. For this purpose the periodical traffic census should prove of value.

Grants are made from the Road Fund to aid in the maintenance of Class I roads on a basis of 50 per cent. of the cost and of Class II roads at a rate of 25 per cent. However, in the case of some of the Highland roads that run through sparely populated counties a special rate of 75 per cent. has been given from the Fund.

All roads in Class I or II have been numbered, those in Class I being distinguished by the initial letter A preceding the route number and those in Class II by the letter B, thus the London–Edinburgh Road has been designated A 1, Manchester–Leeds A 62, and so on. To facilitate through traffic a series of maps showing the various routes and their numbers has been prepared. In addition attention is being paid to the question of adequate sign-posting, by which the route number will be displayed prominently, which it is hoped will be of the greatest service to road users generally. In a form circulated to the various highway authorities of Great Britain by the Ministry of Transport in February, 1921, it was stated that "It is a matter of common knowledge that although the signs recommended by the Local Government Board in 1904 have been extensively adopted, a great variety of other signs and directions, both official and unofficial, have been placed by the sides of highways. The confusing information presented to-day by the variety and number of these signs has undoubtedly created a tendency among road users to disregard them. In the Minister's view this tendency can only be corrected by the general use of an approved series of standard signs, to which road traffic would readily become responsive, with a resulting increase in the convenience and safety of the travelling public." For this purpose the Ministry issued specifications for the consideration of local authorities, so that such notices should be standardized as much as possible throughout the country. It was recommended that Road Direction Posts; Warning Signs against Level Crossings, Schools, Cross-Roads, Corners, etc.; Place and Village Name Signs should be erected, and for all of these specifications were issued by the Ministry as to height, colour, design, shape, etc.

The Problem of Road Maintenance.—That the introduction of new methods and uses of road transport invariably causes a conflict between the new users and the road maintainers is a generalization apparent to any student of the history of our roads. Though it be admitted that the new methods have increased the burden of road repair, and in some cases, owing to the unsatisfactory and very local nature of our road administration, have placed very onerous burdens on rural authorities, it might, however, be urged that this element of opposition has, at times, been unduly stressed. It has been forgotten that all enjoy great advantages from good highways. Every member of the community is interested in cheap and adequate transport, and especially in good road transport. Under modern conditions, before anyone can enjoy the necessaries or amenities of life, transport has to be called upon to play its part, though maybe the important function performed by it is not always apparent, perhaps due to its very familiarity. Nowadays we are all road users. The railway cannot go everywhere, and stations may be far apart. Indeed, the road is complementary to the railway, for without the road the railway would be almost useless. The railways, canals, rivers or steamships may bring goods or passengers to station, dock or depot, but road transport is essential to bring them to the shops, the home and the consumer.

Further, the King's highway is a universal way-leave provider for gas and water pipes, sewers, electricity supply, telephone and telegraph cables.

Consequently it may be urged that everyone should help to bear some part of the cost of road maintenance. This principle appears to have been admitted by Adam Smith, despite the fact that he favoured the imposition of tolls proportionate to tonnage. "The expense," he declared, "of maintaining good roads and communications is no doubt beneficial to the whole society, and may therefore without any injustice be defrayed by the general contributions of the whole society." [1]

[1] *Wealth of Nations*, book v, ch. i, p. 343 (Nicholson's edition).

So far, then, there is some justification that all should contribute something towards the expenses of maintaining the highways, though the amount of that contribution is more open to argument. It may also be urged with justice that the direct user, e.g. the private motorist, the commercial lorry owner, etc., obtains a special advantage, and should thus be called upon to pay a special contribution to defray part of the expense.

The problem of road maintenance has in reality two aspects. In the first place, an equitable solution has to be found for the financial sides of the problem involved in the answer to the questions, by whom are the roads to be maintained and how is the burden to be distributed? Secondly, attention must be turned to the *real* cost of transport, since part of the *total* cost of transport is transferred from road users, if the roadway is provided by the community at the public expense. It has been argued that if a road user does not pay a fair share of the cost of maintenance occasioned by the damage he does to the roadway and of the capital charges involved in the construction of new roads, then he may in effect be subsidized as compared with other systems of transport. In Britain, railways and canals have to charge rates that will cover all the expenses, overhead charges, running cost and interest on capital, and at the present day the competition between road and railway or canal transport has brought the question into prominence. It has been asserted that the lower rates of taxation applicable to commercial vehicles gives in effect a kind of subsidy to traffic carried on the roads. The question does not arise with private motor cars, as they pay at a higher rate, are not so destructive of road surfaces, and maybe use the roads less. Passenger vehicles, either motor buses or motor coaches, also pay higher rates of duty, and in any case they are public vehicles, generally serving the needs of the locality.

Sir William Acworth, for instance, in a suggestive article [1]

[1] *Economic Journal*, vol. xxxii, p. 157.

on "Communication Costs and their Interdependence," proposes and discusses the question, "Why should the user of a railway be expected to pay the total cost of his use, whereas the user of a road is called to pay movement cost only ?"

It has been urged that the railways may thus lose part of their traffic because the road user does not pay the whole of his cost of transport, and that in consequence, since under the Railway Act, 1921, the railway companies are to be allowed to modify their charges so that a "standard revenue" based on that of 1913 may be earned, the result might be that rates would have to be raised on the traffic that remains. Further, it is urged that the railways are important contributors to local rates, and that thus the extraordinary position is being achieved that they are rated to provide a subsidy to a competitive form of transport. Mr. Stephenson declares that "It is actually happening as the result that some traffic is being conveyed by road instead of by railway, with a saving to the sender's pocket, but at a higher cost when the subsidy through the roads is taken into account. Such a condition is only sound business when an industry is in its infancy. Transport by road motor vehicle has surely passed that stage in Great Britain."[1] In another passage the same writer declares, "It would seem, however, a not inequitable proposition that, when two means of transport are in competition, more assistance from the public purse should not be rendered to one than to the other. A departure from this will inevitably result in unduly cheapening one means relatively to the other, thus producing an uneconomic distribution of traffic between them, and one school of thought maintains that road users are already being put in this favourable position."[2]

Mr. Stephenson admits, however, that "It must not be thought that a recognition of the fact that road transport

[1] W. T. Stephenson, *Communications*, ch. xii, pp. 120–1.
[2] *Ibid.*, p. 120.

is receiving assistance from the public in excess of that granted to another means of inland transport carries with it a view that road transport should be discouraged." [1]

A somewhat similar discussion resulted some years ago on the question of State aid for the purpose of reconstructing and improving certain canals and inland navigations, and in the Reports of the Royal Commission of 1906 divergent views were apparent on the question. The advocates of railways held that such State aid to their rivals would be inequitable, since no help had ever been given to the railways either on capital account or on current expenditure.

For the solution of the double problems of the finance of road repair and the question of subsidization of varied types of transport, there appear to be logically three possible and alternative courses of action. These are :—

(1) To drive the new traffic off the roads either by direct legislation or excessive taxation.
(2) To throw the roads open to all traffic without special charges or taxation and to subsidize the capital charges involved in the provision of the specialized way of other forms of transport so that there would be no disparity in treatment.
(3) To make the road user pay a special contribution for the wear and tear he causes to the road.

As regards the first alternative, this historically has been the most popular, though in no case has it been completely successful, at any rate in the long run. Even the early restrictions on steam vehicles imposed by the Turnpike Trusts did not destroy mechanical road traction, but only postponed its development to our own day. To drive particular kinds of traffic off the roads does not appear to be a very economical solution of the problem, unless, of course, it be that the traffic is so very destructive in its nature that the damage done by it to the road surface or

[1] W. T. Stephenson, *Communications*, ch. xii, p. 120.

foundations is out of all proportion to the utility derived. Traffic should rather be encouraged if it pays something towards the cost of upkeep of the road, as roads, and especially modern roads built to suit mechanical traction, are expensive pieces of capital. It pays to work a road hard, because a road is worn out by heavy rains, frost and other weather conditions just as much as by the traffic passing over it. Heavy traffic over well-constructed roads, able to stand up to the weights passing over them, should better enable the costs of upkeep to be met if it be that every vehicle pays something towards the cost. At the present time, it would be in any case an impossible and retrograde solution of the road problem to drive the traffic off the highways. Almost every country in the world is improving or building roads; for instance, in the U.S.A. large sums are being spent for such purposes, while in Norway, Czecho-Slovakia, and even in China extensive road building programmes are under way. Such a policy would mean the arrestment of transport development in Britain; it would entail the loss of a valuable stimulus to efficiency on the part of the railways, for the recent "grouping" has tended to eliminate competition between the railways themselves; the retardation of rural development; the loss of an important contribution to the solution of problems of city and urban transportation, and a setback to slum clearances and housing improvements.

The second alternative—the subsidization of other forms of transport—as a practical proposition, has not a great deal to recommend it in this country. The cost would be too heavy a burden on State funds, since the capital outlay sunk in railways and canals is enormous. Sir William Acworth, speaking of the subsidization of the capital costs of transport concerns, declares that the "practical difficulties are so great that, if the users can and will in practice pay the total costs, it is best to leave them to do so."[1] In new or developing countries it may, of course, be desirable,

[1] *Economic Journal*, vol. xxxii, p. 162.

or indeed necessary, to subsidize railway construction in one way or another, and such a policy has been pursued in many such countries.

We are thus thrown back upon the third solution of making the road user pay in part or in whole for the damage caused. It has been suggested that the entire cost of maintenance should be provided by special taxation levied on road users. But it may be objected that everyone uses the roads, and that such a policy would involve not only the taxation of mechanical and horse vehicles, but also of bicycles and foot passengers, as well as those who utilize the roads as way-leaves. Local taxation, however, provides the best way of taxing the foot passenger or the cyclist, and thus the question becomes what proportion ought to be charged against mechanical road transport ?

Adam Smith, as indicated on a previous page, was in favour of payment according to road usage by means of tolls. "When the carriages which pass over a highway or a bridge, and the lighters which sail upon navigable canal, pay toll in proportion to their weight or their tonnage, they pay for the maintenance of those public works exactly in proportion to the wear and tear which they occasion of them. It seems scarcely possible to invent a more equitable way of maintaining such works . . . It seems impossible to imagine a more equitable method of raising a tax." [1]

In practice, however, turnpike tolls, after an extended experience, proved unsuitable and altogether unsatisfactory, and have in consequence been completely abandoned.[2] The details of taxation, however, under the present and other proposed systems, which avoid the main evils of the turnpike toll, are discussed in the following chapter. Here we are concerned not so much with the details of taxation or the incidence between particular road users as with

[1] Adam Smith, *Wealth of Nations,* book v, ch. i, p. 303 (Nicholson's edition).

[2] For an account of the Turnpike Trusts and their failure, see S. and B. Webb, *The Story of the King's Highway,* and the same author's *Statutory Authorities for Special Purposes.*

questions of principles upon which contributions to the cost of maintenance are to be based.

Since the whole community obtains considerable advantages, direct or indirect, from road transport, and since all use the roads in one way or another, the community can justly be called upon to bear some of the expense of the cost involved in the capital outlay on road construction and in the work of repair and maintenance. To find any general principle, however, upon which an apportionment can be made between the road user and the community seems practically impossible, and the difficulty is rendered the greater by the unco-ordinated nature of our road administration. It might be based on a contribution on a definite percentage basis, and during the discussion of the Finance Act, 1920, as well as during subsequent consideration of a fuel tax, some such idea seems to have been acted upon, for it was decided that motor vehicles should contribute a definite amount towards the expenses connected with highways. Alternatively it might be urged that a suitable and perhaps better policy would be to charge against the new traffic the increased cost of maintenance, allowance being made for changed values of money, or for the performance of work neglected during certain years, such as the war period. Another suggestion made has been that the community should provide any capital outlay required, while the road user should pay for the maintenance. This proposal, however, would involve logically a contribution from all types of road users, from foot passenger to traction engine.

Lord Montagu of Beaulieu and others have urged that a system of highway loans should be utilized to bring roads up to the new standard now required. It would be cheaper in the end, they declare, to rebuild the roads subject to heavy traffic according to modern methods than to go on continually frittering away money year after year on patching up a road that has not been built and was never intended for heavy traffic of the modern type. It may be cheaper to increase capital expenditure in order to save money on annual expenditure. If the interest charges, allowing for a sinking fund, are less than the difference in the cost of maintenance, a saving would be effected. Once the roads were brought up to the new standard required,[1] through the provision of adequate foundations and by the use of reinforced concrete, bitumen or asphaltic slag—these materials being in the opinion of the Seville meeting of the International Roads Congress best suited for modern motor traffic—the annual cost of repair would be much lower. Engineers declare that the technical side of the road problem has been solved, and that they can build a road that will stand up to the heaviest traffic. The difficulty, however, lies in the large initial capital cost. Hence the attraction to many of the proposal for building out of special highway loans. In a time of financial difficulty, however, there are objections to pledging the national credit, and local authorities might not regard any further loans raised on the security of the rates with any great degree of favour, even if it probably meant a curtailment of their annual expenditure in later years. A further difficulty is presented again by the local nature of our road administration, since they are not in as good a position to raise the money required as would a larger or national authority; and further, they may not in the case of the smallest areas have the required technical staff, since the salaries they can afford to pay engineers and surveyors do not always attract the best men. But though it may be admitted that there are difficulties, it must be conceded that a correct appreciation of the problem of obtaining a balance between capital expenditure on real improvement and high annual maintenance expenditure is of the first importance, and upon

[1] A difficulty is presented where a road is used by both horse and motor traffic, since the surface suitable for heavy mechanical vehicles is sometimes dangerous and unsuitable for horses. Experiments have, however, been tried on the Great North Road between London and York by riders on horseback to evolve horseshoes more suitable to modern roads than the usual type.

it depends the possibility of bringing our roads up to the best standard without wasted expenditure.

It will be remembered that in the nineteenth century the problem of road maintenance which had then become of outstanding difficulty was solved by the labours of the great road engineers, notably Telford and Macadam, who reconstructed many roadways and introduced better methods. The conflict of opinion between Telford and Macadam is also interesting in the light of present-day discussions, for Telford advocated good and solid foundations necessitating a high initial capital expenditure, while Macadam pinned his faith to a good surface which could be provided at a lower cost. Eventually Macadam won the day, and his method became the more generally adopted. Are we now to see a reversal of the solution as the result of the growth of heavy mechanical transport capable of travelling at high speed, necessitating a better and a more solid roadway ?

Developments in directions other than those of purely technical and engineering improvements of highway construction, it should not be forgotten, may also contribute to the solution of the road problem. One line of attack that has been indicated above is through the reform of road administration by the inception of a more uniform and co-ordinated system. Another is that of technical improvements in the vehicles themselves, so that they will be less destructive of road surfaces and foundations. Such improvements should be encouraged in every feasible way, legislative or otherwise. Some relief, for instance, might be found in the use of multi-wheeled vehicles, provided they spread the load over more wheels and gave lower axle weights ; through the more general adoption of resilient or cushion tyres, or, better still, the further evolution of the giant pneumatic tyre. A great development has recently taken place in these large pneumatics, but so far their use has been confined to a few motor coaches or an exceptional motor omnibus. Further development of these and of low-pressure tyres might lead to more general adoption with a consequent decrease in road damage. Better chassis springing would help also to lessen the destructive effects of heavy vehicles, and in this direction even the casual observer will recognize that much yet remains to be achieved. For undeveloped countries where roads are not "made" the use of creeper track vehicles is often advocated, and it has been said that these improve a road rather than wear it out, as they act as a sort of miniature steam roller and tend to consolidate the surface. The further increase in the use of private cars should also enable a greater revenue to be raised, and since the cost of road maintenance would not increase in proportion the burden would be lessened on each user. It is remarkable that in Britain the proportion of the population using motor vehicles is still much smaller than in the U.S.A. or even in Canada, with a much smaller road mileage suited to motor traffic. The motor car is still somewhat of a luxury in Britain, though in the U.S.A. or in Canada a cheap car is possessed by many artisans.

During recent years the problem of road maintenance in Britain has appeared to be more acute than is actually warranted by the facts, though this has been often neglected by the antagonists of road transport. This has been due to a variety of circumstances. In the first place, it should be remembered that war-time arrears of repairs had to be made up. During the war as much work on road repair as possible was postponed, and in many areas heavy traffic unsuited to the roads passed in considerable bulk as a result of war activities. Further, the high level of prices and inflated costs made the increase in expenditure more apparent than real, hence any comparison between pre-war and post-war years that ignores this nominal inflation of costs is more startling than is really justified. Finally, some of the present expenditure on road reconstruction has been undertaken, at least partially, for other purposes than those of sheer traffic necessity, since road work has been found especially suitable for providing relief work to the unemployed. There have been cases where the reconstruction of roadways already existing would have been better justified than the construction of new highways on which the amount of traffic to be carried has been highly problematical. Here again road administration has not been based on the needs of traffic so much as by the necessities of local authorities to provide work in their own areas. Maybe, of course, wider considerations, outside the scope of the present work, have determined the choice, but the fact should be remembered in considering the burden of present-day road charges, though perhaps in the future the construction may be more fully justified from the narrow economic and traffic point of view.

Another point that may be made is that in future years the reconstructed roads will, or at least should, cost less to maintain, and hence the burden of the present years is to some degree temporary.

The work now being performed by the Ministry of Transport in their traffic censuses should provide valuable data for the road administrator, and the tackling of the road problem in the light of this statistical material should enable the best distribution of the money available to be made.

But perhaps the most encouraging sign has been the continued fall in expenditure on roads and at the same time the continued expansion in the money received from motor taxation. The maximum expenditure reached in any one year was about £50,000,000, but it soon fell, and in 1922 it was about £37,000,000, while from that year it has continued to fall. The revenue from the taxation of vehicles has been continuously rising since the imposition of the new method of taxation under the Finance Act of 1920. In 1921 the revenue received from motor taxation was £9,735,832, in 1922 it rose to £11,013,861, and in 1923 to £12,757,550, while for the first nine months of 1924 it was £13,892,879.

CHAPTER XVIII

TAXATION OF ROAD VEHICLES

MUCH discussion has centred round the question of motor taxation and the methods by which the required revenue is to be obtained. But before passing on to a consideration of this controversy, the present system of taxation must be briefly examined. The basis of the present regulations is determined by the Finance Act of 1920, which came into force from January 1, 1921. In the second schedule to this Act the rates of duty payable are set forth for each particular class of vehicle. The main provisions of this schedule are as follows :—

Invalids' vehicles and certain agricultural vehicles, such as tractors, locomotive ploughing engines, etc., pay at the rate of 5s. per vehicle per year.

Motor cycles, side-cars, tractors used for road haulage, and certain other vehicles, specifically mentioned, pay duty at various but moderate rates.

Other than in these cases, the main and in consequence more important rates of duties are determined in the case of—

1. Motor omnibuses and hackney carriages by seating capacity ;
2. Commercial goods vehicles by unladen weight ;
3. Other vehicles, principally private cars, on a horse-power basis.

As regards the first class, two separate rates are enforced, one for the Metropolitan Police area and any other district determined subsequently by the Ministry of Transport, the other rate being applicable to all other parts of Britain. The Metropolitan rate is the higher, the excess ranging from £3 to £14, according to seating capacity. For example, vehicles seating not more than six persons pay £15 per year in the Metropolitan Police area, but elsewhere £12; for vehicles seating over 20 but below 32 persons, the respective rates are £72 and £60; those seating over 32 pay £84 or £70.

In the second category—the commercial goods vehicles—the rates applicable range from £6 to £30, the latter being levied on the heaviest vehicles exceeding 4 tons in unladen weight.

In Class 3 the minimum rate is £6, but if the vehicle is over 6 horse-power, there is an additional rate of £1 per unit or part of a unit of horse-power. For the purposes of taxation the horse-power is determined by a Treasury formula.[1]

In brief, then, the private motor car pays at the heaviest rate of £1 per horse-power; the motor bus or motor coach at a rate of £70 if seating over 32; and the commercial lorry at the lowest rate, according to unladen weight, with a maximum of £30.

Quarterly licences may, however, be obtained, while if the licence is taken out on or after the first day of the second month of a quarterly period, two-thirds of the quarterly rate of duty only is charged, and similarly for the third month only one-third is charged. These modifications along with certain others, however, involve payment at a slightly higher rate of duty than the proportionate fraction of the ordinary rate for a full year, while no facilities are given for taking out a licence for less than three months at the commencement of any quarter. The modifications are applicable to the three types of vehicle above enumerated.

In 1924 two concessions were obtained which, though

[1] See Note at end of chapter.

not very great in themselves, did something to relieve certain hardships of the tax. In the first place quarterly licences were issued at a reduced rate, and more nearly equivalent to the fraction of a whole year licence, while in the second place the right to surrender a licence and to claim the return of the tax paid was granted where a vehicle is temporarily out of use.

In many quarters the present system has evoked a storm of abuse because it has no relation to road usage, and bears unequally on the various types of vehicle. Thus in the 1924 *Handbook of the Automobile Association*, it is stated that "three years' experience of the £1 per unit and other vehicle taxes has amply justified the attitude consistently maintained by the Association, which is now fighting for the substitution of a system graduating the individual payment in proportion to the extent of road use. The present tax is earmarked solely for road costs, but, despite this, the present system results in the extraordinary anomaly of the smallest user of the road being compelled to pay the largest tax per mile, and correspondingly the largest user pays the least tax per mile and escapes his proper contribution to the costs of road maintenance and improvement." [1]

The present controversy on motor taxation turns not so much on whether or not road vehicles should bear a special burden, as on the question of the incidence of the tax between the different classes of road users. Under the present arrangement, the same tax is paid whether the vehicle runs 300 or 10,000 miles per annum, except that some reduction can be effected if the vehicle is laid up for part of the year, and quarterly or half-year licences be taken out.

One effect, therefore, of the system has been a tendency to create a more marked seasonal use of vehicles with consequent undesirable reactions on certain phases of the motoring and allied industries. Further, the present

[1] *The Automobile Association Handbook*, 1924, p. 182.

system tends to influence design in the case of private cars along certain lines, since a designer attempts to squeeze an engine of high actual horse-power into a lower category of taxation, and this he is able to do under the Treasury formula, referred to above, by increasing the piston stroke. In some respects this appears to have had a bad effect on the motor manufacturing industry, since production for overseas markets is hindered by the home market requirements.

Mass production and standardization of parts is an essential requirement in automobile manufacture if a cheap car is to be produced, but such large-scale production depends on the possibility of a large market. The " Ford " works give a striking example of the interconnection of standardization, mass production and the capture of large markets.

The main objection against the vehicle and horse-power tax remains, however, that it is not based on road usage, because mileage run, does not affect the amount of tax paid. It thus violates the principle laid down by Adam Smith that vehicles should pay in proportion to the wear and tear they occasion of the roads.

To meet these objections against the present system of taxation, many alternative schemes have been proposed, with the object of bringing taxation into more direct relation to road usage.

The main alternatives proposed fall into one or another of six classes :—

(1) Tolls.
(2) Taxation of motor spirit.
(3) A combined motor spirit and modified vehicle tax.
(4) A modified vehicle tax.
(5) Tyre tax.
(6) A tax based on the average load carried per wheel.

Of these the first proposal may be dismissed as impracticable, though it had the support of Adam Smith in his day. The history of the Turnpike Road Trusts and their tolls has clearly demonstrated their unsuitability, which under modern conditions of fast traffic would be intensified. The reimposition of a system of tolls on a general scale would be altogether undesirable.

Of the other alternative systems by far the most popular is the third, the combined motor spirit and modified vehicle tax.

The first feature of this proposal is that every vehicle should pay an annual registration and licence tax of, say, 5s. or 2s. 6d. per horse-power. Secondly, for the purpose of bringing in the greater part of the required revenue, a flat rate duty per gallon on all imported motor spirit other than alcohol is suggested. The duty would be levied at the port of entry at a flat rate of about 5d. per gallon. Motor spirit used for other purposes, e.g. aviation, industrial processes, etc., it is suggested should be duty free, and to prevent evasion of motor taxation by the unscrupulous, who might be tempted to utilize industrial spirit for their motor vehicles, it is suggested that all duty free spirit should be distinctly coloured.

Whether home-produced fuel, e.g. benzol, should be taxed is more debatable, and the question turns on two points :—

(1) Whether or not home producers should be given what practically amounts to a bounty, and
(2) Whether the amount of home-produced fuel is sufficient to warrant the expense of excise administration.

For those mechanical vehicles that do not derive their power from liquid fuel in the form of motor spirit, e.g. "steamers," "electrics," producer-gas driven motors, etc., the horse-power tax, unladen-weight tax, or seating-capacity tax, would have to continue in use, though some adjustment might be made in the licensing regulations to allow of a more equitable incidence of the duty.

If it were thought desirable to grant rebates for commercial vehicles, this could be done in a simple manner by the adjustment of the vehicle tax part of the duty. The idea of granting a commercial vehicle rebate was no doubt the reason for the combination of the two types of tax in this scheme, for otherwise a fuel tax simpliciter would perhaps be the most advantageous, as well as the least complex, and would eliminate the administrative expenses connected with vehicle licence duties.

Commercial transport users would resist very strongly any proposals to increase the taxation they have to bear, and, indeed, they are against any modification at all of the present system of duties.

In favour of a rebate, under the alternative scheme, it is urged that the ton-mileage per gallon of fuel is less in the case of the commercial vehicle than in that of the private car, on account of the less favourable conditions under which such commercial motors have to operate.

A further reason urged in favour of the rebate is the simple one, that commercial road transport affects the interests of the public, since cheap transport would mean a reduction in the cost of all articles, and since industry is stimulated by adequate and cheap transport facilities. The rebate, however, is attacked from three points of view :—

1. The owners of private motor cars object to the differentiation against them which they declare is too great. They assert that they are shouldering an unfair portion of the burden of road maintenance and improvement.
2. The rebate is said to be undesirable from the point of view of road administration. It is urged that the financial aspects of road construction and maintenance do not warrant the grant of such a privilege, since it is an undoubted fact that a considerable portion of the cost of road repair is due to the heavy commercial motor, shod with solid tyres.

The commercial vehicle, it is asserted, does most damage to the roads, and in the future the use of trade vehicles is likely to increase greatly, with a consequent increase in the cost of road maintenance. In a recent article on the subject it was stated that "at present the private motorist pays about four times as much per ton per mile as does the owner of the heavy commercial lorry, which causes nine-tenths of the damage to the roads."[1]

3. The Railway and Canal Interests, approaching the question from the point of view of the total costs of transport and their relation to State aid, declare that the lower taxation of vehicles engaged in the commercial transport of merchandise means that the full cost of transport is not borne by these enterprises, and that in reality commercial road transport of goods is a subsidized industry.[2]

Some commercial users retort that the greater permissible legal and actual speed of the private motor car is responsible for considerable damage, but while this may to some extent be true, it would be difficult to believe that the damage done is so very great, that the difference in taxation does not serve to cover much more than the difference.

From another point of view, but not that of road usage, an extra tax might be placed on private motor cars. Such an increased rate of taxation might be thought desirable as a kind of "luxury tax," or it might be urged that the possession of a motor car denotes ability to pay. It is interesting to note that Adam Smith would appear to have approved of such grounds for differentiation. "When the toll upon carriages of luxury, upon coaches, post-chaises, etc., is made somewhat higher in proportion to their weight than upon carriages of necessary use, such as carts, wagons, etc., the indolence and vanity of the rich is made to con-

[1] The *Scotsman*, July 3, 1924.

[2] See previous chapter.

tribute in a very easy manner to the relief of the poor, by rendering cheaper the transportation of heavy goods to all the different parts of the country."[1]

In practice, it is not easy, nowadays, to differentiate between the pleasure and business use of private cars. To many busy professional men the motor is becoming more and more a necessity in their everyday work. Again, the same vehicle may be used at one time for pleasure purposes, and at another for business or professional calls. The questions involved would, however, necessitate a study of taxation principles from a wider point of view than can be attempted here.

In favour of a modified vehicle and fuel tax, it is urged that it would mean a more equitable distribution of the burden over all classes of vehicles, graduated according to road usage ; that it would avoid penalizing those who use motor spirit for other purposes, and that it would meet all the requirements of the Ministry of Transport. A fuel tax would, it is argued, vary automatically with the mileage run, and would take some account of speed and weight as well as horse-power. Users would thus pay in proportion to the wear and tear they inflict on the roads, or, at any rate, to a far greater extent than they do under the present system of taxation.

It is argued that the cost of administration and collection need not be heavy, since the greatest bulk of our supplies of motor fuel come to our ports in "tankers" from abroad, and thus the imports could easily be dealt with by the present Custom Officials. Evasion, it is said, should not be any greater than is usual in any system of taxation.

Further arguments advanced in favour of the new tax are that it would be a boon to occasional road users, that the "long mileage interests" would not escape their fair share of road burdens, and that the attention of constructional engineers would be turned towards economy of fuel

[1] *Wealth of Nations*, book v, ch. i, p. 303 (Nicholson's edition).

consumption, which would be to the advantage of the industry.

The motor user would find it easier to pay his contribution to the tax, since the tax would be levied as he went along, instead of being demanded in one lump sum at the beginning of the year or quarter. Thus the commercial user would be enabled to pay it out of revenue, instead of having to lock up a considerable amount of capital. In this respect the proposed tax is more in accordance with Adam Smith's third canon of taxation than is the present vehicle tax, for it would be levied "at the times and in the manner in which it is most likely to be convenient for the contributor to pay it."[1]

That the simple criterion, "taxation in proportion to road usage," seems to be the best principle for apportioning the burden that is to be laid on road users will no doubt be generally admitted. The opponents of the proposed modification of the present tax declare that a fuel tax is impracticable, and that it would not realize the claims made on its behalf. Some, however, go further and declare that even as a principle, fuel consumption is not the best criterion, because it does not necessarily discriminate between destructive and less destructive traffic. It is, for instance, upon such grounds that taxation according to load carried per wheel, irrespective of the number of wheels, has sometimes been advocated.

The opponents of the fuel tax group their arguments under various heads :—

1. That the price of fuel would be raised by an amount greater than the amount of the tax;
2. That it would differentiate against the commercial vehicle;
3. That it is not proportional to road usage;
4. That the cost of collection would be excessive and evasion rife;

[1] *Wealth of Nations*, book v, ch. ii, part ii, p. 347 (Nicholson's edition).

5. That it is impossible to define "motor spirit";
6. That industrial users of "motor spirit" for purposes other than propulsion of road vehicles would be inconvenienced; and
7. That a certain and definite revenue would not be obtained.

As regards the first head, it is asserted that the oil companies would put up the price by more than the amount of the tax, in order to recoup themselves for their incidental expenses, and to pay interest on their capital locked up when the fuel was taken out of bond. The retailer, too, it is said, would add something further to the retail price in order to recompense himself for his extra outlay. Thus the result would be on this reasoning, that instead of the foreign producer bearing some of the tax, the price to the consumer would be increased by an amount greater than the amount of the tax.

The case, however, is not so simple as it might seem to be at first sight, because a great variety of considerations have to be taken into account before an opinion can be given as to the probable effect of the tax on the price of the product. As a matter of fact, the incidence of the tax as between consumer and producer is not as easily determined as some seem to think. In the first place, the "elasticity" of the demand must be considered. If the demand is "elastic"—i.e. if on a rise in the price of motor spirit there should be a considerable falling off in its use, or a reversion to other types of vehicle, such as the "steamer," or to other types of fuel, as for example "producer-gas" systems of power propulsion—then the oil companies might have to bear some of the tax to prevent their sales falling off. Whether they would do so or not under the above circumstances depends on the relative importance they assign to the British market as compared with the rest of their world markets, and also to the degree of monopoly they possess. Have they alternative markets that could absorb the surplus at a better price than that possible in the British market after the imposition of the tax? If they had, the incidence would tend to be on the British consumer, and possibly the price would rise by an amount greater than the tax. The question of monopoly is also important, because if the oil companies have a monopoly, they might prefer to curtail production rather than bear part of the tax, if this would mean that their profits would be greater. It is doubtful, however, if they would in fact, under the present organization and technique of the industry, be inclined to curtail production to any considerable extent, and this conclusion is reinforced when it is remembered that there is a growing amount of competition due to the exploitation of oil fields outside the control of the American Oil Trusts.

As regards the second argument—that the modified fuel tax would differentiate against the commercial vehicle—this can be best considered along with the third proposition, that the new system of taxation would not in effect be proportional to road usage. The opponents of the fuel tax declare that while the private owner can make long non-stop journeys, the trade vehicle cannot do so. Much of the work done by commercial motors is of the nature of collection and delivery work, and it is often performed in busy or even congested streets. The engines have to be kept running, and consequently fuel is consumed during the waiting periods, and by the continual stopping and starting of the vehicle. This applies also to passenger vehicles employed on city transport work.

The private owner may often be able to choose his road, the time, the length, and frequency of his journeys; but the trade vehicle or motor bus is tied down to a definite route, and must perform its duties, irrespective of weather or other conditions. Again, the commercial motor requires a larger proportional reserve of horse-power, which involves lower efficiency, especially when unladen or when working in hilly districts. As compared with the industrial vehicle, the modern light car with a low horse-power engine is of high efficiency, and the engine is generally working near to the maximum of its capacity, as it is now possible with the aid of a three or four speed gear-box to do so with a high speed engine propelling a light car.

It must be admitted that there is something to be said in favour of these contentions. But while those upholding the other side might admit that the new scheme of taxation is not perfect, they would assert that a fuel tax is much more proportional to road usage than the present vehicle tax, which bears no relation whatever to that factor. Further, many would admit of a rebate being granted in the flat rate part of the new tax, to act as a compensation for the less exact proportion of fuel consumpt to road usage in the case of trade or commercial vehicles. For example, some suggest the vehicle proportion might be at 2s. 6d. per horse-power for commercial motors and 5s. per horse-power for private cars.

A more general argument in favour of the commercial rebate is often advanced, for it is declared that since these commercial vehicles are utilized not so much for individuals as for public or industrial services, they are entitled to special consideration. "The interests of the public must also be considered, and any charges that would result in increased rates for freight or passenger fares would be unwelcome and unfortunate." [1]

This, however, is an argument that does not appeal to all private motorists or the railway companies.

The fourth count against the new proposal is that it would involve a considerable cost of collection, and that thus any slight advantages that it might possess would be outweighed. This, however, is a doubtful point; but it is a question to which a layman can hardly give a definite answer, since it requires to be decided by expert administrators. It is a matter, however, which should receive careful consideration before any change is made.

[1] The *Scotsman*, July 8, 1924.

The fifth objection against the modified vehicle and fuel tax likewise requires impartial and expert consideration. Can motor spirit be adequately defined, and from this definition can specifications be framed for revenue purposes ? The difficulties involved are apparent when the evidence of the expert witnesses before the recent Committee that investigated the question of revising the tax is studied.[1] The difficulty lies in the fact that whatever test be utilized—" flash point " or other—it is not easy to determine what is motor fuel and what is not. If the definition be wide, then spirit required for other commercial and industrial uses will be included, and this would mean a hindrance to its use for these other purposes. Thus we are led to consider in conjunction with this objection the further and sixth objection to a fuel tax enumerated above. The majority of the Committee, it would appear, were of opinion that " no method of administering a motor spirit duty can be contrived which would not inflict grave inconvenience and additional expense upon a considerable number of consumers of motor spirit." It has been argued that conditions have altered considerably since the petrol tax was abolished in 1920, because the use of motor spirit for commercial, industrial and agricultural purposes has greatly increased.

On the other hand, if only high-grade spirit be included, evasion and abuse by motor users would be encouraged, since substitutes for taxable motor fuel with but small losses in engine efficiency would be easily available.

The question is thus seen to be a difficult and rather technical one, on which the experts themselves differ considerably.

In view of the difficulties of a fuel tax, a *via media* has been advocated in certain quarters. The advocates of the compromise would retain the present system of vehicle taxation, but would introduce certain modifications in the

[1] This Committee—the Committee on the Taxation and Regulation of Road Vehicles—considered the question for over two years, and at the time of writing is at length about to present a report on the subject.

periods for which licences are issued, and would modify the present incidence between the various classes of vehicles to some extent. It is suggested that licences should not be confined to fixed periods, but should be issuable from any date for a year, quarter or a month, and that the charge for the shorter periods should be fixed at a proportionate, not at a higher rate, as at present. To motor coach owners, it is suggested, facilities should be granted so that proprietors might be able to take out a weekly or even daily licence, to enable them to run an occasional trip during the off season. It is also suggested that facilities should be granted for the transference of a licence from a vehicle laid up to an unlicensed substitute.

It is declared that if the above facilities were available, the hardships and inequalities of the present system of vehicle taxation would be considerably mitigated.

NOTE.

Treasury Regulations for calculating the Horse-power of Motor Cars.—1. For the purposes of these regulations the horse-power of any mechanically propelled vehicle deriving its motive power wholly from an internal combustion engine worked by a cylinder or cylinders shall be taken to be :—

(*a*) In the case of a single-cylinder engine the horse-power attributable to the cylinder of the engine.

(*b*) In the case of an engine having two or more cylinders the sum of the horse-powers attributable to the separate cylinders.

2. The horse-power attributable to any cylinder of an internal combustion engine shall be deemed to be equal to the square of the internal diameter of such cylinder measured in inches divided by a numeral :—

(*a*) In the case of a cylinder having a single piston, the numeral used as divisor shall be 2·5.

(*b*) In the case of a cylinder having two pistons, the numeral used as divisor shall be 1·6.

3. The horse-power of any mechanically propelled vehicle deriving its power wholly from a steam engine shall be taken to be proportional to the effective heating surface of the boiler supplying steam to such engine, at the rate of one horse-power for every 3 square feet in such effective heating surface, and the effective heating surface shall be taken to be :—

(*a*) In the case of a boiler having horizontal or approximately horizontal tubes, the whole of that surface of the tubes which is exposed to the flame or hot gases.

(*b*) In the case of a boiler having vertical or approximately vertical tubes, half of that surface of the tubes which is exposed to the flame or hot gases.

4. Any mechanically propelled vehicle deriving its motive power from an electric motor or motors shall be deemed to be of 6 horse-power.

5. In measuring cylinders and boilers and in calculating horse-power, fractions of inches and feet and fractions of a unit of horse-power are to be taken into account. Provided that in the final calculation of horse-power a resultant fraction of less than 0·1 of a unit of horse-power shall be omitted.

6. Where it appears that, in consequence of the exceptional design or construction of the engine of any mechanically propelled vehicle, the horse-power as calculated under this regulation is substantially less than the average power which the engine would develop in continuous use on the road, if there were no restrictions on speed other than those imposed by the vehicle itself, then such average power shall be taken as the power of the vehicle.

APPENDIX A

MOTOR TRANSPORT COSTS AND RECORDS[1]

The keeping of cost records is a matter of vital importance to all owners of motor transport. Without such records, it is impossible to check the performance of the individual vehicles or to discover if the fleet is working at a maximum efficiency. Records are also essential to the correct determination of rates and fares.

The records kept should give a complete view of the costs of the fleet, and to obtain these it is necessary that all the items of both running costs and standing charges should be tabulated.

To ascertain running costs, the following or similar records should be kept :—

1. A daily log prepared by the driver of each vehicle, showing the nature of the work performed, the tonnage carried, the time taken, etc.
2. Daily mileages obtained from speedometer readings.
3. The quantities and cost of fuel, oil, etc., issued to each vehicle.
4. A special book recording the cost of tyres.
5. The value of spares, materials, etc., debited against the particular vehicles.
6. Weekly wage sheets.[2]

As regards overhead or standing charges, care must be taken to include all items such as depreciation, insurance,

[1] See Chapters VI and XV.

[2] Wages may, however, be regarded as a standing charge, not a running cost.

interest, tax, etc.; while expenses such as those for garage, salaries, etc., must be divided amongst the several vehicles.

Depreciation can be dealt with in one of several ways. Thus a "life" of so many thousand miles could be given to each vehicle, and from this the depreciation could be calculated in pence per mile. A more usual method, which has the merit of simplicity, is to assign a "scrap value" to the machine at the end of a period of years, say 5, 8 or 10, according to an estimate of its life, depreciation per year being calculated on the first cost without tyres less the "scrap value." There is a danger, of course, that the vehicle's life may be overestimated, while on the other hand, if it is underestimated to any considerable extent, the apparent cost per ton-mile for transport will be too high during the period while depreciation is being written off.

Since concrete examples of cost records may prove more useful than abstract statement of the problems involved, the following tables have been inserted with the kind permission of Messrs. William Younger & Co., Ltd., Edinburgh, and Messrs. Hovis, Ltd., Battersea.

It is to be appreciated that motor vehicle costs are of necessity dependent on the nature of the work performed, the loading factor, the topography of the routes traversed, the current prices of fuel, the rate of wages, etc., and many other local or special circumstances. The records of costs here inserted are only intended to give a practical indication of the manner in which competent traffic managers keep their records. The figures can give no guide as to the probable costs of a motor fleet working under different conditions or in other places.

Fleet Records of Messrs. William Younger & Co., Ltd.

[*See Fold-in Table.*]

Messrs. William Younger's fleet is employed on various kinds of work, though originally intended only to deliver beer to customers' premises in Edinburgh. This work is somewhat peculiar, in that the runs are short (about 1–1½ miles), and much time is required for loading and especially off-loading, since the casks have to be "set up" in cellars, often awkwardly situated. The fleet is also used to transport beer to the company's siding, about 1⅛ miles from the works, or to the docks at Leith.

Return loads are often obtained in bringing back malt or empty casks, while grain, it has been found, can be carried from the docks to the works more cheaply by the fleet than by contractors. A certain number of long-distance runs of from 30 to 45 miles are made to Glasgow or Border towns. The annual tonnage carried is considerable—indeed, one Leyland lorry may handle as much as 90 tons in a day.

The cost of the fleet, it is stated, has been saved in 4½ years. Moreover, since the vehicles are well kept, the fleet has a considerable publicity value. The firm's drivers become skilled in the "setting up" of casks, while being accustomed to the yards, etc., they can perform more journeys per day than could be effected by hired vehicles with drivers, strangers to the layout of the works.

The following running costs and particulars are kept:—

Mileage.—Speedometer reading taken daily and entered in a Day-book kept by the storeman.

Tonnage.—Each driver records the tonnage carried, trips run, and the articles transported in his Tonnage-book.

Petrol and Benzol.—Issued twice a week from Bowser tanks, fitted with meters, a separate account being kept for each vehicle.

These three items are collected in the Monthly Book, from which the costs are made out.

A special book is kept for tyre costs, while spares and other items are charged against each lorry as required.

Fleet Records of Messrs. Hovis, Ltd.

Messrs. Hovis, Ltd. employ a large fleet of road vehicles, the different types—steam, petrol, or electric—being utilized on the work best suited to their special characteristics. Thus the "electrics" are used to serve an area of about 10 miles radius and only cover a small mileage per week. Though the cost per ton-mile may appear to be high, the special work allotted to them is performed more cheaply by this type of vehicle than it would by any of the other types.

It will be noticed that wages are not included in the costs as tabulated. The men are remunerated in a manner peculiar to the milling trade, a standing wage plus an allowance based on tonnage being paid to both the driver and the carrier, since both assist in the unloading.

No charge is made in the records against garage or office expenses.

In the following tables the costs of two machines of each type are tabulated for six-week periods.

STEAMERS

Garrett No. 51.

Week ended	Tons.	Miles.	Ton-Miles.	Running Costs. Tyres.	Running Costs. Fuel.	Running Costs. Maintenance.	Standing Charges. Depreciation.	Standing Charges. Licence, Insurance, Interest.	Total Cost.	Cost per Ton-Mile.
1924.				£ s. d.	£ s. d.	£ s. d.	£ s. d.	£ s. d.	£ s. d.	Pence.
Aug. 26	95¾	248	1316·74	2 7 4	2 19 2	2 0 0	2 1 10	2 0 0	11 8 4	2·1
Sept. 2	69	305	1671·62	2 18 5	3 7 4	2 0 0	2 1 10	2 0 0	12 7 7	1·7
Sept. 9	75¾	196	739·25	1 9 2	2 10 11	2 0 0	2 1 10	2 0 0	10 1 11	1·9
Sept. 16	64¼	203	765·50	1 18 10	2 14 9	2 0 0	2 1 10	2 0 0	10 15 5	3·3
Sept. 23	73½	167	607·61	1 3 5	2 16 4	2 0 0	2 1 10	2 0 0	10 1 7	3·9
Sept. 30	80	211	956·75	2 0 5	2 17 3	2 0 0	2 1 10	2 0 0	10 19 6	2·9
Total..	458¼	1,330	6057·47	11 17 7	17 5 9	12 0 0	12 11 0	12 0 0	65 14 4	15·8

Average Cost per Ton-Mile per Week = 2·6 Pence.

Garrett No. 58.

Week ended	Tons.	Miles.	Ton-Miles.	Running Costs. Tyres.	Running Costs. Fuel.	Running Costs. Maintenance.	Standing Charges. Depreciation.	Standing Charges. Licence, Insurance, Interest.	Total Cost.	Cost per Ton-Mile.
1924.				£ s. d.	£ s. d.	£ s. d.	£ s. d.	£ s. d.	£ s. d.	Pence.
Aug. 26	96½	212	1044·25	2 0 7	2 17 0	2 0 0	2 1 10	2 0 0	10 19 5	2·5
Sept. 2	82½	190	984·37	1 16 5	2 16 2	2 0 0	2 1 10	2 0 0	10 14 5	2·6
Sept. 9	74	316	1556·75	3 0 6	3 3 2	2 0 0	2 1 10	2 0 0	12 5 6	1·2
Sept. 16	91¼	351	1764·25	3 7 3	3 10 3	2 0 0	2 1 10	2 0 0	12 19 4	1·7
Sept. 23	91¾	204	796·25	1 2 1	2 5 0	2 0 0	2 1 10	2 0 0	9 8 11	2·7
Sept. 30	76¾	329	1441·49	3 3 0	2 19 9	2 0 0	2 1 10	2 0 0	12 4 7	2·0
Total..	512¾	1,602	7587·36	14 9 10	17 11 4	12 0 0	12 11 0	12 0 0	68 12 2	12·7

Average Cost per Ton-Mile per Week = 2·1 Pence.

4-TON LEYLAND LORRY COSTS.

Messrs. William Younger & Co., Ltd., Brewers and Maltsters, Edinburgh.

January to June, 1924.

Number of Lorry.	Number of Days on Road.	Miles Run.	Average Load (Tons).	Ton-Miles.	Fuel. Used Gallons	Fuel. Cost.	Drivers' Wages.	Oil and Grease.	Interest and Depreciation at 5 % and 20 %.†	Maintenance and Repairs.	Tax, Garage and Insurance.	Cost of Tyres.	Painting and Body Repairs.	Miscellaneous.	Total Cost.	Cost. Ton-Mile.	Cost. Lorry-Mile.
						£ s. d.	£ s. d.	£ s. d.	£ s. d.	£ s. d.	£ s. d.	£ s. d.	£ s. d.	£ s. d.	£ s. d.	d.	d.
1	143	3,679	2·26	8,314	715	54 19 5	160 11 9	4 18 2	2 10 0	35 7 9	26 17 0	14 2 1	5 12 2	4 12 0	309 10 4	8·93	20·19
2	151	3,942	2·08	8,200	798	60 11 8	166 9 2	4 18 2	2 10 0	32 12 4	26 17 0	15 2 4	1 17 3	4 12 0	315 9 11	9·23	19·2
3	130	3,428	2·16	7,404	679	51 1 10	162 7 10	4 18 2	2 10 0	35 19 0	26 17 0	13 2 10	0 4 8	4 12 0	301 13 4	9·77	21·12
4	144	3,385	2·39	8,180	660	50 7 6	165 9 7	4 18 2	2 10 0	32 0 8	26 17 0	12 19 7	3 7 1	4 12 0	303 1 7	8·88	21·48
5	134	3,621	2·32	8,400	600	45 19 5	156 0 4	4 18 2	2 10 0	37 4 10	26 17 0	13 17 7	12 9 4	4 12 0	304 8 8	8·69	20·17
6	148	3,801	2·3	8,742	679	51 18 4	166 7 2	4 18 2	2 10 0	30 18 0	26 17 0	14 11 4	0 4 8	4 12 0	302 16 8	8·31	19·12
7	144	3,919	2·1	8,329	750	57 7 8	168 14 8	4 18 2	48 0 8	36 6 0	26 17 0	15 0 5	0 4 8	4 12 0	362 1 3	10·55	22·17
8	151	3,679	2·19	8,057	677	51 14 9	165 11 3	4 18 2	67 18 6	40 5 7	26 17 0	14 2 0	2 15 3	4 12 0	378 14 6	11·28	24·7
9	147	3,868	2·36	9,128	655	50 0 1	165 11 6	4 18 2	35 10 11	31 6 2	29 17 0*	14 16 6	0 4 8	4 12 0	336 17 0	8·85	20·9
10	117	2,906	2·34	6,700	592	46 10 9	163 5 2	4 18 2	47 18 7	54 4 8	29 17 0*	11 2 9	20 2 7	4 12 0	382 11 8	13·7	31·59
11	119	3,174	2·17	6,887	668	50 8 11	170 14 9	4 18 2	89 13 3	47 18 11	28 15 9*	12 3 4	25 17 6	4 12 0	435 2 7	15·16	32·9
12	96	2,516	2·3	5,786	467	37 6 0	163 8 4	4 18 2	111 14 6	31 15 1	26 17 0	9 12 10	0 4 8	4 12 0	390 8 7	16·19	37·24
13	18	496	2·28	1,030	104	8 17 8	12 15 9	0 14 3	17 11 11	—	4 15 11	1 18 0	—	0 1 10	46 15 4	10·89	22·62
Total ..	1,642	42,414	29·25	95,157	8,044	617 4 0	1,987 7 3	59 12 3	433 8 4	445 19 0	334 18 8	162 11 7	73 4 6	55 5 10	4,169 11 5	—	—
Average Twelve ‡ Vehicles	135	3,493	2·25	7,844	662	50 13 10	164 11 0	4 18 2	34 13 0	37 3 3	27 10 2	13 7 10	6 2 0	4 12 0	343 11 4	—	—

* Licensed as private cars to carry passengers for "firm's outings," etc.
† A "scrap value" of £100 is assigned to each vehicle at the end of a five-year life.
‡ No. 13 a new vehicle, not included in average. Standing and Running charges are based on total mileages, costs, etc., of all the vehicles.

STANDING CHARGES—per Mile.	Pence.	Pence.
Wages	11·25	
Interest and Depreciation	2·46	
Tax, Insurance and Rent	1·90	
Establishment Charges and Repair Shop Wages	2·08	
		17·69
RUNNING CHARGES—per Mile.		
Fuel	3·49	
Lubricants	0·34	
Tyres	0·92	
Spares	0·43	
Painting, etc.	0·41	
Miscellaneous	0·31	
		5·90
Total		23·59

COST PER LORRY-MILE	1s. 11½d.
COST PER TON-MILE	- 10½d.
TOTAL TONS ACTUALLY HANDLED	49,502
TONS HANDLED PER LORRY, DAILY	30
TOTAL TRIPS	21,943
TRIPS PER LORRY, DAILY	13

1-TON FORD LORRY COSTS.

Messrs. William Younger & Co., Ltd., Brewers and Maltsters, Edinburgh.

January to June, 1924.

Number of Lorry.	Number of Days on Road.	Miles Run.	Average Load (Tons).	Ton-Miles.	Fuel. Used Gallons	Fuel. Cost.	Drivers' Wages.	Oil and Grease.	Interest and Depreciation at 5 % and 25 %.	Maintenance and Repairs.	Tax, Garage and Insurance.	Cost of Tyres.	Painting and Body Repairs.	Miscellaneous.	Total Cost.	Cost. Ton-Mile.	Cost. Lorry-Mile.
						£ s. d.	£ s. d.	£ s. d.	£ s. d.	£ s. d.	£ s. d.	£ s. d.	£ s. d.	£ s. d.	£ s. d.	d.	d.
1	146	3,921	0·47	1,842	316	24 2 9	97 2 9	6 10 0	23 15 1	34 0 2	14 7 6	4 18 0	—	0 11 4	205 7 7	26·75	12·57
2	126	3,707	0·58	2,150	298	23 1 6	95 0 9	6 10 0	36 16 5	48 11 6	16 12 0	4 12 0	6 10 9	0 11 4	238 6 3	26·6	15·96
3	143	4,786	0·63	3,015	343	25 12 11	94 14 9	6 10 0	23 16 7	33 15 11	17 17 6	5 19 0	—	0 11 4	208 18 0	16·62	10·47
4	136	4,622	0·57	2,634	331	24 0 9	94 18 9	6 10 0	24 1 1	33 14 0	13 2 0	5 15 0	8 14 0	0 11 4	211 6 11	19·25	10·97
Total ..	551	17,036	2·25	9,641	1,288	96 17 11	381 17 0	26 0 0	108 9 2	150 1 7	61 19 0	21 4 0	15 4 9	2 5 4	863 18 9	—	—
Average Four Vehicles	138	4,259	0·56	2,410	322	24 4 5	95 9 3	6 10 0	27 2 3	37 10 5	15 9 9	5 6 0	3 16 2	0 11 4	215 19 8	—	—

STANDING CHARGES—per Mile.

	Pence.	Pence.
Wages	5·38	
Interest and Depreciation	1·53	
Tax, Insurance and Rent	0·87	
Establishment Charges and Repair Shop Wages ..	1·74	
		9·52

RUNNING CHARGES—per Mile.

	Pence.	Pence.
Fuel	1·36	
Lubricants	0·37	
Tyres	0·3	
Spares	0·37	
Painting, etc., Miscellaneous	0·25	
		2·65
Total		**12·17**

Cost per Lorry-Mile	**1s. 0d.**
Cost per Ton-Mile	**1s. 9d.**
Total Tons actually handled	2,952
Tons handled per Lorry, Daily	5·35
Total Trips	5,276
Trips per Lorry, Daily	9·5

[*To face p.* 242

PETROL

LEYLAND NO. 48.

Week ended	Tons.	Miles.	Ton-Miles.	Running Costs. Tyres.	Running Costs. Fuel.	Running Costs. Maintenance.	Standing Charges. Depreciation.	Standing Charges. Licence, Insurance, Interest.	Total Cost.	Cost per Ton-Mile.
1924.				£ s. d.	£ s. d.	£ s. d.	£ s. d.	£ s. d.	£ s. d.	Pence.
Aug. 26	54½	301	597·62	0 11 3	3 18 6	3 0 0	1 11 5	1 19 3	11 0 5	4·4
Sept. 2	46¼	356	760·87	0 13 4	3 14 5	3 0 0	1 11 5	1 19 3	10 18 5	3·4
Sept. 9	45¾	338	706·37	0 12 8	3 17 11	3 0 0	1 11 5	1 19 3	11 1 3	3·7
Sept. 16	46	355	847·49	0 13 4	4 5 9	3 0 0	1 11 5	1 19 3	11 9 9	3·2
Sept. 23	44¼	384	832·61	0 14 4	3 10 11	3 0 0	1 11 5	1 19 3	10 15 11	3·1
Sept. 30	49	316	686·86	0 11 10	2 5 9	3 0 0	1 11 5	1 19 3	9 8 2	3·2
Total . .	285¾	2,050	4431·82	3 6 9	21 13 3	18 0 0	9 8 6	11 15 6	64 14 0	21·0

Average Cost per Ton-Mile per Week = 3·5 Pence.

LEYLAND NO. 36.

Week ended	Tons.	Miles.	Ton-Miles.	Running Costs. Tyres.	Running Costs. Fuel.	Running Costs. Maintenance.	Standing Charges. Depreciation.	Standing Charges. Licence, Insurance, Interest.	Total Cost.	Cost per Ton-Mile.
1924.				£ s. d.	£ s. d.	£ s. d.	£ s. d.	£ s. d.	£ s. d.	Pence.
June 10	34	222	592·62	0 8 4	2 19 2	3 0 0	1 11 5	2 0 11	9 19 10	4·0
June 17	49½	302	627·00	0 11 3	5 9 11	3 0 0	1 11 5	2 0 11	12 13 6	4·5
July 1	37	247	503·25	0 9 3	3 8 11	3 0 0	1 11 5	2 0 11	10 10 6	5·0
July 8	48	350	688·99	0 13 1	4 17 5	3 0 0	1 11 5	2 0 11	12 2 10	4·2
July 15	41½	326	666·25	0 12 2	5 1 5	3 0 0	1 11 5	2 0 11	12 5 11	4·4
July 22	37¾	281	594·50	0 10 6	4 1 6	3 0 0	1 11 5	2 0 11	11 4 4	4·5
Total . .	247½	1,728	3672·61	3 4 7	25 18 4	18 0 0	9 8 6	12 5 6	68 16 11	26·6

Average Cost per Ton-Mile per Week = 4·4 Pence.

ELECTRICS

WALKER NO. 42.

Week ended	Tons.	Miles.	Ton-Miles.	Running Costs.			Standing Charges.		Total Cost.	Cost per Ton-Mile.
				Tyres.	Fuel.	Maintenance.	Depreciation.	Licence, Insurance, Interest.		
1924.				£ s. d.	£ s. d.	£ s. d.	£ s. d.	£ s. d.	£ s. d.	Pence.
Aug. 26	65¼	108	366·75	0 4 0	1 13 6	1 5 0	3 9 6	2 7 5	8 19 5	5·8
Sept. 2	73	165	375·12	0 6 2	1 14 6	1 5 0	3 9 6	2 7 5	9 2 7	5·8
Sept. 9	68¾	141	345·00	0 5 3	1 14 0	1 5 0	3 9 6	2 7 5	9 1 2	6·3
Sept. 16	53¾	142	368·50	0 5 4	0 19 10	1 5 0	3 9 6	2 7 5	8 7 1	5·4
Sept. 23	59¾	135	352·00	0 5 0	2 0 6	1 5 0	3 9 6	2 7 5	9 7 5	6·3
Sept. 30	55½	111	271·00	0 4 2	1 17 8	1 5 0	3 9 6	2 7 5	9 3 9	8·1
Total ..	376	802	2078·37	1 9 11	10 0 0	7 10 0	20 17 0	14 4 6	54 1 5	37·7

Average Cost per Ton-Mile per Week = 6·3 Pence.

WALKER NO. 45.

Week ended	Tons.	Miles.	Ton-Miles.	Running Costs.			Standing Charges.		Total Cost.	Cost per Ton-Mile.
				Tyres.	Fuel.	Maintenance.	Depreciation.	Licence, Insurance, Interest.		
1924.				£ s. d.	£ s. d.	£ s. d.	£ s. d.	£ s. d.	£ s. d.	Pence.
Aug. 26	60¾	68	313·82	0 2 6	1 14 0	1 5 0	3 9 6	2 7 5	8 18 5	6·8
Sept. 2	74	126	278·50	0 4 9	1 8 6	1 5 0	3 9 6	2 7 5	8 15 2	7·5
Sept. 9	62	150	378·62	0 5 7	1 13 0	1 5 0	3 9 6	2 7 5	9 0 6	5·7
Sept. 16	56½	209	363·25	0 7 10	1 2 10	1 5 0	3 9 6	2 7 5	8 12 7	5·7
Sept. 23	69½	153	319·87	0 5 8	2 3 9	1 5 0	3 9 6	2 7 5	9 14 4	7·1
Sept. 30	73	176	424·00	0 6 7	1 16 3	1 5 0	3 9 6	2 7 5	9 4 9	5·2
Total ..	395¾	882	2078·06	1 12 11	9 18 4	7 10 0	20 17 0	14 4 6	54 2 9	38·0

Average Cost per Ton-Mile per Week = 6·3 Pence.

APPENDIX B

SELECT BIBLIOGRAPHY

In the following list, which does not pretend to be a complete bibliography, the author has only included those works and sources which he has found most useful in the compilation of the present book :—

Bibliographies.

The Readers' Bulletin. Coventry Public Libraries, 1923.

The Glasgow Public Libraries Joint Technical Catalogues. Motor Vehicles, 1922.

Ballen. Bibliography of Road-making.

Blessing. List of Books on Automobiles and Motor Cycles. [Mainly American.]

Official Publications.

Reports of Royal Commissions.

Royal Commission on Local Taxation. Final Report (1901).

Royal Commission on London Traffic (1905), Vol. I, Cd. 2597.

Royal Commission on London Traffic (1906), Vol. IV, Cd. 2987.

Royal Commission on Motor Cars (1906), Cd. 3080.

Royal Commission on Canals and Inland Navigations (1909), Vol. VII, Cd. 4979.

Royal Commission on London Government (1923), Cmd. 1830.

Reports of Select Committees, etc.

Transport in the Metropolitan Area (1913), H.C. 278.

First and Second Reports on Transport (1918), $\frac{130}{136}$.

Shortt Committee Report (1918), Cmd. 5.

Rural Transport (Scotland), (1919).

Transport (Metropolitan Area), (1919), 147.

Gattie Committee Report (1920), Cmd. 580.

Agricultural Tribunal of Investigation, Final Report, Cmd. 2145, 1924.

Linlithgow Committee Report, 1924.

Ministry of Transport Departmental Committee Reports.

Advisory Committee on London Traffic (1920), Cmd. 636.

Road Conveyance of Goods by Railway Companies (1921), Cmd. 1228.

Inland Waterways (1921), Cmd. 1410.

Taxation and Regulation of Road Vehicles, Second Interim Report (1922).

DEPARTMENTAL REPORTS AND PUBLICATIONS.

Board of Trade.

London Traffic Branch. Annual Reports.

Handbook on Road Transport (1918).

Ministry of Transport.

Road Board Transfer of Powers.

Annual Traffic Returns.

Tar Treatment of Roads, 1921.

Traffic Census 1922 (1924).

Tramways and Light Railways and Trackless Trolley Undertakings. Annual Reports.

Standardization of Road Direction Posts and Warning Signs. Form 39 (Roads).

ACTS OF PARLIAMENT.

Carriers Act, 1830.

Locomotive Act, 1861.

Locomotives Act, 1865.

Tramways Act, 1870.

Highways and Locomotives (Amendment) Act, 1878.

Locomotives on Highways Act, 1896.

Light Railways Act, 1896.

Locomotives Act, 1898.

Motor Car Act, 1903.
Development and Road Improvements Funds Act, 1909.
Finance Act, 1910.
Finance Act, 1915.
Local Government (Emergency Provisions) Act, 1916.
Ministry of Transport Act, 1919.
Roads Act, 1920.
Finance Act, 1920.
Railways Act, 1921.
London Traffic Act, 1924.

STATUTORY RULES AND ORDERS.

Statutory Rules and Orders, 1903, No. 998.
The Heavy Motor Car Order, 1904.
Road Vehicles (Registration and Licensing) Order, 1921, No. 221.
Road Vehicles (Registration and Licensing) Regulations, 1921.
Road Vehicles (Part Year Licensing) Order, 1921.
The Heavy Motor Car (Amendment) Order, 1921, No. 906.
The Heavy Motor Car (Amendment) Order, 1922, No. 556.

BOOKS.

Commercial Road Transport.

CONRADI. Mechanical Road Transport.
GRUPP. Economics of Motor Transportation.
LANE. Motor Truck Transportation.
LISSENDEN. Traffic Management.
MAIRET. Trade Transport and Finance.
PHILLIMORE. Motor Road Transport for Commercial Purposes.

YEAR-BOOKS.

A. A. Hand-book.
Canada Year-book.
Motor Transport Year-book.
Municipal Year-book.
Railway Year-book.

General.

Acworth. Elements of Railway Economics.

Acworth. The Railways and the Traders.

Colson. Cours d'économie politique.

Fowler. Transport and its Indebtedness to Science (British Association Report).

Kirkaldy and Evans. History and Economics of Transport.

Macdonald. The Road Problem (British Association Reprints).

Marshall. Principles of Economics.

Marshall. Industry and Trade.

Nicholson. Principles of Political Economy.

Porter. Progress of the Nation.

Pratt. English Canals.

Adam Smith. Wealth of Nations.

Stephenson. Communications.

Venn. Foundations of Agricultural Economics.

Historical.

Cannan. History of Local Rates in England.

Clark. Tramways (1878).

Jackman. Transportation in Modern England.

Knowles. Industrial and Commercial Revolutions.

Parnell. Treatise on Roads (1833).

Pratt. A History of Inland Transport and Communications in England.

Thorold Rogers. A History of Agriculture and Prices in England.

S. and B. Webb. Story of the King's Highway.

S. and B. Webb. Statutory Authorities for Special Purposes.

Young. Steam on Common Roads (1860).

Miscellaneous.

Percy Ashley. Local Government.

Belloc. The Road.

Bulkeley. Mechanical Appliances for Handling Railway Traffic.

Watson Grice. National and Local Finance.

WEBB and FREEMAN (Edited). Seasonal Trades.
WHYTE. Electricity in Locomotion.

PERIODICALS, JOURNALS, ETC.

The Autocar.
The Commercial Motor.
The Electric Vehicle.
Engineering.
Manchester Guardian Commercial.
Modern Transport.
The Motor.
Motor (New York).
Motor Transport.
The Scotsman.
The Sunday Times.
The Times.
The Times Trade Supplement.
The Tramway and Light Railway Journal.
The Tramway and Railway World.

Note.—The contributed articles and summarized reports of papers printed in the above periodicals furnish a valuable source of information on current transport topics. It would however, be an impossible task to attempt to enumerate all these articles, though the Author wishes here to express his indebtedness to this important source of information.

HOUSE JOURNALS, ETC.

Edinburgh Corporation Tramways Department Journal.
The Road-maker (published by the British Reinforced Concrete Company, Ltd.).
Shepherd's N.E.W.S. (Published by Wm. Shepherd & Sons, Ltd.).

PROCEEDINGS, REPORTS, JOURNALS, ETC.

The Economic Journal.
Journal of the Institute of Transport.
Proceedings of the Municipal Tramways Association.
International Road Congress Report (Seville Meeting, 1923).

INDEX

PRINTED BY UNWIN BROTHERS, LIMITED, LONDON AND WOKING, GREAT BRITAIN